Agates

Inside Out

Designed, Written, and Compiled by **Karen A. Brzys**
Photography by **Thomas P. Shearer**

Research Assistance by **Candace Prill**

Cover Photograph: An intricate Lake Superior agate.
Figure 1 (above): A condor agate from Argentina.

Published by the Gitche Gumee Agate and History Museum
Grand Marais, Michigan
First printing March 2010

15 14 13 12 11 10   1 2 3 4 5 6 7 8 9 10

Printed in China

ISBN # 978-1-891143-97-7

For information about obtaining additional copies of this book, please contact Gitche Gumee Agate and History Museum
PO Box 308, Grand Marais, Michigan (MI) 49839
Office: (906) 494-2590, Museum: (906) 494-3000
www.agatelady.com — Karen@agatelady.com
NOTE: All sales of this book benefit the Gitche Gumee Museum.

DVDs, photography reprints, calendars, and other products will be available in the future. Check the webpage www.agatelady.com for further information.

Please give us your opinion and let us know which photographs in this book are your favorite. Find out how to vote by going to page 244 in this book, or go to the www.agatelady.com webpage.

Unless noted otherwise, Karen A. Brzys created all of the diagrams. Except as noted here, Thomas P. Shearer took all of the photographs. The exceptions are: Figures 31, 77, and 265 (Karen A. Brzys), Figure 51 (Stephen W. Morris), Figure 52 (ANDRÁS BÜKI), Figure 56 (K.L. Milliken), and Figure 75 (Graham Wilson). See the captions of the figures for more information.

We would like to thank the following people for loaning us specimens or lending lapidary assistance: Dave Ault, Gary Braun, Mark Anderson (www.DifferentSeasonsJewelry.com), Keith Bartel (Beaver Bay, MN, Agate Shop), Mary Collings, Elaine and Jerry Elness, Brett Fogelberg, Kelly Madigan, Jill Phillips, Eric Powers, Terry Roses (Fragments of History, Duluth, MN), Sharon Smith (www.Agatesrock.com), Jim Watson, and Scott Wolter.

TABLE OF CONTENTS

DEDICATION

Those of you who have spent time at the Gitche Gumee Museum in Grand Marais, Michigan know that its operation is a labor of love. For the past decade, it has truly been a privilege to carry on the legacy of the founder, Axel Niemi. As thanks for your support, which has come in many forms, I would like to dedicate this book to all of the museum faithfuls, especially those who have contributed time and resources. Without you, the museum, the mineral art, and this book would not be possible. Thanks to all of you who have "rocks in your head."

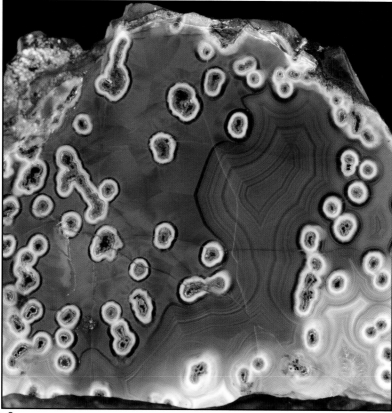

Figure 2
A very unusual Michipicoten (mĭsh–ĭ–pĭ–cō–ten) tube agate from Ontario, Canada.

"Underneath the surface appearance, everything is not only connected with everything else, but also with the Source of all. Even a stone can show you the way back to the Source and to yourself. When you look at it or hold it and let it be without imposing a word or mental label on it, a sense of awe, of wonder, arises within you." [1] FROM ECKHART TOLLE'S *A NEW EARTH.*

ACKNOWLEDGEMENTS

I was helped by many people during the effort to research, write, and compile this reference guide. I would like to thank my rockhound friends who have endured countless hours listening to me ramble on about agate genesis. Next I would like to acknowledge and express gratitude to Tom Shearer. The agate story could not be told effectively without his outstanding photography. I would like to thank those who contributed editing time including Lynne Kane, Kim Amthor, Susan and Paul Bennett, Diana Mavis, Gerald and Jill Phillips, Renee Beaver-Stocking, Candace Prill, and Tom Shearer (who can do more than just take wonderful pictures). Candace also needs to be singled out because she helped compile data. Sam Speigel and Julie Taylor at Partners Books provided sound advice, final production assistance, and help with distributing this book. Anna DeVault from Imago Sales, New York, provided valuable help in working with the printer. I was aided significantly by an article published in August, 2009. It represents a lifetime of research by Eckart Walger, a German geologist. Walger passed away in 2003, but his family, notably Helga Walger and Burkhard Walger, and researchers Georg Matthess, Volker von Seckendorff, and Friedrich Liebau, published the paper on his behalf. This article helped me to understand agate genesis in a new and thought provoking way.

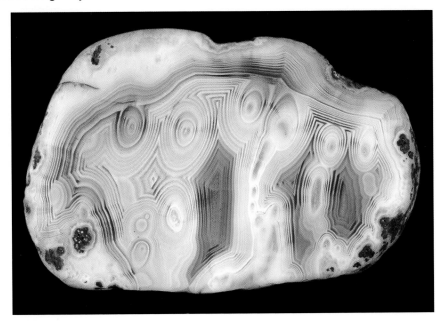

Figure 3
This Lake Superior shadow and tube agate was picked up on the beach by the museum founder, Axel Niemi, in Grand Marais, Michigan.

INTRODUCTION

Two years ago I decided to write another agate book. The first book, *Understanding and Finding Agates*, was written as a quick reference source to help people to be more successful in their search for the elusive agate. The feedback about the book was extremely positive, but people told me that they want to know more. It became clear that a book is needed that includes comprehensive information about how agates formed, how to find them, and what they look like. This book evolved from a lifetime of agate hunting and a decade of interacting with rockhounds at the museum. Beginning agate hunters want the basics, and those with more experience want the detail. This book has been compiled to meet both sets of needs. It will help you to "think like an agate" so that you can be more successful in finding them.

A database was created with information from more than a hundred academic articles, dozens of agate books, and countless web sites. With the help of modern research technologies, I was able to even obtain translations of articles published in foreign journals. Once the research was underway, I had to start thinking about the photography.

A magic moment came when Tom Shearer came into my mineral art booth at a show in Minnesota. He offered free color photographs in exchange for borrowing some of my "Wowser" agates. When he returned the next day with my agates and corresponding photographs, I realized that my dilemma regarding photography was possibly solved. We met again in July when Tom agreed to help with the book. During more than three decades of research, I had never seen such outstanding photographs of agates. Tom has exclusive techniques that he developed to capture the intricate beauty of agates. One technique proved useful in photographing three-dimensional rocks for this book. Tom took several different photographs of each rock, setting a different plane of focus for each picture. He then combined and "stacked" the photographs merging only the portions that were in focus. This technique allows you to see a two-dimensional photograph of a three-dimensional agate with all of the rock's sections in focus. This book will not be the last time you see Tom's work. There will be other products. Watch the www.agatelady.com web page for announcements about additional products.

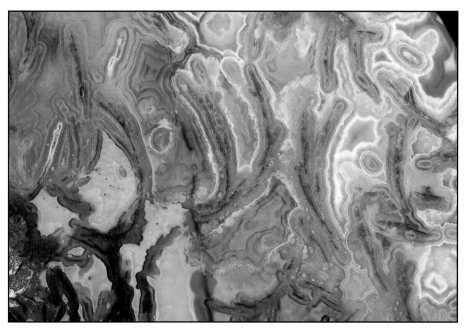

Figure 4
This detailed picture demonstrates the close-up detail that photographer, Tom Shearer, can achieve using his special techniques. This slab was sold as a Lake Superior agate even though it appears to have characteristics more typical of Mexican agates.

For the remainder of the book, I will write from the perspective of "we" to acknowledge the team effort that this project has required. The book has been organized as follows:

Chapter 1 defines what agates are, reviews agates and human history, details agate characteristics, and describes the different types of quartz minerals.

Chapter 2 discusses how agates formed. This chapter is intended for those of you who live and die agates and want to understand everything about them. If you simply want to learn how to be a more successful agate hunter, and you don't really care about the detailed scientific aspects, you may want to skip this chapter and go on to Chapter 3. However, in my experience, the more you understand agate formation, the more successful you will be in differentiating between an agate and an agate-want-to-be. This chapter reviews the relevant geology, agate forming influences, agate formation theories, types of host rock, and the timing of agate genesis.

Chapter 3 presents information about the specific characteristics you should look for when rockhounding for agates. Information in this chapter was compiled from communications with rock club representatives, library and internet research, our own hunting experiences, and examination of agates from all over the world. There are also general agate hunting tips, information about how to clean agates, and suggestions for assessing the value of agates. A summary with agate hunting suggestions is included on the flap inside the front cover.

Chapter 4 includes descriptions of 31 different types of agates, based on their developmental structures.

Chapter 5 has information about agates from different geographical locations. Since there are more than 3,000 named agates in the world, we cannot be comprehensive. However, we do list the types of agate structures found in each state and describe agates from several states and other countries.

In the back of the book there is a list of reference cites, index, information about the museum, and invitation for you to vote for your favorite photographs in this book. We hope you enjoy learning about agates "inside out."

Figure 5
This Mexican crazy lace agate is a perfect example of how ornate agates can be.

CHAPTER 1 What Is An Agate?

A BASIC DESCRIPTION

One of the most intriguing forms of quartz produced by nature is the semi-precious gemstone, agate. It is a variegated form of chalcedony (pronounced kal-sed'-nee), which is a type of microcrystalline quartz made of silicon dioxide (SiO_2).[2] Microcrystalline means that the crystals are so small that they cannot be seen with the naked eye or with a normal optical microscope.[3] In fact, the only way to see actual agate crystals is to use powerful technology such as a transmission electron microscopy TEM or a scanning electron microscopy SEM.[4]

Agates naturally develop when empty pockets or veins inside host rock fill in molecule-by-molecule and layer-by-layer as quartz microcrystals self-organize to form concentric bands or other patterns. Agates can be found in igneous, sedimentary, and metamorphic rocks and have been discovered on every continent.[5] They can be collected from deserts, mountains, rivers, shorelines, gravel pits, prairies, and fields.

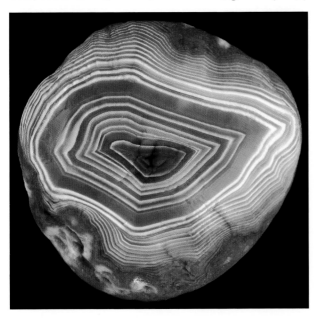

Figure 6
Most of the world's agates have concentric bands that fill in host rock pockets. This prime example is a Lake Superior agate.

Agates are technically classified as sedimentary because they are deposited in empty pockets with silica from mineral-rich fluids or gels.[6] The colors and arrangement of microcrystals are influenced by changes in pressure, temperature, and mineral content that occur during the formation process.[7] Unlike other gemstones, each agate is unique. Even slabs cut from the same specimen will vary.

AGATES AND HUMAN HISTORY

Agates have attracted attention for eons. They have been discovered with the remains of the original rockhound, Stone Age man, that date between 16,000 and 20,000 years ago.[8] Because of their colorful concentric patterns, as well as other unique properties, agates were one of the first geological specimens collected. Therefore, it is not surprising that some of the names that we use today are quite ancient. Pliny and Theophrastus used names such as chalcedony and agate during the first millennium (77 A.D.). This was before any kind of systematic naming was devised and long before the science of mineralogy was born.[9]

The name agate comes from the Achates River in Sicily, which at one time was a source for these gemstones. However, the exact location of the original agate river is disputed by some.[10,11] Given the passion and commitment of most agate pickers, it is interesting that in Greek, Achates means "a faithful companion or friend."[12] Because agates are extremely hard (a hardness of 7 out of 10 on the Mohs Scale), they can easily be polished. Thus, agates have been used to make decorative artifacts and useful tools for thousands of years. In the Khambat region in India, skilled craftsmen made agate beads during the Paleolithic era 10,000 years ago.[13,14] Artifacts dating back as far as 9,000 years ago have been recovered in Mongolia and in Western Asia.[15] Agates were used to make jewelry, wine goblets, urns, and seals by the Mongolians, Egyptians, Sumerians, and Babylonians.[16] Eye agates adorned the carvings of Idols in ancient Egypt. For centuries, agates were used to make mortars and pestles and fulcrums for balances.[17]

Figure 7
This is a hand-carved carnelian agate urn from Asia. It now resides at the Gitche Gumee Museum.

The first recorded description of agates appeared in the writings of Greek philosophers around 300 B.C.[18] The power of the agate bug was evident with Mithradates (171-138 B.C.), the fifth king of Pontus, who collected over 4,000 agate bowls.[19] Albertus Magnus (Albert the Great, 1193-1280 A.D.), a theologian, alchemist, and politician in Germany, was responsible for the development of the modern understanding of agates. He was the first to describe the cryptocrystalline quartz structure of agates.[20] The first large-scale mining of agate took place in the Nahe River valley in Germany in 1497, which later gave rise to the agate cutting operations in Idar-Oberstein, Germany. These lapidary masters used river currents to power their grinding wheels.[21,22] One of the first scientists to propose an agate genesis theory was Cosimo Collini in 1776. In 1850, Jokob Noeggerath presented the idea that the bands formed one at a time when silica-saturated waters percolated through vesicles in basalts.[23]

The popularity of agates took a big step forward in the late 1800s. Although toy marbles had been around for thousands of years, they were expensive and time consuming to produce until Sam Dyke invented machinery to mass-produce toy marbles made out of clay in 1884. Soon thereafter, when toy marbles became the new craze, manufacturers began using agate. The marble players who were lucky enough to have an "aggie" had a distinct advantage due to the hardness and density of agate over softer clay marbles. There was even an agate lapidary industry in Michigan during the late 1800s and early 1900s that used Lake Superior agates to make beads and marbles.[24] Even modern glass marbles are designed to look like agates.[25]

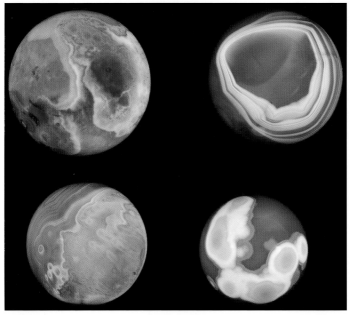

Figure 8
These "aggies" were carved from Lake Superior agates.

Today, the agate industry is a worldwide venture worth billions of dollars. Agates are mined, collected, sold, and traded in nearly every country. They are cut into thin sections, polished, and fashioned into jewelry, beads, bookends, and other objects. Agate mines and factories exist in Brazil, Uruguay, Germany, Botswana, India, Australia, Madagascar, Argentina, Mexico, Canada, and the U.S.

During the past decade, the internet has created new opportunities to connect collectors with sellers and suppliers. If you insert the word "agate" into an internet auction site, you will have to sort through many thousands of listings. People are pulling agates from their attics and basements to sell on the internet. In some cases these specimens have been passed down many generations. One Fairburn agate nodule sold on eBay a few years ago for $13,000! Dealers in Argentina, India, Australia and other countries can reach collectors in the United States and Europe. After a few decades of declining interest since the last big agate push occurred in the 1950s and 1960s, agate collecting is again on the rise. Perhaps people living in this fast-paced, technologic society are benefiting from the handsome, mysterious, and powerful agate.

AGATES AND THEIR "FIRST COUSINS"

Quartz is a chemical compound made up of silicon dioxide (SiO_2), which is also known as silica. Silicon, a non-metallic element, is the second most abundant element comprising 28 percent of the earth's crust. (Oxygen is the most abundant at 47 percent.) Thus, it is not surprising that silicon dioxide is the most plentiful compound on earth.[26] Silica comes in many forms. Molecules of silica can be suspended in water, precipitated out of solution to form non-crystalline gels or solids (such as opals), or grown into crystalline quartz.

Macrocrystalline Quartz

The quartz form of silica comprises 12.6 percent of the Earth's crust.[27,28] Interestingly, the Earth's mantle and core are completely void of quartz.[29] When quartz is pure without trace minerals contained in its structure, it is colorless, transparent, and very hard—almost glass-like. In fact, quartz minerals are harder than most types of steel. Only about 30 other minerals exceed it in hardness.[30]

The ancient Greeks thought that "rock crystals" must be made of a material that is frozen so deeply that it can't melt.[31] The word "quartz" was first seen in European mining literature in the 14th century. The word is probably either German or Slavic in origin.[32] Until 1823, scientists classified quartz as an element, which is a material that cannot be subdivided because all of its atoms have the same atomic number. However, at that time, Swedish chemists Torbern Bergmann and J.J. Berzelius discovered that quartz is instead a chemical compound made up of oxygen and what they determined to be a new element, silicon.[33]

When most people think of quartz, they envision the six-sided crystals with six-sided pyramids at their ends. Macrocrystalline quartz comes in a number of colored varieties like amethyst (violet), citrine (yellow), or smoky quartz (gray or brown). The colors are due to inclusions of other minerals or trace elements that are contained within their structure. For those of you who love your colored quartz specimens, it is best to store these away from sunlight. The ultraviolet radiation in sunlight can cause the color in amethyst, citrine, and smoky quartz to pale.[34,35]

Figure 9
This is a macrocrystalline quartz crystal.

Macrocrystalline means that you can see the crystal with your unaided eyes.

Most of the world's quartz is either found in "miniature rocks," or sand, which is formed when larger rock erodes into minute pieces. There is also a lot of quartz hidden in granites, which are made up of between 5 and 50 percent quartz. In some nodular pockets and geodes, macrocrystalline quartz can dominate. These are often called "sugar quartz."[36] To be considered agate, more than 50 percent of such specimens would have to contain banded microcrystalline chalcedony.

Quartz has many uses in modern society. It is the primary component of concrete (quartz sand and gravel). It is also used in manufacturing glass and ceramics. Quartz has unique properties that allow it to be used in piezoelectric and pyroelectric generators. When you strike or heat quartz crystals, mechanical or heat energy can be converted into electrical energy. It is because of these characteristics that quartz is used to make watches, computer chips, electric lighters, and starters in your grills, stoves, and gas heaters.[37]

Quartz occurs in a great number of varieties that differ in form and color. The varieties of quartz can be subdivided into two groups. Macrocrystalline includes quartz with crystals that you can see with the unaided eye. Microcrystalline includes quartz with crystals that require a powerful microscope to see them. The table below lists the most common types of quartz varieties.

Table 1: Quartz Varieties[38]

Macrocrystalline		Microcrystalline	
		Fibrous	**Granular**
Amethyst	Rock Crystal	Agate	Chert
Ametrine	Rose Quartz	Carnelian	Flint
Aventurine	Smoky Quartz	Chalcedony	Jasper
Citrine	Tiger's Eye	Chrysoprase	
Milky Quartz		Sardonyx	

Another difference between macrocrystalline and microcrystalline quartz is the way in which the crystals grow. Macrocrystalline quartz grows by adding silicon dioxide molecules to the crystal's surface, layer by layer to make intact larger crystals. Microcrystalline quartz minerals form when separate individual miniature crystals bond together.

When agate hunting, it is common to find milky quartz and other macrocrystalline specimens of quartz. Milky quartz is white and translucent to almost opaque due to numerous evenly distributed gas or fluid inclusions.[39] You can differentiate these from microcrystalline quartz varieties with a close examination. Hold each rock in the sun or under a bright light and determine whether you can see individual crystals sparkle when you move it back and forth. If you can see sparkling quartz crystals, the specimen is macrocrystalline.

Figure 10
When you find macrocrystalline quartz such as these beach pebbles, look at them closely and determine whether you can see individual crystals sparkle as you move the specimens back and forth under a bright light.

Another macrocrystalline quartz variety that can be confused with agate is tiger's eye, as well as the related varieties hawk's eye and cat's eye. These specimens have a silky shine with wavy patterns of parallel lines that seem to move when the stone is turned. This optical character is called chatoyance because it resembles an eye of a cat. ("Chat" is French for cat.) The chatoyance results from the fibrous structure of the quartz crystals. These minerals form when blue-gray crocidolite asbestos fibers are partially or totally replaced with silica and other minerals. Asbestos is a hazardous material, but its dangerous fibers are well embedded or completely replaced, and thus not a health threat.[40] Below is a photo of Marra Mamba Tiger Iron, which contains tiger's eye, red jasper, and black hematite. This specimen is from Mount Brockman in Western Australia. It is known for its rippled wavy bands of color that often resemble a scenic view.

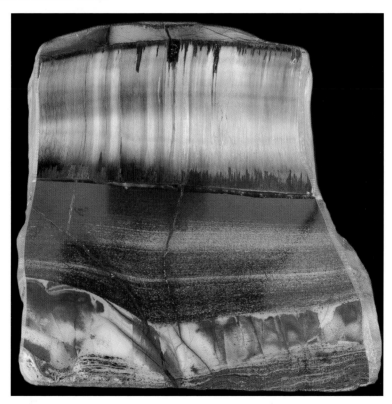

Figure 11
Marra Mamba tiger iron contains wavy patterns of gold tiger's eye, red jasper, and black hematite.

NOTE: The other varieties of macrocrystalline quartz listed in Table 1 will not be discussed here since they are not easily confused with agate. For more information on these other quartz varieties, go to the web page <u>www.quartzpage.de</u>.

Fibrous Microcrystalline Quartz

As you can see in Table 1, the microcrystalline quartz varieties are subdivided into two groups. The distinction between "fibrous" and "granular" is based on the size and shape of the microcrystals.[41] Microcrystalline quartz reveals the nature of its crystal structure when sections are ground down to transparency and examined with a powerful polarizing microscope.[42] A representation of these shapes is depicted in the graphic below. Chert, flint, and jasper have small, spherical microcrystals that pack together like BB pellets in a jar. Because the crystals pack together so tightly, granular microcrystalline quartz is opaque. Fibrous microcrystalline quartz, on the other hand, has longer crystals that allow it to be translucent in most cases.[43]

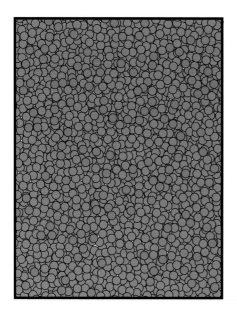 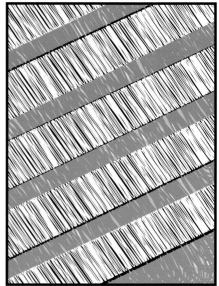

Figure 12
The above graphic illustrates the general shape of the two main subgroups of microcrystalline quartz. Chert, flint, and jasper (left) have granular microcrystals, whereas chalcedony agate (right) has fibrous microcrystals. In both diagrams, the orange color represents iron oxide impurities. The gray represents the silica quartz crystals.

There are several different types of fibrous quartz. Pure chalcedony is a dense, translucent material that is white, gray, or blue and is homogeneous in appearance. Thus, pure chalcedony with no mineral impurities does not have any pattern or variation in color.[44] Chalcedony can be differentiated from macrocrystalline quartz because of its density. Very often macrocrystalline quartz specimens have small random stress fractures that develop when the quartz, which forms at high temperatures, cools off. The density of the microcrystalline structure of chalcedony, combined with the fact that it forms at lower temperatures, results in a more uniform, fracture free appearance. Since chalcedony is microcrystalline, it will not exhibit any of the sparkling crystals that are evident in macrocrystalline quartz.

Figure 13
Chalcedony microcrystalline quartz

When chalcedony is non-banded but is red or brown, due to iron compound inclusions, it is classified as either carnelian or sard. Carnelian is a translucent, bright orange to deep red form of chalcedony. Sard is a translucent brown form of chalcedony.[45] (For more information about carnelian, refer to Chapter 3.) Similarly, chrysoprase is a green chalcedony with nickel oxide inclusions that alter the color. This is quite a rare form of quartz; thus, it has more value than most other varieties. The commercially available chrysoprase comes from Australia.[46] Finally, banded chalcedony is classified as agate.

Granular Microcrystalline Quartz

There are also several forms of granular microcrystalline quartz. Chert, flint, and jasper are dense, granular forms of microcrystalline quartz that are almost always opaque. There is apparently no clearly defined line that classifies one from the other. Flint and chert are usually grouped together, with flint being darker in color. They grade into jasper as the impurities, particular iron oxide, increase.[47] All have a range of color caused by mineral inclusions that includes black, gray, yellow, orange, brown, and red. These forms of microcrystalline quartz occur as solid masses in sedimentary rocks, as well as filings in cracks of all rock types. Usually, the silica is of a biogenic (biologic) origin made up of countless skeletons of tiny marine organisms such as radiolaria and diatoms.[48] Three billion old chert has been found at Lake Magadi in Kenya. This African chert is unusual, though, since it appears that it had a non-biogenic origin.[49] The oldest fossils in the world are stromatolites, which are reported to be 3.5 billion years old. These primitive organisms formed rock-like buildups of microbial mats. The communities of microorganisms such as bacteria and algae trapped particles and built up mounds that stuck up above the seafloor. Jasperized stromatolite formations have been found in Australia, Minnesota, and other locations.[50]

Although chert and flint can have some color variation, they cannot compete with jasper, which often has patterns that rival those in agate. In some cases, chert, flint, and jasper can actually have some agatized sections, and all three can have crystal pockets with macrocrystalline quartz. Pictured below are specimens of gold chert and red jasper.

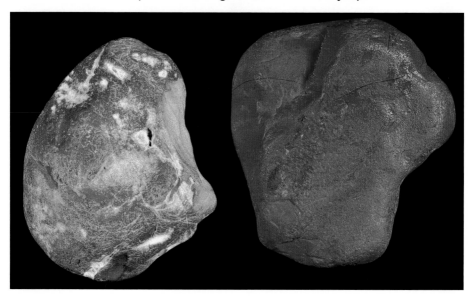

Figure 14
Opaque gold chert and red jasper found on a Lake Superior beach.

Because chert, flint, and jasper are "first cousins" to agate, they can have some of the same characteristics. This is especially true for specimens that have been weathered. For more information about the similarities and differences between agate and its chert, flint, and jasper first cousins, refer to the Agate-Want-To-Be section in Chapter 3.

Silicified Fossils

Other rocks that can be confused with agate are silicified fossils. Just as microcrystalline quartz can form agate, it can also replace organic structures. Pictured on the next page are some examples of silicified fossils.

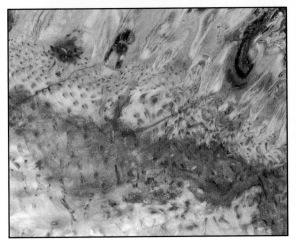
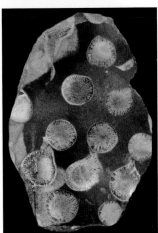

Figure 15 (top) Fossil sponge from Florida.
Figure 16 (lower left) Petrified palm root from Louisiana.
Figure 17 (lower right) Fossil reeds from Michigan.

Fossils are formed from a petrification process, which is a geologic term describing the method by which organic living material is converted into stone. Usually this happens when the organic remains are buried in lava or sediments before they can decay. Petrification can take place in two related ways: replacement and permineralization. Replacement occurs when water dissolves the original hard parts and replaces them with mineral matter. The most common replacement minerals are calcite, silica, pyrite, and hematite. When the original organism is replaced quickly the fossil usually loses the detailed structure, leaving behind just the original shape. Permineralization occurs when ground water carrying dissolved minerals infiltrates the microscopic pores. The minerals in this case replace the detail of the original organism.[51]

The most famous example of petrification is the Petrified Forest in northern Arizona. This is not the only area known for petrified wood since it is also found in nearly every state and in many foreign countries. It is not known for certain who the first Europeans were to see the great display of petrified wood in Arizona. It was probably Spanish explorers during their expeditions in the 1500s. The earliest written record dates from 1851 when an army officer mentioned petrified wood in a report.[52]

Figure 18
This is a close up of petrified wood that shows how quartz filled in and replaced the original wood fiber.

The story of how the Petrified Forest developed is quite interesting. At one time the northeast part of Arizona was lowland with numerous rivers and streams. In the basin there was a lush forest with conifer trees up to nine feet in diameter and over 200 feet tall. During the Triassic Period (200 to 250 million years ago), the area that is now Arizona was located near the equator. During that period all of the continents had combined to form one super-continent called Pangea.[53] Trees in the area died and were deposited by rivers in flood plains and streambeds. Most of the trees decomposed, but a few were buried so deep that there was not enough oxygen to allow decay. West of this area massive volcanoes spewed ash into the atmosphere. Wind currents carried the ash and deposited it with the silt that buried the trees. Ground water dissolved silica from the ash and carried it into the buried logs. Over time, the silica in solution either replaced cell walls, crystallizing as quartz, or deposited in the air spaces within the wood tissue. This petrification process explains how cell structure, annual rings, and other features of the original trees were preserved.

As the petrification process continued, other minerals combined with quartz to create the brilliant rainbow of colors often found in petrified wood. In some cases minerals infiltrated later during the millions of years of burial as a secondary deposit in the cracks, checks, or other openings in the petrified or partially petrified wood. Iron oxides produced the great variety of shades of red, brown, and yellow. The black color was probably due to manganese oxide or carbon.[54]

At first the now petrified trees remained buried under 3,000 feet of sediment.[55] However, around 60 million years ago this area was uplifted along with the Rocky Mountains. With the uplifting came erosion from streams and rivers that removed the overburden layers and exposed the petrified trees.[56]

Some scientists classify petrified wood as agate; others do not. The determination comes down to two issues. First, the type of quartz needs to be identified. Most of the quartz in petrified wood is macrocrystalline, although there may also be some microcrystalline replacement. For those specimens that contain mostly microcrystalline crystals, the second issue is whether petrification was a replacement process, or whether it may have involved an agatization process. If the wood tissue was directly replaced by silica so that the wood fibers defined the structure, then these specimens of petrified wood are not agate. If, on the other hand, the individual pore spaces self-organized and filled independently to create separate agatized pockets, then these specimens of petrified wood are made up of "colonies" of agates. Depending on the specimen, there could be some of both structures.

QUARTZ PROPERTIES

The physical properties of macrocrystalline and microcrystalline quartz varieties are listed in Table 2.

Table 2: Properties of Quartz Minerals [57,58,59]

Property	Macrocrystalline	Microcrystalline
Chemical Formula	SiO_2	SiO_2
Color	None if pure, otherwise any	Any
Light Transmission	Transparent to translucent	Translucent to opaque
Luster	Vitreous	Waxy to dull
Luster of fractured surface	Vitreous to fatty	Dull
Streak	White	White to slightly colored
Refractive Index	1.544 to 1.553	1.533 to 1.539
Specific Gravity	2.6481 g/cm³	2.4 to 2.7 g/cm³
Hardness	7	6.5 to 7
Fracture	Conchoidal, sometimes uneven	Conchoidal, sometimes uneven
Water Content	<0.1%	0.1 to 4%
Non-Silica Impurities	0.01 to 0.5%	1 to 20%
Formation Temperature	1063°F (573°C)	122 to 572°F (50 to 300°C)
Melting Point	3038 to 3115°F 1670 to 1713°C	3272 to 3632°F 1800 to 2000°C
Tests	Insoluble, unless placed in hydrofluoric acid	Insoluble, unless placed in hydrofluoric acid
Porous	No	Yes
Formation Pressure	Up to 19 PSI	0 to 5 PSI

The differences between macrocrystalline and microcrystalline quartz are in part attributable to tiny spaces that are filled with water, and possibly air. Macrocrystalline quartz has a consistent internal arrangement with molecules packed so tightly that no air or water-filled pockets exist. The needle-like crystals in fibrous microcrystalline quartz, on the other hand, tend to trap air and water. The granular forms of microcrystalline quartz can have some of these pockets, but not as many as the fibrous varieties.[60]

The physical properties of microcrystalline quartz varieties can be affected by the mineral impurities contained within or between the crystal structures. It is because of these impurities that most microcrystalline quartz specimens cannot actually be classified as minerals, which are naturally occurring, homogenous inorganic solid substances with a definite chemical composition. Chert, flint, jasper and agate, which have mineral impurities in addition to silica, are classified as "textural varieties of quartz." They are more similar to rocks, which contain more than one type of mineral.[61]

It is interesting to note we often find agate, jasper, and quartz in separate vesicle pockets within the same basaltic lava flow. To form these different quartz varieties, the conditions across the lava flow must have varied. The temperatures, pressures, and minerals in one area of the rock matrix may have favored the formation of agate, wherein a short distance away chert or quartz may have developed. The upwelling of molten dikes also produced variations in conditions within the lava flows.[62] The deeper a vesicle or seam within the flow, the higher the pressure and temperature, which caused quartz to form rather than chalcedony.

Figure 19
This incredible agate has a seemingly infinite variety of microcrystalline quartz formations. The source location is unknown since this slab was purchased out of a bargain bin.

CHAPTER 2   How Did Agates Form?

THE EARTH — IN THE BEGINNING

Sometime more than 4 ½ billion years ago, subatomic particles, element atoms, and grains of dust arrived in the space that is now occupied by our solar system. It is thought that this material came here from an exploding supernova that took place somewhere else in our galaxy. These materials gravitated and compressed, becoming hotter and hotter, until nuclear reactions began to take place. The result of this compaction was the birth of our sun. As the sun grew in size, it started to exert a gravitational pull on the remainder of particles, dust, and gas. The "space debris" formed infant planets, called plantesimals, which began to orbit around the sun.[63] At that time our newborn sun was only 73 percent of its present day intensity.[64]

The Earth began as one of these small planetesimals, gaining mass and size each time another planetesimal collided with it. When one of the larger asteroid-sized planetesimals collided with the Earth, the impact created heat that caused the Earth's surface to turn molten.[65] For approximately 100 million years, more material continued to accumulate, a process called accretion, to increase the size of the Earth. Finally, as the accretion slowed, the Earth's surface began to cool. Some of the elements combined, forming the first rocks in the Earth's crust. These very first rocks were igneous, derived from the Latin word meaning "from a fire." In fact, all rocks on Earth had igneous origin, since the elements that formed them were once in a molten state.[66]

Modern geologists and geophysicists accept that the Earth's age is around 4.567 billion years. This estimate was determined by radiometric dating of meteorite material and is consistent with the ages of the oldest known terrestrial and lunar samples. The oldest surviving terrestrial minerals analyzed to date are small zircon crystals from Western Australia, which are at least 4.404 billion years old.[67]

During the next few hundred million years, the now cooled Earth surface looked similar to the surface of the current day moon, with thousands of impact craters imbedded in the newly formed igneous rock. There was not yet an atmosphere, nor were there any oceans. In time, the interior of the Earth started to heat up from the decay of radioactive elements, reaching the melting point of the igneous rocks that made up the newborn Earth. As the rocks melted, the iron and nickel deposited by the meteorites sank to the center of the Earth, forming its core. The lighter weight materials, such as the silicates, rose to the surface, erupting as an almost endless string of volcanoes. The volcanic lava cooled and a new basaltic crust formed on the surface, separated from the center core by a partially molten mantle comprised of somewhat heavier magnesium-rich minerals.[68]

This basaltic crust formed around 4 billion years ago. At that time, during the height of the great meteorite bombardment, a massive asteroid hit the area that is now central Ontario, Canada. Scientists think that the impact created a crater up to 900 miles wide. They also think that the force of the collision triggered the formation of even more continental crust by melting vast amounts of basalt and converting it into granite.[69]

Only three sites located in Canada, Australia, and Africa have rocks that have not changed significantly throughout geologic time. Most other rocks have eroded, metamorphosed, or melted entirely. Few rocks on the present day Earth date beyond 3.7 billion years.[70] In 1999 geologists found what they thought was the oldest rock outcropping on Earth in Canada's Northwest Territories, called Acasta gneiss. It was dated at 4.031 billion years old. Then, in 2008 they discovered even older rock in the Nuwuagittuq belt on the east coast of Hudson Bay, in northern Quebec, which dates from 3.8 to 4.28 billion years old.[71] Scientists have studied these ancient outcroppings and determined that by the time the rock formed, the continental crust had already covered around ten percent of today's landmass.[72] These continent "seeds" are called cratons. The map below illustrates where scientists think that the original cratons existed (shown in red), relative to today's landmasses (shown in white). On the map, the west blue dot marks the location of the Acasta gneiss; the east blue dot marks the location of the Nuwuagittuq belt.[73]

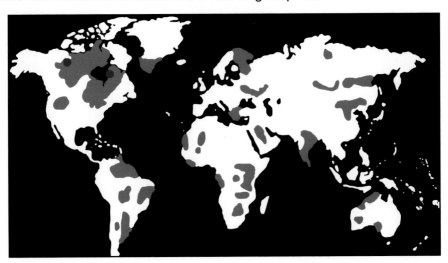

Figure 20
The red areas on this map mark the craton locations three billion years ago. The blue dots in Canada represent the locations where scientists have found the oldest rocks on Earth.

During this period of continent growing, tremendous quantities of gas and steam were released to form a primordial atmosphere. The icy asteroids and comets that hit the Earth during its formation supplied the water, which was released as steam. It didn't take long for the water vapor to condense and fall back to Earth as rain. There was so much water vapor that when it started to rain, it rained for hundreds of millions of years without stopping. Since the young rock was totally exposed, it quickly eroded to form the first sedimentary rock on Earth. The rainwater filled in the depressions on the rocky surface, spread out, and deepened to form the first oceans.[74] Once there was water, it didn't take long for life to evolve. The earliest known evidence of organic life was discovered in 3.85 billion year old sediments on Greenland. In 1999, evidence of bacteria and blue-green algae was found in 3.5 billion year old greenstone in Western Australia.[75,76]

As the thin craton sections of crust floated and moved freely on top of the molten mantle, these continent seeds started to collide and combine. You can think of it as giant blocks of crust being welded together (accretion). In many cases, the impact edges of the cratons formed parallel mountain ranges, some that are still visible today such as the Barberton Mountains in southeastern Africa.[77,78]

Volcanoes were extremely active on the cratons. The thinness of the craton crust did not produce much of a challenge for the upwelling magma. Volcanoes located at the leading impact edges of the cratons spewed lava and ash, causing the cratons to grow and spread out. In the center of the cratons, magmatic intrusions also forced their way to the surface, increasing the height and thickness of the cratons. Throughout this period of continent growth, rain continued to pour down, eroding the igneous rock and breaking it into smaller pieces, which piled up and consolidated to form new sedimentary rock. The collisions of the cratons happened with such force that rock was also metamorphosed as a result of the heat and pressure. Scientists have estimated that the average rate of continental growth for each craton during this period was around one cubic mile a year.[79]

About 2.5 billion years ago, nearly three-quarters of the present landmass had formed.[80] The North American continent was assembled from the joining of seven cratons, a process that completed around 2 billion years ago.[81] As the continents enlarged in size, they become more stable and eventually started to slow their erratic wanderings.

Although the total landmass was spreading out and continents had now developed, the Earth's crust was still relatively thin. On several of the continents, cracks (rifts) formed in this thin crust, which created an avenue for molten lava to spill out onto the Earth's surface. Gas bubbles coalesced in this lava, which created vesicle pockets in which agates later formed. Lake Superior agates, for example, were "born" in basaltic lava that flowed out of a rift zone that ran from what is now southeast Nebraska to Thunder Bay, Ontario. This rift zone, called the Keweenawan rift, was active around 1.1 billion years ago.[82] Its geologic chapter started when a "hot spot" developed beneath the current Lake Superior region. Upwelling of basaltic magma accumulated beneath this spot, forcing up the crust into a dome-like formation. The doming produced large-scale tensional forces, which eventually split the crust and caused opposite sides of the rift to move apart. This Keweenawan rift was believed to have been over a thousand miles long. Compare this with the Grand Canyon, the largest canyon on Earth today, which is only 277 miles long! Geologists have studied the remains of the Keweenawan rift zone. The most surprising thing they discovered is how productive this rift was in producing lava. Researchers estimate that successive flows spilled out of this rift piling lava over 65,000 feet tall and over 125 miles wide![83,84] This is more than twice the size of Mount Everest. In fact it was so productive that the lava pile eventually choked off and stopped the rifting. That is a good thing for those living in the United States because if the rifting had continued, the North American continent would have split in half.[85]

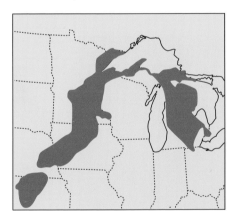

Figures 21 and 22
A graphical approximation of the Keweenawan Rift Zone is shown on the left. Lake Superior agates formed in the western part of this rift zone. A rift zone diagram is depicted below.

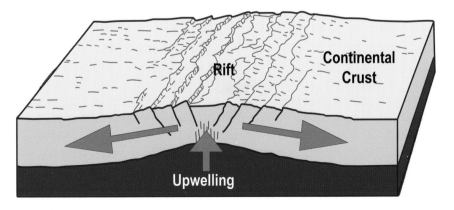

Similar rift zones existed all over the planet. There were tremendous outpourings of basalt that covered Washington, Oregon, and Idaho. Extensive volcanism also covered the Colorado Plateau, the Sierra Madre region in northwest Mexico, various areas in Africa, Madagascar, and Brazil. In fact, the lava flows in southern Brazil "paved" the area with 750,000 square miles of basalt, which is the largest lava field in geologic history. It is probably not a coincidence that many of today's agate rich areas correlate with the locations of these ancient rift Zones.[86,87,88,89,90]

For the past billion years, the continents, which sit on top of plates that are floating on the semi-molten mantle, have continued to move around, join together, split apart, and move around some more. Today, there are eight major tectonic plates and many more minor plates. All of these plates are moving in their respective directions between 2 to 4 inches per year. Over the eons, the movement of these plates has shaped the continents, formed mountains, and changed the surface of the Earth over and over again. Tectonic plates are able to move because the Earth's lithosphere (top layer) has a higher strength and lower density than the underlying asthenosphere. Their movement is driven by heat dissipation from the mantle. The areas where plates come together today define the places where geologic activity is taking place, including volcanoes and earthquakes.[91,92]

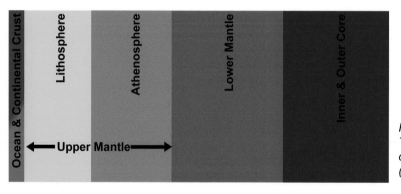

Figure 23
The layers
of the Earth
(not to scale)

The crust now makes up less than 1 percent of the Earth's radius and about 0.3 percent of its mass. This is significantly less than the shell of a chicken egg, which comprises 11 percent of an egg's weight. The continental crust is assembled like a layer cake with sedimentary rocks on top, granite and metamorphic rocks in the middle, and basaltic rocks on the bottom. If you include continental margins, the continental crust today covers about 45 percent of the Earth's surface. The continental crust varies from 6 to 45 miles thick and rises on average about 4,000 feet above sea level.[93] This contrasts with the oceanic crust that averages only four miles thick. Also, the oceanic crust is very young geologically. Most oceanic crust is younger than 170 million years old. The difference in ages is due to the recycling of oceanic crust into the mantle at the intersections between ocean plates and continental plates. In the battle of plate tectonics, the continental plates win every time.[94]

AGATE FORMATION

The remainder of Chapter 2 is intended for the intellectually curious and for those who want to get to the next level of understanding about agates. These semi precious gemstones have been studied for almost 250 years. At the end of the 18th century J.F. Hoffman (1761) and U.F.B. Bruckmann (1773) both published articles on agate formation.[95] Despite considerable research, most people agree that the agate formation process is still not yet completely understood. One reason, perhaps, is that no one has documented agate formation in real time, nor have agates been successfully manufactured in the laboratory.[96,97] It is amazing that we cannot make agate, but we can make diamonds, rubies, sapphires, and emeralds.[98,99]

There are reasons why scientists have tried to "break the agate formula." When developers install hot-water geothermal systems, for example, they often encounter problems with the precipitation of silica that causes scaling on the equipment. Oil well rigs also encounter problems with silica build up.[100,101] They could avoid these problems if they better understood how microcrystalline quartz forms. Although many of us rockhounds want to understand agates, we also hope that it is never possible to manufacture artificial agates.

We think that our species is the most highly evolved on Earth. Perhaps we are, but not on all levels. We cannot fully manipulate the formation of the mineralization phases of quartz, but there are at least five taxonomic phylums of organisms with members who can. Some species of algae, sponges, diatoms, bacteria, and radiolaria accomplish biomineralization, or the use of silicates to harden or stiffen body parts. Further study of the methods used by these organisms may provide new understandings about agate genesis.[102,103,104]

The subject of agate formation is complex. There are numerous variables and factors to consider. One recently published article influenced the content of this book. German geologist, Dr. Eckart Walger, began studying agate formation in the early 1950s. Both his master's thesis and doctoral dissertation involved agates. However, he made a living teaching and researching marine geology; agate research was something he did on the side. His professional life involved transport processes of beach sands. He was an expert not only in geology, but also in paleontology, sedimentology, fluid dynamics, and mathematics. He was known for his passionate teaching and the thoroughness of his research. All of his training and experience contributed useful skills that helped him investigate agate genesis.

After retiring, Dr. Walger decided to compile his life's work on agate formation and was in the process of publishing when he unexpectedly passed away on February 8, 2003.[105] His interests not only involved the optical appearance and mineralogical features of agates, but also the fundamental physico-chemical and hydrodynamical processes that formed agates. Dr. Walger's widow and sister knew that he had been preparing the manuscript, so they turned over his fragmentary computer files and handwritten documents to three other researchers: Georg Mattheiss, Volker Von Seckendorff, and Friedrich Liebau. The article entitled "The formation of agate structures: models for silica transport, agate layer accretion, and for flow patterns and flow regimes in infiltration channels" was published in August 2009 in the *Neues Jahbuch fur Mineralogie.*[106]

Figure 24
This Laguna Mexican agate has a dramatic connective channel as well as vivid colors, due to the mineral impurities supplied by the environment during its formation.

The remainder of this chapter is what evolved from the agate genesis research. When possible, diagrams, photographs, and non-technical language have been used to tell the agate formation story. Rather than mention the authors of the different concepts, we have only presented the concepts. This decision is not intended to take away from the tremendous contributions of all agate genesis researchers. The focus of this chapter is to present the concepts, not to serve as a comprehensive literature review. If you would like to identify the authors of the various theories, please refer to the corresponding cites in the list of references.

There are two main agate genesis theories. One suggests that agates formed from the inflow of mineral-rich aqueous solutions into empty vesicle pockets. This theory will be discussed first. The second is the silica gel theory, which suggests that agates formed from silica gel clumps in molten lava.

Since the subject of agate genesis is complex, we have taken the advice of Dr. Walger:

The situation suggests some fundamental considerations to the solution strategy of the enigma. Generally it holds true for a problem too big and too complex to be solved in total that it should be divided into separately treatable sub-problems, and the total solution is gained by synthesis of the sub-problems.[107]

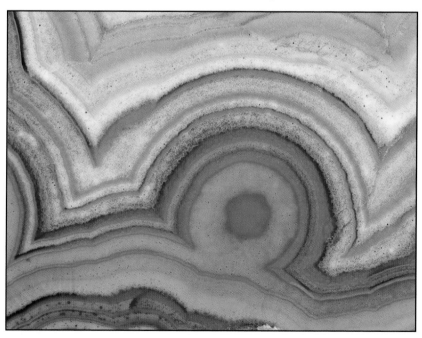

Figure 25
Sometimes nature can make the best art such as depicted in this spherulite formation in a Montana dry head agate.

INFLOW AGATE GENESIS THEORY

Agates are found on all continents and inside pockets of all three types of rock including igneous, sedimentary, and metamorphic.[108] When there were empty pockets inside host rock, sometimes they never filled in with secondary minerals. If the pockets did fill in, there were many factors that determined whether agate, some other type of quartz, or another mineral resulted. To generate agate, there had to be the right geologic structures, rock layer formations, environmental conditions, and chemical components.[109] Some hot springs in areas with geothermal activities and the white smokers on the ocean floor can deposit chalcedony, but agates do not seem to form in these environments because all the required conditions do not exist.[110]

The first agate genesis hypothesis is called the inflow theory. Those in this camp believe that silica rich fluids entered the empty vesicle pockets and supplied the minerals needed to form agate. They list the following factors as those that influenced agate formation.

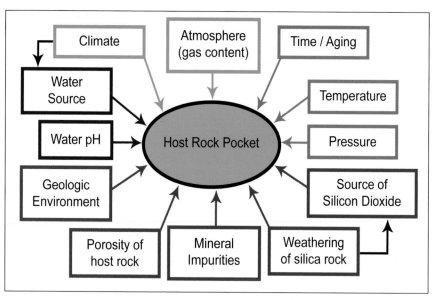

Figure 26
Several factors influenced agate genesis according to those who support the inflow theory. The light blue boxes are atmospheric influences, the dark blue boxes are water influences, the brown boxes are influences on or in the host rock, and the red boxes are other time and physical influences.

Carbon Dioxide → Carbon dioxide from the atmosphere mixed with water to form carbonic acid that weathered and eroded silica out of overlying silica-rich rock.[111,112] It appears that during most of the agate forming periods in Earth's history, the carbon dioxide levels were between 5 and 20 times higher than today's atmospheric levels.[113,114] These higher carbon dioxide levels were due at least in part to the extensive volcanic activity. In a recent study of the Kilauea volcano in Hawaii, the localized amount of carbon dioxide was over 24 percent, compared to the average in today's atmosphere of 3 percent.[115]

Climate-Supplied Water → The climate supplied rainwater mixed with carbon dioxide to form carbonic acid, which weathered silica out of overlying silica-rich rock. [116]

Water Transport → Water transported silica into rock pockets and seams. This water was usually meteoric, which is ground water that originated from precipitation. Water not only percolated down from rain, but also hydrothermal water, heated by volcanic hot spots, rose from deep within the Earth to fill the pores in host rock and vesicle pockets.

Water pH → If the pH of the water in the agate forming environment increased to between 7.5 and 8, due to the existence of alkaline lakes in the area, the silica would have: become more soluble, been more mobile in solution, and been able to more easily attach to each other to grow fibrous microcrystals and bands within the agate pocket.[117-122]

Source of Silicon Dioxide → Since agates are made of at least 98 percent silica, enough had to be available to initiate the self-organizing banding process. Inflow theorists think that silica was provided through the weathering and chemical breakdown (devitrification) of volcanic ash, rhyolitic tuff, and other rock that contained shards of volcanic glass or silica (e.g. sandstone and bentonite). Some believe that silica-rich sponges and other marine organisms could have also been a source.[123]

Weathering of silica rock → Carbonic acid, formed when carbon dioxide mixed with water, broke down source rock to supply silica.

Porosity of host rock → The pores in the host rock around the agate pocket would have had to become supersaturated with silica water. The supersaturated pores would then have served as a supply source for the silica that was transported into the pocket to form agate.

Geologic Environment → The majority of the world's agates formed in rhyolitic ash flow tuffs, basaltic lava flows, andesite rock formations, marine carbonate deposits, and continental claystone deposits.[124]

Mineral Impurities → Mineral impurities such as iron and aluminum played a significant role in the formation of agate. Not only did they interact with silica and influence the chemistry of the banding, they also contributed color to the agate bands.

Pressure → Within a single host rock area, the pressure could have varied from the top of the rock formation to the bottom. Since agate formed under low-pressure conditions, if there was a variation in pressure, agates would have formed near the top of the formation.

Temperature → Much work has been done to determine the temperature constraints on agate formation. The consensus seems to be that agates formed at lower temperatures (122-572°F, 50-300°C). Toward the upper end of this range, it appears that the silica molecules were able to combine to form small particles, or colloids, which are what accumulated to generate agate bands.[125] Higher temperatures also influenced the ability of the penetrating fluids to chemically weather the rock.[126] The fact that microcrystalline quartz contributed to the silicification of petrified wood, agatized coral, and sedimentary agates seems to verify that the temperatures must have been in the lower range, at least as compared to the temperature of molten lava which was greater than 2000°F (1093°C).[127]

Time / Aging → No one knows for sure how long it took agates to form. The conditions would have had to remain within the required parameters for the duration of agate genesis.

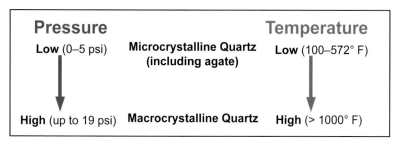

Figure 27
This chart shows the relative pressure and temperature influences on quartz formation.

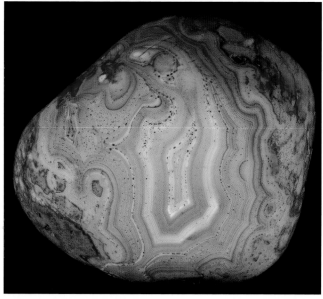

Figure 28
An intricately formed Lake Superior agate.

The inflow agate genesis theory is summarized below.

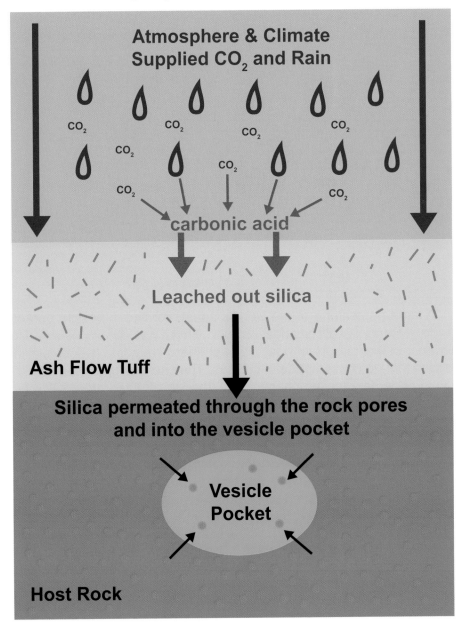

Figure 29
Agates formed in pockets inside host rock when the right conditions existed. Carbon dioxide mixed with water to form carbonic acid, which eroded silica out of overlying ash flow tuff or other silicified rock. The pores in the host rock filled with silica-rich fluid and became supersaturated. The silica-rich solution then flowed from the pores in the rock into the pocket. With the right temperature, pressure, and level of mineral impurity, agate filled in the pocket.

Possible Sources of Silica

Nature could not have made agate, or other quartz rocks for that matter, without silica (silicon dioxide). Most agates comprise around 98 percent silica.

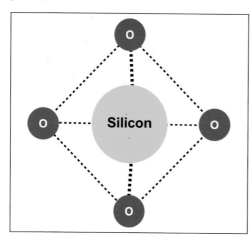

Figure 30
In the vast majority of silicates, there is a tetrahedral arrangement with four oxygen atoms surrounding a central silicon atom. Two of the oxygen atoms are shared with other molecules.

A large percentage of the world's agates formed in vesicle pockets inside volcanic basalt or andesite rock. These igneous rocks are usually poor in free silicon dioxide, although there are some hypocrystalline basalts that do contain silica inclusions. Thus, to free up silicon dioxide, it was necessary for the chemical weathering of other, more silica rich rocks. There may have been many different sources of silica, depending on the geologic environment and conditions. The following are some source possibilities:

- **Volcanic Ash** Volcanic ash may have spread great distances from explosive volcanoes, with the help of wind currents and rivers. In continental and marine sedimentary environments far removed from volcanic sources, air-fall-ash is thought to have been the source of silica for agate formation.[128] Some of the ash generated by pyroclastic flows contains up to 24 percent silica by weight.[129,130] Many of the agate producing areas in the world had active volcanoes that supplied ash during or before the agate formation period.[131] For example, the agates found in New Mexico were formed from silica supplied by volcanic ash.

- **Bentonite** This is a clay-like mineral that develops from the weathering of volcanic ash. The Khur agates in Iran are thought to have formed from the chemical weathering of silica out of bentonite.[132] The same is thought to be true for agates found in Nebraska.[133]

- **Rhyolitic Tuff** Many volcanoes were prolific in the amount of ash that they spewed out. Much of this ash compacted to form a welded tuff, such as rhyolite, which has a high silica content between 59 and 69 percent.[134-137] Thunder egg agates in Oregon formed in rhyolitic tuff.

- **Sandstone** Researchers in Queensland, Australia, have studied the geology of the area in which Agate Creek nodules are found. They determined that a large inland sea covered the basaltic lava flow, which caused thick layers of sandstone to be deposited. They feel that silica was leached from the sandstone and fed into the pockets to supply the agate-making material.[138,139]

- **Organic Sources** Agates that formed in sedimentary rock may have acquired silica from organic sources such as sponges, diatoms, and radiolaria.[140,141] Tampa Bay agatized coral from Florida may have formed from biogenic silica supplied by these organic sources.

- **Ground Water** Even though natural groundwater and streams have lower amounts of silica, given the geological time scale, it could be argued that the larger volume of water required to carry enough silica would not have been a problem.[142]

- **Hydrothermal Fluids** It is possible that hydrothermal fluid, which is groundwater heated by magma or a volcanic vent deep below the surface, could have leached silica out of rocks and become supersaturated. Later, these hydrothermal fluids could have risen up through fractures, fault lines, or porous rock to supply vesicle pockets with silica.[143-145] Direct crystallization of chalcedony is possible in certain hydrothermal conditions.[146] It has been found that rates of cooling and evaporation are slower with hydrothermal fluids, which would have given time for micro crystals of quartz to form.[147]

Figure 31
This photo shows ash flow tuff in Bandelier National Monument near Los Alamos, NM. The tuff was spewed out of two eruptions of the Jemez Volcano.

Whatever the source material, a chemical weathering (devitrification) process took place when carbon dioxide mixed with water to form carbonic acid, which then chemically decomposed the source rock to free up silica and other minerals. Decaying humus in the soil may have also contributed acids to make this process even more effective.[148]

Usually, silica took the form of silicic acid, which is comprised of silicon, hydrogen, and oxygen. Fluids within the rock pores become supersaturated with silicic acid. But since this form of silica is inherently unstable, it would have rapidly condensed and eliminated water to form polymer colloids. These at first were small particles floating in the fluid between the pores of the host rock. Over time, the colloids would have joined together. This occurs because silica molecules love their friends. You can think of the polymerizing process as lots of silica molecules "holding hands" to form longer chains of silica molecules.[149-151] This is an important step for agate genesis because it appears that under normal agate forming conditions, quartz does not crystallize directly from single molecules of silicon dioxide suspended in an aqueous solution.[152]

This polymerization process was most effective when there was a high degree of supersaturation (lots of silicon dioxide molecules), lower temperatures (<212°F, 100°C), and pH levels above 7.5.[153] Also, it is thought that if there was a slow rise in supersaturation, a slow decrease in temperature, and a slow increase in pH—which was a likely scenario—then there was an increase in the development of silica polymers.[154] It is these polymer colloids of silica that were transported into the vesicle pockets to make agate.

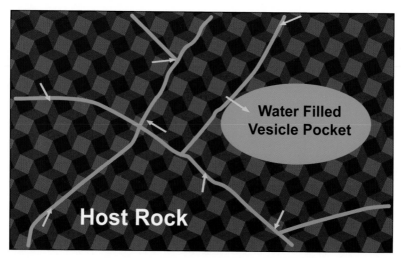

Figure 32
This diagram illustrates the relationship between the matrix host rock, the capillary fractures, and the agate pocket. Silica rich fluids moved from the inter-granular pores in host rock into the capillary fractures and then into the vesicle pocket.

Silica Transport

Once the pores in the host rock became supersaturated with silica colloids, the next step in the agate genesis process was for silica to be transported into the vesicle pocket.[155] When the host lava rock first began to cool and solidify into rock, contraction took place throughout the matrix, producing a network of cracks called "fractures." At the top of the lava flow, there tended to be more cooling-induced fractures as well as more vesicle pockets, since the gas bubbles within the flow rose to the top. Over time, these fractures served as a conduit and facilitated the movement of fluids throughout the host rock. There was not only meteoric water from precipitation that percolated down through the crack system, but magmatic water from volcanic activity and hydrothermal water from deep within the Earth also were transported through the network of cracks.[156]

In many cases, at least one of these fractures happened to connect with the vesicle pocket. What developed was a system of interconnected pores, capillary fractures, and larger vesicle pockets within the host rock—all of which were filled with water.[157]

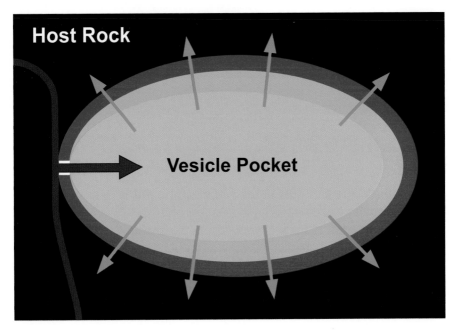

Figure 33
This diagram shows how silica-rich fluid entered from the capillary fracture in the host rock into the vesicle pocket (dark blue arrow). To satisfy the law of continuity (inflow must equal outflow), silica-depleted water recycled back out of the pocket and returned to the host rock through the semi-permeable layers of the agate (light blue arrows).

Even though all the voids in the host rock were filled with water, the silica concentrations varied. The silica saturation in the smaller pores of the host rock attained a higher concentration, for various complex hydrologic reasons, while the concentration in the larger vesicle pockets was significantly lower. Consequently, a difference in concentration level (gradient) developed between the inter-granular pore solution and the fluid within the "agate" pocket.[158] This gradient was the driving force that caused the higher saturated solution in the pores to move into the vesicle pocket either through the capillary fractures or directly through the pores of the outer husk of the vesicle. The driving force of this fluid movement was the need to equalize the silica concentration levels.

Figure 34
This close up of an agate from Michipicoten Island in Lake Superior clearly shows the capillary fracture in the host rock that "fed" the agate pocket.

Once the silica-rich fluid started to flow into the pocket, the concentration of silica in the cavity fluid increased and equilibrium of the supersaturation concentration levels was reached, slowing down the inflow. As the flow slowed, silica colloids precipitated out of solution and attached to the walls of the pocket to form a membrane. When the precipitated membrane formed, it took up space, causing some of the water to be forced back out of the agate pocket. This outflow was distributed over the entire agate circumference. This is called the "continuity condition." Basically, what this means is that there has to be an outflow to equal the amount of inflow since water cannot be compressed (See Figure 33.)[160-163]

The silica-poor water was transported up the concentration gradient, escaping through the semi-permeable agate layers and back into the intergranular pores of the host rock. Since the host rock around the pocket was depleted of fluid, the outflow of silica-poor water was in part driven by the need to again equalize concentration levels.[164]

Inside the "agate" pocket, as the silica colloids precipitated out of solution to form the membrane, the silica concentration again declined, causing more silica-rich fluids to enter, and the process repeated itself.[165] The driving force exerted by the concentration gradient was maintained as long as chemical weathering in the surrounding rock continued to supply silica, which would then move through the host rock as "lateral secretion." This is a geologic process by which fluids such as carbonic acid dissolved minerals from rock and re-deposited the minerals in nearby pores.[166-167]

In most cases, fluids entered the agate cavities through capillary fractures that happened to intersect near the outside of the vesicle cavity, as is shown in Figure 34. A chalcedony band always formed first, immediately lining the inner surface of the cavity. If a connective channel perforated this outer band, then that channel delivered fluids to the pocket.[168] If the first agate band was not perforated, or if there was no intersection with a capillary fracture, these agates developed instead by direct diffusion. Silica-rich fluids diffused from the host rock pores through the semi-permeable agate layers directly into the cavity. Proof of agate "porosity" is demonstrated by the fact that agates can be artificially colored by injecting dyes through the semi-permeable agate layers.[169-170] This porosity would have allowed direct diffusion as well as continuity outflow (See Figure 35.)

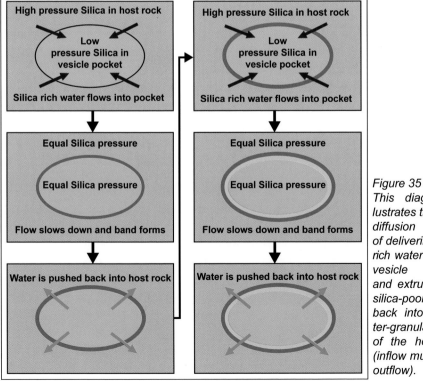

Figure 35
This diagram illustrates the direct diffusion method of delivering silica-rich water into the vesicle pocket and extruding the silica-poor water back into the inter-granular pores of the host rock (inflow must equal outflow).

Infiltration Channels

The tube-shaped connective channels are central to understanding agate formation. They connected the interior of the agate to the exterior. While conducting research for this book, museum staff examined 774 Brazilian agate slabs between 2 and 6 inches in diameter. As we carefully looked at each slab, we tabulated how many showed evidence of connective channels. It is important to point out that these were random slabs, so that in all cases one slab represented only a portion of the original specimen. As an example, for the five-inch diameter agates we estimate there would have been approximately eight slabs cut from each rock. We were surprised to discover channels in 56 percent of the slabs that we looked at! One conclusion you can draw from the occurrence of these channels is that they are not random and must therefore play a role in agate formation.[171]

Those who believe that these connective structures are "exit channels" suggest that on occasion agates must have had to relieve pressure via an expulsion release. We can understand why a lot of researchers have labeled these as "tubes of escape." As can be seen in Figure 36, the bands next to the tube-like channel thin toward the outside of the agate. It appears that this thinning is in response to the material in the center of the agate pushing out.[172] Some researchers believe that the outward extrusion deformed previously established bands, rather than fracturing them, thus proving that the bands had not yet hardened and must have been in a gelatin state.[173] Others suggest that the outward push occurred because as crystallization inside the pocket progressed, the agate would have occupied a larger volume and caused material to be squeezed from inside the agate nodule toward the outside.[174] Still others say that material was extruded out of the pocket by expansion from heat generated by chemical reactions that occurred during crystallization.[175] In some cases, the "tubes of escape" do not extend all the way from the center to the exterior of the nodule, indicating that there was not enough pressure to force a complete tube of escape.[176] Because most of these tubes are wider at the exterior, it has been suggested that just before material was expelled through the husk, it had to break through the resistant skin, causing it to bunch up at the exit point.[177] Those who feel that the channels are "exit tubes" argue that they could not be entrance channels because inflowing silica would have sealed up the channels and not allowed additional material to infiltrate the pocket. Although many of these out-flow enthusiasts stand behind their opinion that the tubes are "exit channels," some admit that they are not really convinced that enough internal pressures would have developed inside the agate pocket to create the need for a pressure release.[178]

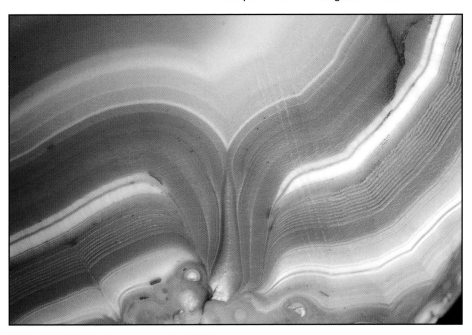

Figure 36
The connective channel with thinning bands connects the interior of the agate to the exterior in this Lake Superior agate found in Copper Harbor, Michigan.

There are also several scientists who support the fact that the channels are inflow in origin. Most of the original researchers did not have access to modern scanning electron microscopes, but only had the tool of observation, felt that the channels are inflow structures. Von Leonhard in 1823, for example, labeled these tubes as "infiltration channels." He defined them as "structures formed by the inflow of the silica-precipitating solution into the cavity in which the agate structure was built up."[179]

There are a few analogies that explain how the channels may have been able to stay open to continuously provide agate pockets with silica-rich solutions. The dynamics of the channels can be compared to keeping a faucet dripping in the winter so that water pipes don't freeze. Another analogy would be the cardiovascular system. As long as there is a positive blood pressure, blood particles are kept from attaching to the walls of blood vessels.[181,182] A third analogy is borrowed from sedimentation flow dynamics involving the impact of flowing water. Picture a river entering a lake. The flow of water keeps the junction point open. This is the concept of "scour," which is the hole left behind when sediment is washed away from the bottom of a river due to the motion of water.[183]

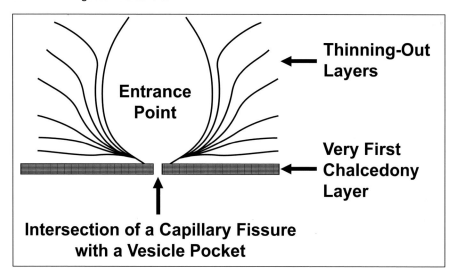

Figure 37
This diagram shows the different components of an infiltration channel.[180]

The geometrical shapes of connective channels can vary. However many take on the shape of a green onion, as depicted in the figure above. The reason why the entrance point into the agate pocket may have stayed open is because of the power of the inflowing fluid, or what is technically called a laminar plane free jet. Let's just say that it is a "jet stream" that forms when fluid is forced through the small opening at the entrance point of the connective channel. This jet stream prevents minerals from attaching near the entrance point:

> *The effect of attachment prevention has its maximum in the immediate vicinity of the entrance point of the jet and is decreasing with increasing distance from that point. Even if being also very faint, when sweeping along the wall the jets are obviously effective enough, to diminish the probability of the colloidal silica particles … that are carried along the wall to be attached to it.* [184]

Scientists haven't just made this statement; they have developed mathematical proofs with equations based on research from a number of experts, including Einstein. The mathematical equations prove that the model "is within an order of magnitude of the cavity dimensions." [185,186] Those that support the concept that the channels are inflow structures summarize the parameters as follows:

> *Many agates exhibit banding that narrows and is sometimes completely cut off. This pinching off of bands usually occurs near the fill hole. One theory about this feature is that the current velocity of solutions entering … the vesicle is fastest at the fill hole. The faster current flow associated with this relatively small*

area carried away the fine-grained chalcedony and accessory iron-oxides from the depositional surface. Pinched-off bands within the vesicle were probably caused by eddy currents similar to those seen in rivers. These high-velocity flow areas prohibited uniform accumulation of chalcedony.[187]

More proof to support the fact that these are inflow channels is the fact that the orientation of the connective channels is random around the pocket. If the channels formed as outflow from pressure release, there would be a tendency for that release to be influenced by gravity. After tabulating 774 agate slabs, but looking at closer to 2,000 agates, we can say with certainty that the orientation of the connective channels is random. We can draw this conclusion because a lot of the slabs had sections with water-level bands that were formed under the influence of gravity. Thus, given that these identifiable slabs told us which way was "up," we determined that the connective channels were completely random.[188]

Figure 38
The infiltration area in the inflow channel filled with water- level banding. If this was an outflow channel caused by pressure release, it would be difficult to explain how the water-level banding would have formed.

Figure 39 shows obstructions within the connective channel. If this were an outflow channel caused by a pressure release powerful enough to burst through the outer husk wall, there would not be random non-deformed crystals growing lazily in the middle of the channel. Instead, these aggregate growths appear to have developed within the channel, changing the flow of incoming fluid. Also, the crystals appear to be growing in toward the center of the pocket. Thus, the mineral aggregate was effective as an obstacle disturbing the inflow system and, accordingly, modifying the spatial distribution of the bands that formed near the channel opening.[189,190]

Figure 39
The infiltration channel in this Mexican Laguna agate has aggregates of mineral impurity (probably calcite) that grew in the channel. The stalks of the aggregate appear to point inward and are not deformed, which would have occurred if the channel formed as outflow from pressure release.

Similarly, if the channels formed from outflow, it seems that they would be solid with material. We observed several connective channels that in fact are hollow. The hollow opening seems to indicate that inflow into the cavity stopped before there was complete filling of the connective channel.[191]

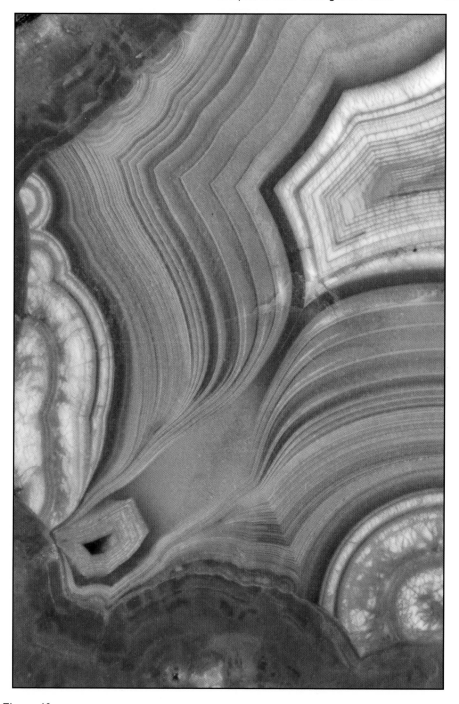

Figure 40
A separate geode-like formation with a hollow center formed in this channel. If the channel was created with outflow pressure release, it is not likely that a hollow opening would have developed. This is a Lake Superior agate that has post-formation staining from iron oxide rich water.

The next series of photos shows
infiltration channels in cross section.

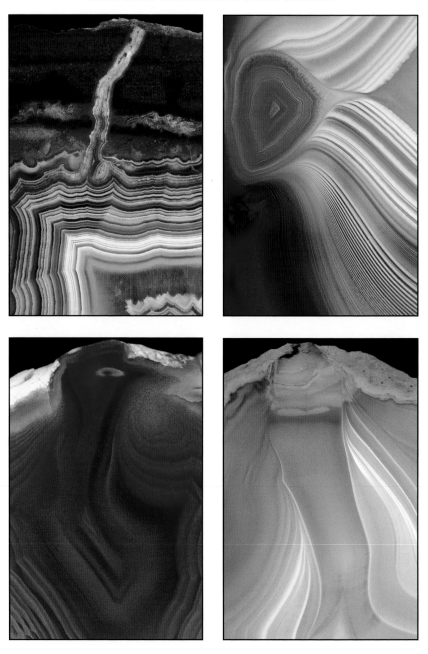

Figures 41, 42, 43, and 44
The upper left photo is a Mexican crazy lace agate. In the upper right is a photo of a Queensland, Australia agate. Notice the new fortification pattern that grew in the channel. The lower left is Mexican Laguna agate. It appears that the channel completed its fill with fortification bands from inflowing fluids. The lower right is a Brazilian agate with an amazing inflow channel.

As the colloidal silica particles entered the infiltration channel, they were carried away by the faint inflow current. That is why after the start of the convection, the first agate bands thinned out at a sharp angle towards the entrance point of the channel. With increasing distance away from the entrance point, the flow dissipated, allowing the silica colloids to precipitate out and attach. As these thinning out layers started to accumulate, the actual entrance point moved increasingly deeper into the vesicle pocket. This caused the thinning-out bands to become more and more inclined toward the entrance point, as shown in Figures 41-44. Eventually, the infiltration channel finished forming and developed a narrow slot that stayed open and continued to feed the pocket. After this stage was reached, significant agate banding conditions existed to add thick sequences of layers.[192,193]

Each infiltration channel is a bit different. This is because the amount of available energy caused by the inflow jet determined the characteristics of the infiltration channel. The channels can also vary when there is growth of mineral inclusions or crystals within the channels, which then impacts the forming of subsequent bands. This variety of infiltration channel configurations may hold the key to understanding agate formation:

> *Infiltration channel structures show so many specific features and spatial relationships, that they cannot be generated by a process which would inevitably bring in a high degree of randomness.... From the approach presented here no exact data can be derived, but it offers a reasonable argument that the model proposed is debatable, and a concept path, along which a further approach to "truth" can be expected.[194]*

There is one more area of proof that connective channels are the result of inflow, and not outflow. If the thinning layers were deformed as a result of pressure release, then it makes sense that the orientation of the silica fibers in the chalcedony bands would have deformed due to the force of the extrusion. Scanning electron microscope pictures of the fibers in the thinning out bands indicate that this is not the case: their orientation is perpendicular to the curvature of the band.[195]

Concentric Banding

Although it is true that no two agates are alike, even slabs cut from the same agate are different, there are control mechanisms that are universal in the formation of all agates. Researchers who have studied agates from all over the world have discovered similarities in texture, microstructure, and rhythmic zoning.[196] Originally it was not known whether the formation of agate banding was due to external control from the surrounding environment, or to some type of internal self-organizing rhythm. Scientists have concluded that the crystallizing process was in fact dictated by certain self-organizing dynamics. In other words, the oscillating textures resulted from internal dynamics of the growth itself, not from changing conditions outside the agate.197 Whatever these internal control mechanisms were, they operated world-wide to form all types of agate.[198] The conditions that surrounded the pocket may not have directly controlled agate banding, but they did have some influence. Temperature, pressure, silica levels, and impurity concentrations also impacted agate genesis.[199] Thus, the internally controlled rhythms were superimposed on the effects of the changing conditions outside the pocket to contribute to the beauty of the banded agate.[200]

There are basically two types of agate banding. First is what some call "common agate banding" that consists of layers that are circumscribed in concentric rings around the walls of the vesicle pocket. There is no consensus on the name for this type of banding, but some of the descriptive names include concentric banding, fortification banding, adhesional banding, and wall-paper banding.[201]

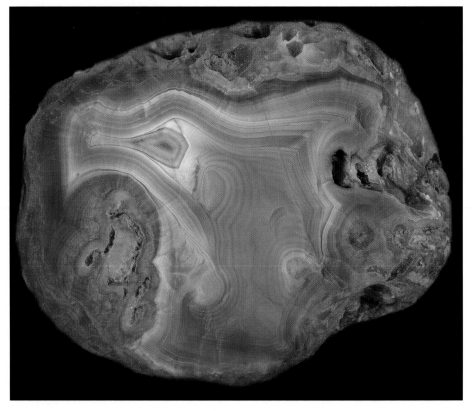

Figure 45
This is a concentrically banded Lake Superior agate. Do you see the eagle?

As presented in Chapter 1, the primary form of quartz that makes up agate is chalcedony. This form of quartz has microscopically fibrous structure, made of elongated silica rods that grew into an interwoven texture that gives chalcedony its great strength and durability.[202] These fibers are actually made up of much finer and nearly parallel fibers, which themselves are composed of a large number of tiny elongated quartz crystals.[203] One of the most interesting things about the way that these crystals and fibers grew is that they developed nearly perpendicular to the orientation of the agate bands.[204]

You can liken the agate crystal formation to a legion of soldiers lining up, shoulder to shoulder. The agate bands developed as fingers of silica that grew progressively from the outside of the cavity toward the inside. The first step was the formation of a coating of silica surrounding the cavity. Many agates have what can be called as "the very first chalcedony layer." This band is distinctly different from that of all the following layers. It is usually not thicker than 3 mm and is often transparent, if weathering or post-formation mineral staining has not altered it.[205-207]

Figure 46
This Mexican agate shows how the very first chalcedony layer on the outside of the agate (bottom section of photo) is different and more translucent than the other banded layers.

An influence on the formation of the first banding layer was the coarse inner surface of the vesicle pocket. This rough surface provided "nucleation centers" on which the silica fibers grew. The undulating nature of the bumpy crust caused the fibers to grow in bundles that oriented inward. As the bundles reached a certain width, they came into contact with other bundles, forming distinct boundary lines. Based on the texture of this arrangement, these are classified as "parabolic, fibrous wall-lining bundles."[208,209] These bundles are shown in the following photo, and graphically illustrated in the diagram below.

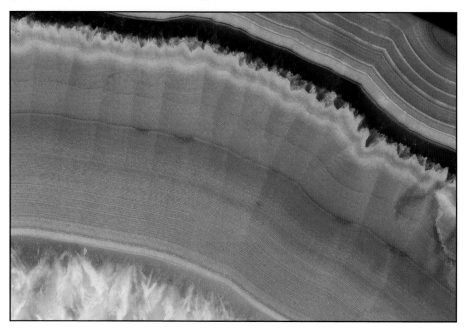

Figure 47
This photo clearly depicts the parabolic, fibrous wall-lining bundles.

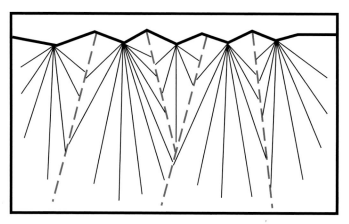

Figure 48
This graphic shows the fiber bundles. The coarse inner surface of the husk is the thick black line on top. The orange dashes are the boundaries between fiber bundles.

Once the agate pocket started to fill in, distinct difference developed in successive bands. The obvious banding variation resulted from dramatic changes that occurred in or around the agate pocket. Less obvious variation developed because of slight differences in the chemical make-up of alternating bands. There are actually a lot more banding layers than what can be seen with the unaided human eye. This high number of bands was first discovered by Sir David Brewster, an English scientist, who was best known for his discoveries of the kaleidoscope and stereoscopic microscope. Using the latter device, Brewster determined that agates have up to 17,000 bands per inch![210] Modern scanning electron microscopes indicate that the actual number of bands is much higher.

The first layer of chalcedony banding usually formed very quickly when the initial super-saturation condition developed in the pocket. If the silica colloids entered the pocket via direct diffusion they had to be small enough to penetrate through the semi-permeable layers. They were probably not long strings of molecules, but instead were chains of only five to ten silica molecules. As the concentration level in the pocket increased, more and more silica molecules started "to hold hands." The kinetics, or the rate of the chemical reaction forming the molecule chains, intensified.[211] Once the concentration of embryonic colloid chains increased to the super-saturation level, there was acceleration of the polymerization process.[212]

As the amount and size of the polymer chains floating in solution inside the agate pocket increased, the colloids started to adhere to the inside wall of the cavity. Since the silica was already in a polymerized state, it took less energy for them to precipitate out of solution and attach.[213] The speed of this attachment was influenced by the saturation of colloids, the size of polymerized particles, the cooling of the solution (that may have paralleled the cooling of the host rock), a decrease in pH, and the presence of trace element ions that acted as coagulants, such as various forms of magnesium, iron, and aluminum.[214,215] As the colloids attached and "found their friends," they formed a thin, gel-like membrane. With increasing thickness of the gel layer, the concentration of "free" silica colloids in the pocket's fluid decreased, and the accretion (attachment) to the vesicle wall slowed down, finally coming to a temporary halt. Because the process stopped, there was never complete closure of the silicified texture in the membrane layer. Therefore, a residual porosity remained that allowed for excess silica-poor fluids to then be extruded back out of the pocket and for new silica-rich fluids to enter during the next membrane-forming part of the cycle.[216,217] The amount of outflow of silica-poor fluid equaled the amount of inflow of silica-rich fluid. Not long after each membrane developed, the gel in the membrane spontaneously formed quartz microcrystals to harden the layer.[218]

Although scientists cannot make agate banding happen in the laboratory, they can measure the intimate detail and chemical components of agate banding. It appears that silica colloids were not alone. In fact, researchers have determined that other minerals contributed to the formation of bands, and ions helped to control the process of coagulation.[219] The boundaries between individual bands were sharply contrasting either because different types of quartz crystals formed, in response to changing temperature, pressure, or silica concentration, or because of the presence of trace element impurities.[220]

In some cases, the mineral impurities, such as iron and copper, simply tried to "get in the way." If these impurities had the same electrical charge as silica colloids, they were incompatible and were pushed to the inside and away from the leading edge of membrane formation, settling in the troughs and at the tips of the crystal fibers as the gel membrane solidified.[221,222] Over time, these impurities built up and somewhat blocked silica colloids from getting to the active membrane surface. When there were enough of the impurities built up, they formed their own bands or spheroid deposits, as shown in Figures 49 and 50.[223] After the impurity's concentration was reduced because the free molecules precipitated and attached, silica growth continued again.[224] It is interesting to note that the spatial distribution of these trace elements decreased from the husk to the center of the agate.[225]

Figure 49
This Lake Superior agate photo shows red bands with iron oxide impurities that precipitated between layers of chalcedony. Note that the iron oxide bands decreased toward the center of the agate (top portion of photo).

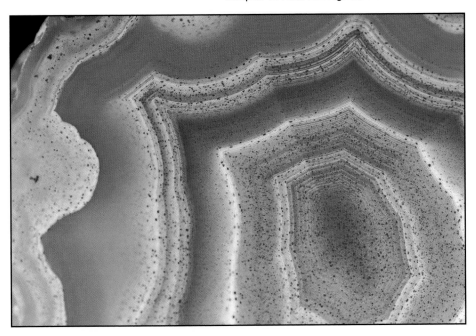

Figure 50
Sometimes iron oxide formed individual polka dot spheroids, rather than forming distinct iron oxide bands, as shown in this Mexican Laguna agate.

This rhythmic process is like a crystal making party. First the silica colloids decided that they wanted to have a crystal making party. One thing about silica, is that it is very discriminatory. Thus, they didn't let the impurities come to their party and kicked them to the inside of the pocket. But the impurities were jealous, so they built up a barrier layer until they had enough to have their own crystal making party. They partied themselves out as they laid down their band, and then the silica started again.

Another way to look at this oscillating process is that an "internal rhythm" developed with alternating stages of inflow, crystallization, and outflow. The differences in silica concentrations between the host rock pores and the pocket caused silica-rich fluids to flow into the pocket. Once the concentrations equalized, the flow stopped, allowing silica colloids to attach to the inner surface and form a membrane layer. As the silica colloids in the pocket were used up, the attachment process stopped and the membrane crystallized. The resulting semi-permeable membrane and crystal layers then allowed silica-poor fluids to flow out of the pocket and silica-rich fluids again started to flow in, beginning the process again.[226]

This oscillating process is sometimes referred to as the Belousov-Zhabotinsky reaction or Liesegang ring reaction. What is most interesting about these reactions is that there is "excitability" that is caused by a chemical reaction, allowing patterns to self-organize. The Liesegang phenomenon has been investigated for over 100 years. Like agate genesis, there is not agreement among scientists about how these self-organized patterns develop. Oscillating patterns can not only be created in the laboratory (see photos below), but they are also seen in nature in the structure of bones, teeth, bacterial colonies, etc. Although the agate genesis process is thought by some to be a type of Belousov-Zhabotinsky or Liesegang reaction, others feel that agate genesis is significantly more complex. These reactions do not in and of themselves describe how agates self-organized to form banding. If it were that simple, scientists would have by now applied these reactions to manufacture artificial agates.[227]

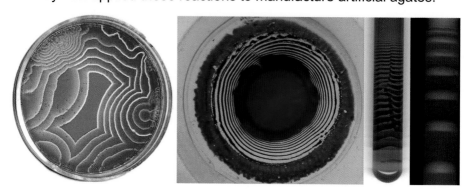

Figures 51 and 52
The left photo is a Belousov-Zhabotinsky reaction. Permission was granted to use this photo from Dr. Stephen W. Morris, University of Toronto Physics Department, www.flickr. com/photos/nonlin/. The right photo is a Liesegang Ring reaction. Permission was granted to use this photo from DR. ANDRÁS BÜKI, www.insilico.hu/liesegang/index.html. Although both reactions can produce concentric rings within a gelatin material, neither method has been successful in producing solid microcrystalline quartz with rhythmic banding.[228A, 228B]

Other trace elements that entered into the agate pocket actually helped the silica to form chalcedony bands. These ions seemed to stimulate coagulation of the silica colloids, which facilitated band formation.[229,230] When the bands were developing, trace element ions entered into the lattice structure of the individual microcrystals of quartz. These trace element molecules were larger than the silica molecules, so they took up more space. The silica fibers tried to maintain their structural continuity while simultaneously making room for the larger ions, which resulted in the fibers growing in a twisted orientation.[231-235] This in turn twisted the lattice structure within the entire band. It is thought that aluminum was usually the catalyst, but potassium, sodium, zinc, barium and calcium ions may have also been responsible. All of these ions were capable chemically of forcing this twisting, plus they occurred in the host rock that usually surrounded agate pockets.[236,237] These catalysts apparently helped to link the negatively charged silica particles. As the silica crystallized, aluminum accumulated at the front of the active crystallization surface. There was an internal rhythm created that alternated between crystal growth, diffusion or infiltration of mineral rich fluids into the agate pocket, and outflow of mineral poor fluids out of the pocket.[238]

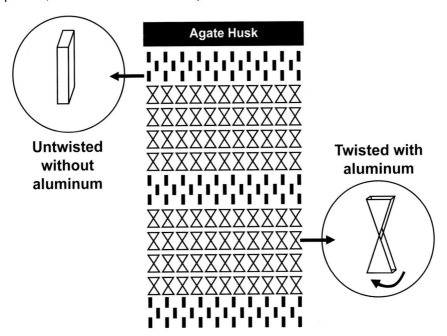

Figure 53
This diagram graphically illustrates the alternating layers of twisted and untwisted bands in the fibrous microcrystalline structure of agate. MODIFIED FROM WANG AND MERINO, 1990.[239]

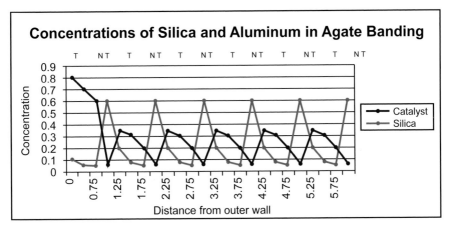

Figure 54
This chart shows the alternating concentration levels in the bands between silica and aluminum. The relative growth of the agate bands is from left to right. Every other band has high aluminum content, which twists (T) the fibers. Those without aluminum were not twisted (NT). MODIFIED FROM WANG AND MERINO, 1990.[240]

As the agate bands formed in this oscillating fashion, due to the alternating layers of twisted and nontwisted layers, a zigzag appearance resulted. This "wrinkle banding," also called "Runzelbanderung," was influenced by the crystallization temperature as well as by the inclusions of ions in the fibrous structure. This banding pattern can be seen with the naked eye because the nontwisted fibers are coarser than the finer, twisted fibrous bands, which changes their optical properties.[241]

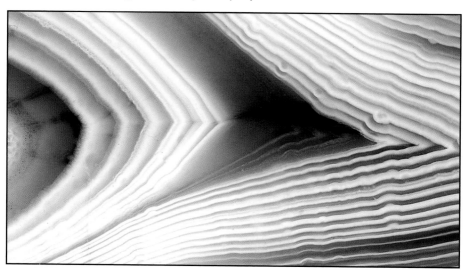

Figure 55
The optical differences in the twisted and nontwisted agate bands can be seen in this Botswana, Africa, agate photograph.

This beautiful wrinkle banding can also be seen in the scanning electron microscope photo of agate banding below.[242] Another name for this banding pattern is zebraic chalcedony.

Therefore, the optical character of agate banding can be caused by the inclusion of mineral impurities between the agate bands, as well as from the inclusion of catalyst ions that twist alternating layers, changing their optical and physical characteristics. Depending on where the bands are within the agate, and the specific conditions that existed when each band formed, the width of a band can vary from 8 to 100 nanometers. (A nanometer is equal to one billionth of a meter.)[243]

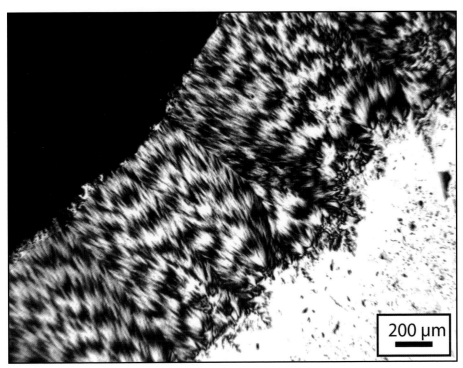

200 µm

Figure 56
This scanning electron photo shows the wrinkle banding that forms because mineral impurities twist some of the agate fibers. Used by permission from Dr. K.L. Milliken, University of Texas at Austin.

During formation, the width of the bands usually changed between the outer husk and the center of the pocket. Bands on the outer edge averaged around 50 microns (one micron is one thousandth of a millimeter, or one thousand nanometers), increasing to over 400 microns in the center. This change in band width is not a constant, and varied considerably from agate to agate.[244,245] This band width trend probably occurred because, as the agate developed, the amount of trace elements in the surrounding host rock was depleted, thus reducing the amount fed into the pocket. When the trace element concentration decreased, twisting of the chalcedony fibers decreased, causing a subsequent decrease in the oscillating switch between twisted and nontwisted bands. This increased the size of the crystals, which increased the width of the band. Also, as the size of the pocket became smaller because it was filling in, the potential for osmotic pressure differences decreased, slowing the inflow of new fluids.[246] The tighter the pocket opening became, the more contorted were the bands. The fibers never seemed to "collide" with each other, however, even when there was not enough space.[247]

Figure 57
The lower right side of this Black River agate from Argentina clearly shows the band width increase from the outer husk (bottom right) into the center of the agate. It has a hemispherical formation on the bottom left side, too.

In most agate specimens from all over the world, there is a progression of banding types that developed. The type of silica crystal progressively grades from cryptocrystalline silica at the husk to fibrous chalcedony to larger macrocrystalline quartz crystals. This occurs because, when the silica first started to crystallize, the process happened so quickly that cryptocrystalline silica formed first. This is microcrystalline quartz, but the crystals are small and somewhat disorganized. The rapid growth of microcrystals would have resulted in decreasing silica concentrations in the pocket, which would have led to progressively slower growth of chalcedony fibrous crystals. This is the section of agate with the typical concentric bands. Gradually, the level of silica concentration and trace elements became sufficiently low so that macrocrystalline quartz began to form. This progression is illustrated in Figure 58.[248,249]

Another thing that changed the characteristics of agate bands is the amount of water that was caught within the bands. When the agate bands first started to form, the process happened so quickly that more water tended to get trapped within the crystalline structure. As the agate filled in, the process slowed down and water was more efficiently recycled back into the host rock's pore spaces, with less water becoming trapped. In fact, when macrocrystalline quartz filled the center of the agate, it had almost no water content. The relative amounts of water are depicted in Figure 59.[250,251A]

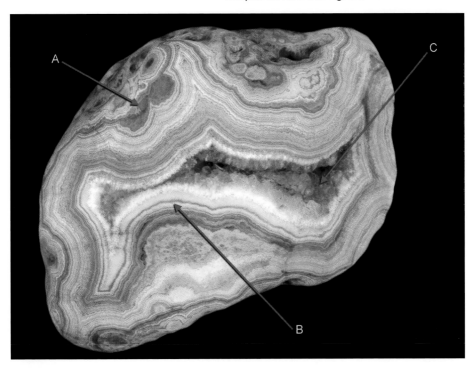

Figure 58
The three zones of formation are shown in this photo of a Crowley Ridge agate from Arkansas: (A) cryptocrystalline quartz (nearest the husk), (B) chalcedony fibrous banding, and (C) macrocrystalline center fill.

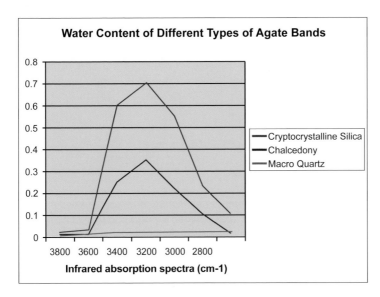

Figure 59
As the agate pocket filled in, the amount of water in the three main types of banding decreased. This chart was modified from an unpublished paper written by David R. Lee.[251B]

As the agate pockets filled in, the influxes of compositionally diverse fluids with respect to silica saturation and trace elements could have varied, forming a variety of different types of bands.[252] Also, varying crystallization conditions may have upset the chalcedony banding, causing the formation of non-fibrous microcrystalline quartz layers, or even intervening macrocrystalline quartz layers. Sometimes, these non-fibrous layers served as new nucleation centers when the fibrous conditions became favored again.[253] If there was enough silica, the vesicle pockets become completely filled. If not, geodes with hollow centers and macro crystals with termination points developed.[254] The agate pictured below shows several different periods of genesis, including chalcedony that grew over the macro crystal points.

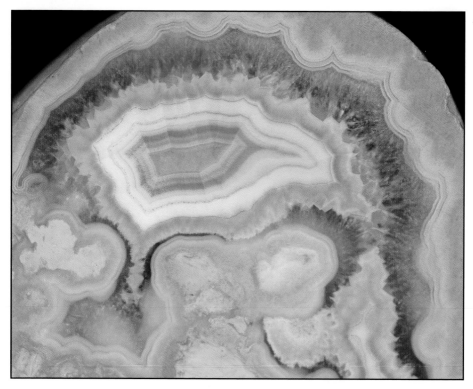

Figure 60
This complex Lake Superior agate shows several different agate genesis stages including quartz termination points that were later covered up with additional chalcedony banding.

One final point to make about agate banding is that sometimes things did not go according to plan, and bizarre banding patterns developed. This could have happened for several reasons, but one is that the host rock areas supplying different agate pockets may have overlapped. When there was a pocket that had its own section of host rock from which to draw fluids, a feedback situation was created between silica-rich fluids flowing into the pocket, and silica-poor fluids recycling out of the pocket. If there were vesicle pockets that were close together, there may have been an overlapping of drainage/supply areas that disrupted the normal feedback mechanism. In this case, the corresponding processes of agate formation in adjoining pockets became unpredictable, creating bizarre banding patterns in adjoining agates.[255]

Horizontal Banding

The other main type of agate banding, although less common, has straight parallel bands instead of concentric rings. Again, there is no consensus on the name for this banding pattern but some are horizontal banding, Uruguay banding, gravitational banding, onyx banding, parallel banding, water-line banding, and water-level banding.[256] A typical example is shown in the figure below:

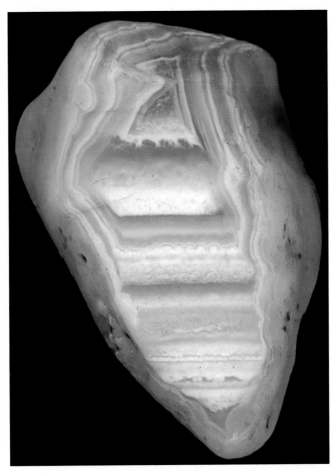

Figure 61
This agate started filling in with concentric banding. Then, larger silica colloids grew in the fluid within the pocket and settled out with gravity to form horizontal water-level banding.

Agates with horizontal banding formed when silica particles settled out by the force of gravity, mostly at or near the bottom of vesicles. Occasionally horizontal bands developed in other places within the agate nodule as conditions changed to favor this type of banding.[257] It seems that gravitational banding mostly formed during the early phase of agate genesis. At this stage, chemical weathering of the silica source rock was most active, supplying the largest amount of silicic acid. As the silica initially infiltrated or diffused into the pocket, it quickly formed large silica colloids that settled out by gravity into the bottom of the vesicle pocket.[258] Just as it is true with the formation of concentric agates, trace element ions played a role in helping to stimulate the coagulation/precipitation of the silica colloids into horizontal bands.[259]

These rarer types of agate are usually found in continental flood basalts, associated with large fissure eruptions. This lava resulted from hotspots or upwelling plumes within the mantle. Because of the deep origin of this lava, the temperature of the molten mass was higher, resulting in lower viscosity lava flows that spread out over vast areas.[260]

Horizontally banded agate differs from the concentric banded agate in many ways. First, the bands tend to be much thicker and can have less regularity. In some cases individual bands can break apart along their "bedding planes," or they can merge and continue as thinner concentric bands that circumscribe the cavity.[261] The silica crystals are also different. Unlike concentric banded agates with their fibrous structure, the microcrystals in horizontally banded agates are granular in texture. As the particles settled out, there was stratification due to the variation of grain size. Depending on the conditions during formation, macrocrystalline quartz layers may have formed between the microcrystalline quartz layers. Also, the larger crystal grains settled out first, grading to smaller ones on top, which is opposite the crystal size pattern that developed in concentrically banded agates.[262,263]

Figure 62
This Lake Superior agate shows horizontal bands with breaks in the "bedded planes."

One of the most interesting things about horizontally banded agate is that they are "geopetal" rock structures that indicate the direction of up and down within the host rock. Their bands deposited like sediments from aqueous solutions in a horizontal pattern that was indicative of the initial orientation of the cavity in the parent volcanic rock.[264-266]

Probably the most important aspect of horizontally banded agate is that their very structure may prove that these agates formed from aqueous solutions.[267] Some researchers suggest that the bands had to form in an aqueous environment to allow for the microcrystalline quartz to develop into flat bedded planes.[268] They studied horizontally banded agates that also have infiltration channels and noticed that the inflow current through the infiltration channel did not influence the formation of the horizontal layers. This means that the settling velocity of the particles forming the horizontal layers was higher than the velocity of the inflow current.[269,270] It is not a coincidence that horizontally banded agates formed most often in subtropical or tropical regions with significant rainfall. These areas with considerable supplies of meteoric water, as well as the higher amounts of silicic acid, favored the formation of horizontal banded agates.[271,272]

SILICA GEL AGATE GENESIS THEORY

The second theory explaining how agates may have formed is the silica gel theory. This camp believes that lumps of silica within molten lava developed into agate nodules.

There are a few different versions of this theory. One hypothesis is that agates formed when the host magma was still hot and fluid. This group suggests that the silica colloids in the magma clumped together (agglutinated) into a mass. Surface tension caused the silica to form into spheres, and then the banding and other internal structures formed "according to the geophysical and geochemical laws."[273] Another group believes that silica gel clumps in the magma separated into hydrous and anhydrous layers.[274] Other silica gel supporters believe that when molten lava flowing across the Earth's surface came into contact with water, the water instantly went supercritical. This occurred when water was pushed beyond the boiling point. The temperature and pressure of the water went beyond 705°F (374°C), and 300 PSI (pounds per square inch). The liquid and gas phases of water merged into a supercritical fluid. The water was lighter than liquid, but denser than vapor. When the water went supercritical, it "flashed" into the magma and reacted with the silica lumps contained in the lava. A hydrous silica-rich gel resulted.[275]

As the basaltic lava flow stopped moving, it began to cool down and solidify. The silica gel also cooled and then began to solidify and self-organize to form agate. The trace minerals in the vicinity of the gel served as a catalyst to facilitate the repetitive banding patterns. Chalcedony fibers formed due to instability at the crystallization front caused by cations that acted to accelerate and facilitate crystal growth. The self-organizing oscillations that resulted caused the alternating twisting (silica crystals with ion impurities) and non-twisting (silica crystals without ion impurities). In summary, supporters of this silica gel theory believe that their model explains the "repetitive layering, fibrosity, alternate trace-element content … and alternate-band fiber twisting," as well as the tendency that agates had to finish filling in with macrocrystalline quartz fill.[276,277]

One measure of proof, claims the silica gel supporters is that a basaltic lava flow they examined in Brazil had agates that formed in only the bottom three meters of the flow, leaving the vesicle pockets in the upper 11 meters empty. This, they say, shows that the agate forming process took place from the bottom up within the flow. The gel supports also suggest that the area around the agate pockets were often altered, compared to the rest of the host rock matrix, due to the impact of the supercritical flashing of the water.[278]

Another factor that supports the silica gel theory is that the aqueous solutions, according to the gel supporters, could not have had high enough concentrations of silica to support agate genesis.[279,280] They also suggest that as the gel crystallized, with aluminum and other catalysts exerting their chemical assistance, the concentration of silica would have had to be higher than what could have been supplied by an aqueous solution.[281]

One more point that gel enthusiasts make is that the center fill of macrocrystalline quartz in many agates gives support to their theory. This camp believes that as the agate self-organized and crystallized from the gel, the center of the pocket became richer in water with a lower silica concentration. Once the silica concentration dropped below the threshold needed to form microcrystalline quartz, a non-banded macrocrystalline region developed instead. Thus, the boundary between chalcedony and macrocrystalline quartz marks the line where the silica gel changed from being saturated to under-saturated.[282] As the gel crystallized into agate, giving off water as a byproduct, the water concentration in the center of the pocket increased. They believe that either the pressure built up, or that the water was converted to steam, producing the escape channels.[283] This camp obviously feels that agates formed under high temperatures, which would have been required to cause the initial supercritical flashing of the water, as well as the later production of steam that formed the connective channels.

One final observation made by the silica gel theorists is that the host rock may not have had open pathways that would have been large enough to transport silica-rich aqueous fluids.[284] The most problematic aspect of the fluid-based theory is that initial crystalline deposits of chalcedony may have blocked the inflow of additional silica solutions. The only way there would have been enough silica for agates to form was to have the source (e.g. silica gel) in the pocket to begin with.[285]

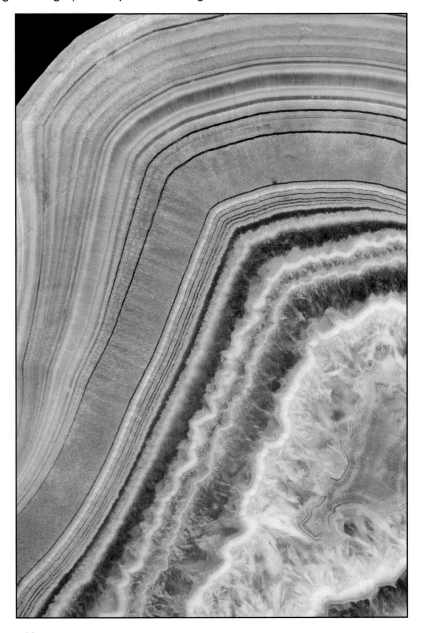

Figure 63
This Lake Superior agate shows the typical fibrous growth of the microcrystal "fabric,"
which developed perpendicular to the bands.

AGATE GENESIS CONCLUSIONS

Since human beings were not around when agates formed, and because we cannot replicate the agate genesis process in the laboratory, perhaps we will never completely solve the mystery of agate formation. Since there are more than 3,000 named varieties of agates that developed over three billion years of Earth's history, perhaps both of the main genesis theories explain how at least some of the agates formed.

After significant reading, studying, evaluating, and pondering, we have summarized what we learned about agate genesis in the list included in the following pages. Some of the explanations given by researchers are lacking in scientific proof. Given the controversy about agate genesis, it is hard to take researchers at their word when they make blanket statements such as "formed according to the geophysical and geochemical laws," without explaining these "laws" or otherwise proving them. Many of the agate genesis studies contribute valuable data, but their interpretations sometimes are based on one or another set of observations such as chemical, crystallographic, textural or isotopic, while disregarding others.[286] Some theories were based on the examination of a limited number of agates or on the assessment of a limited number of host rock venues.[287] Still other researchers focused on the agate attributes that supported their theory and disregarded agate characteristics that their theory did not explain.

The list below evaluates the issues involving agate genesis and the claims made by the agate genesis theorists.

Silica Gel Theory

- If there were blobs of silica within the molten lava, then there may have been sufficient silica to support agate genesis. The exact source of these silica deposits in the lava is not known. Others question whether there would have been enough silica gel clumps to create all of the world-wide agates that we now see.

- Some believe that during crystallization there would have been compaction of the gel that would have caused the mass to shrink. Since this compaction would have required as much as 18 to 20 percent more silica to complete the filling in of the pocket, from where did this additional silica come?

- Gel supporters claim that the connective channels formed from pressure or heat that built up in the pocket due to the crystallization process or from the flashing of water that accumulated in the center of the agate pocket. They claim that the thinning out of the bands near the entrance of the channel is proof that the channels must have formed from an outflow process.

- If there was compaction when the silica gel crystallized, leaving extra space within the pocket, then it doesn't make sense that enough pressure would have built up during the crystallization process to force material out of the pocket and create "exit channels," as the silica gel theorists have argued.

- Another point put forth by gel enthusiasts is that some of the connective channels did not extend all the way to the husk exterior, suggesting there was some but not enough pressure. However, it is possible that diffusion conduits could have formed part way through the filling-in process to open up a new channel. Another possibility is that a fracture may have developed in the previous bands due to geologic or other stresses, creating a new pathway and entrance channel with laminar jet flow part way into the agate.

- The hypothesis that water in the center of the agate reached a super-critical stage and "flashed" out of the pocket to form the connective channel doesn't make sense. Why would the water have accumulated, without supercritical phase flashing, only then to all of a sudden reach this stage to create an exit channel?

- Some do not feel that chunks of chert or other original source material for the silica blobs would have survived the ordeal of burial, melting of the surrounding rock, and extrusion without being dissolved, dissipated, or destroyed.

- The silica gel theory does not explain how agates formed in sedimentary and metamorphic rock.

- Proponents of the gel theory suggest that the "onion" shape of the channels resulted from the pressure that built up behind the agate husk when the husk resisted allowing the pressure to extrude out of the cavity.

- If the channels were formed via pressure release, it would seem that gravity would have played a role causing more channels to form at the bottom of the pocket. When museum staff examined dozens of agate slabs with both connective channels and horizontal banding (which told us what direction was "up"), we determined that the orientation of the channels was completely random and not influenced by gravity.

- It does not seem possible that horizontal bands could have formed from viscous gels.

- It may have been possible for impurities caught within the gel to have formed other agate structures. Stalk aggregates, for example, may have developed in the gel, similar to how stalagmites form in a cave. There is evidence that they grew upward since they developed when a material of lower density rose up through the vicious, gelatinous medium of higher density.288 It has been suggested that some of the tubes and other structures would have needed a viscous medium to support and suspend them throughout the cavity. Otherwise they would have settled down to the bottom of the pocket.

- The hypothesis that trace elements served as catalysts to help generate the oscillating banding patterns seems very plausible. The proof that this process did occur lies in the detailed analytical results that scientists have gained by measuring the chemical composition of agate bands. There is no question that bands alternate relative to those with twisted fibers (Silica contains impurities.) and those that are not twisted (Silica does not contain impurities.)

- Some silica gel enthusiasts argue that the inflow process could not have occurred since the first bands of chalcedony would have blocked further inflow of fluids. Other scientists have proven mathematically that the porosity of fibrous chalcedony would have allowed diffusion from the surrounding host rock. Proof lies in the fact that agates today are often dyed by taking advantage of this porosity. Also, scientists have shown that the connective channels could have stayed open to supply an inflow of fluids, due to the velocity of the inflow movement itself (laminar jet).

Inflow Theory

- Various researchers proved by mathematical calculations that it would have been possible for the saturation rate of silica to reach high enough levels in the pores of host rock to supply the vesicle pockets.[290,291] Scientists studying Brazilian amethyst geodes, some of which have agate bands, determined that the amount of silica in the surrounding rock was sufficient to produce the siliceous rims without requiring extraneous silica supply.[292] One gel supporter suggests that a relatively small agate nodule of 50 g would have required several thousand liters to deposit all the silica as chalcedony.[293] This argument was meant to convince us that the inflow process does not explain agate genesis. However, because geologic time is very accommodating, this argument actually supports the plausibility that agates could have formed via the inflow process, although according to a slower timeline than what we are used to in our human experience. More research is needed, however, to verify whether an osmotic difference in silica concentration levels developed to the degree needed to drive flow between the supersaturated silica concentrations inside host rock pores, as compared to the lower silica levels inside agate pockets.

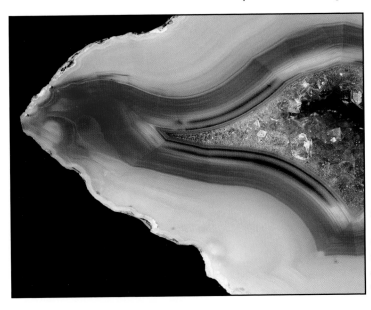

Figure 64
The inflow channel can be seen on the left side of this Argentina condor agate.

- If some agates did form from a silica gel that compacted during crystallization, additional silica would have been needed to complete the agate. It makes sense that the only source for additional silica would have been from diffusion inflow through the semi-permeable agate layers. If this inflow could have finished off the formation of agates that started from silica gel blobs, then why couldn't agates have formed entirely from an inflow process?

- Researchers examined the fibrous structure of the crystals in the thinning bands surrounding the connective channel and found that they were not deformed by an outflow, which would have occurred if the channels were created via pressure release. In fact, the orientation of the fibers stayed true to the perpendicular growth angle, conforming to the curve of the sidewalls of the channel.

- The museum staff's examination of 774 agate slabs showed indication of channels in 56 percent of the slabs. This percentage seems high if the channels were formed when the occasional gel-created agate needed to relieve pressure. It seems more likely that the channels served as the conduit for inflow, delivering silica-rich fluids into the pocket.

- As for the onion shape of the connective channels, researchers observed that the shape is indicative of a laminar flow jet that prevented accumulation near the entrance of the channel. The dynamics of this flow, they say, is similar to leaving a faucet dripping in cold weather to prevent water pipes from freezing or the way a tributary keeps its channel open at the junction with a river.

- There are aggregate crystal growths of mineral impurities that formed in connective channels, some of which clearly have an inward growth pattern. Other channels have aggregates that show how the inflow was disrupted, causing changes in the formation of subsequent bands. Still other channels have hollow areas that did not completely fill in. These developmental tendencies would not have resulted if the channels were formed from outward pressure release.

- Assuming that horizontal agate bands accumulated as the larger colloids settled out first, followed vertically with bands made up of progressively smaller colloids, the formation of this type of banding, claim the inflow supporters, had to occur in an aqueous environment.

- Inflow enthusiasts suggest that the fluid inside agate pockets would have provided not only the impurities needed to form eye, sagenite, and tube agates, but would have also served as a conducive environment for such growth to take place. In many cases, these impurity structures formed first, and subsequent agate banding grew around the structures.

- The aqueous inflow model would apply not only to agates formed in igneous rocks, but also to those that formed in sedimentary and metamorphic rocks.

- Although the influence of impurities on the twisted and non-twisted banding pattern of agates was proposed by silica gel enthusiasts, it is possible that this process could also explain banding formed during the inflow process. Scientists have hypothesized that silica colloids in aqueous solutions accumulated to form a temporary gel membrane. The mineral catalysts could have acted on the temporary gel membrane, which then crystallized into chalcedony with alternating twisted and non-twisted fibers, just as they would have influenced banding in an entire pocket filled with silica gel.

- Analysis of fluid inclusions caught within agate banding has indicated that the bands formed at low temperature and that meteoric water at least in part served as a supply for these inclusions. The results seem to indicate that at least these agates were not formed in hot molten lava from silica gel blobs.

- Another bit of proof comes from a study of the origin of agates in volcanic rocks from Scotland. Researchers found that bound waters in the agates preserved their "hydrogen isotope ratios." Devices measured the isotopic ratio of hydrogen and determined the probable source of water. They identified the source of water in the agate as having at least a component of meteoric origin (from precipitation), which means that the agates could not have been formed from silica gel blobs in molten lava.[294,295]

- Some scientists suggest that if an entire pocket of silica gel went through the aging/crystallization process, there would be unavoidable internal stresses caused by the unavoidable shrinking. These stresses would create macroscopic as well as microscopic shrinking fissures. The fact that these shrinking fissures are not seen within agate banding seems to indicate that the development of the agate banding involved only a small amount of fresh, highly hydrated shrinkable silica gel, rather than an entire mass of silica gel.[296]

- Scientists have determined that the amount of rare earth elements in agates and their surrounding host rocks are similar, suggesting that the elements are mobilized by circulating fluids. If agates instead formed from closed-system silica gel blobs, there would more than likely be different amounts of rare earth elements. [297]

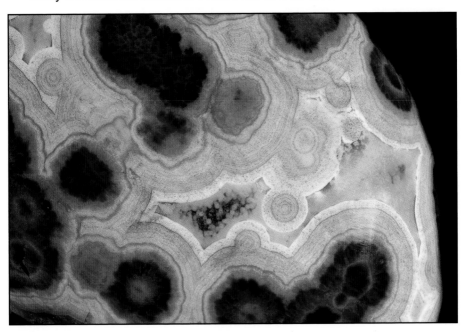

Figure 65
Sometimes it is hard to tell what a specimen really is. This is ocean jasper from Madagascar. It is opaque and is technically classified as jasper. However, it certainly has some agate-like banding.

TYPES OF HOST ROCK

Of the approximately 3,000 varieties of agate in the world, the vast majority formed as secondary deposits inside igneous rock. There are also some that formed in sedimentary rock pockets. Although there is mention in numerous publications and web sites that agate formed in metamorphic rock, these examples are rare. The only agates that formed in metamorphic rock in the Gitche Gumee Museum's collection is an iron lace agate from the Republic Mine in Ishpeming, MI. Most of these were found during the 1970s when the mine was active. These agates formed within the seams of metamorphic iron formation. Two other agates found in metamorphosed rock are those found at Stockdale Beck, Cumbria, England and the ancient agates found in the Pibara Craton area of Western Australia.[298-300]

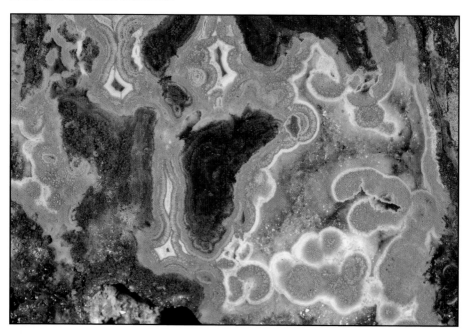

Figure 66
This is iron lace agate from Ishpeming, Michigan. It formed inside metamorphosed banded iron formation.

Other than the rare metamorphic rocks, there are five major agate-forming environments:

1. **Thunder eggs that occur in rhyolitic, welded ash-flow tuffs.** These are the first agates to form in the agatization cycle. The silica source is from devitrified (chemically weathered) volcanic ash. An example is the thunder egg agate from Oregon.

2. **Amygdaloidal agates that occur in vesicular tholeitic (contains little to no olivine) basalts with their silica source derived from overlying rhyolitic ashes.** Examples are plume agates from Cottonwood Spring and Sheep Canyon basalts in Brewster County, Texas, and Lake Superior agates from late Precambrian basalts in Michigan, Minnesota, and western Ontario.

3. **Amygdaloidal agates that occur in vesicular andesitic rocks.** The silica source is overlying rhyolitic ash. An example is the Montezuma agate from andesitic rock in Chihuahua, which is in northern Mexico.

4. **Nodular or vein agates that form in continental sedimentary rocks such as claystones.** The silica source is air-fall volcanic ash. An example is the blue agate from Nebraska.

5. **Nodular agates that form in marine sedimentary rocks.** The silica source has been considered to be organic (sponges, radiolarians), but could have been air-fall volcanic ash. Examples are Tampa Bay agatized corals in Florida and dry head agates in Montana.[301]

Igneous Rock Agates

Two different types of agate formation occurred in igneous rocks. Amygdaloidal agates formed in vesicle pockets within both basalt and andesite. Thunder eggs formed in rhyolitic tuff.

AMYGDALOIDAL AGATES

Basalt is the most abundant of all lava rocks. This fine-grained igneous rock forms from the cooling of highly mobile lava flows. Because of the fluidity of these flows, basalt can spread over great distances. When the continents were first forming, basaltic lava flows extruded from rift zones, which were cracks in the shallow crust of the embryonic continents (see Figures 21 and 22). As already reported earlier in this chapter, there were basaltic lava flows in the Lake Superior region.[302] An even bigger flow occurred in Brazil which spread basalt over 191,950 cubic miles! Just for reference, this Brazilian lava flow would have been enough to cover the entire state of Minnesota with a pile of lava over two miles high.[303]

As the lava cooled, there were bubbles of various gases that moved up through the lava. Gases included around 90 percent steam, with the source being ice from the comets and asteroids that hit the Earth during its formation.[304-306] In addition to water vapor, there were also carbon dioxide, chlorine, hydrogen fluoride, and sulfur dioxide gases.[307]

Much of the gas escaped into the atmosphere. Other bubbles coalesced on their way up, forming large vesicle pockets called amygdules (which means "almond shape," pronounced a-myg-dule).[308] In some cases, the pockets would orient vertically, reflecting the upward rise of the gas bubbles through the lava. In other cases, they were horizontally oriented, reflecting the lateral movement of the lava that stretched and elongated the pockets.[309] Since the top of the lava flow cooled and hardened first, the bubbles of gas became trapped.

Fragmentation of the lava flow's top sometimes formed a splintered surface because of the movement of the still-molten lava underneath. These fractured zones, or what can be called "frothy zones," sometimes filled with agate, other forms of microcrystalline quartz, macrocrystalline quartz, calcite, thomsonite, stilbite, or copper. When cracks filled in with agate, rather than oblong-shaped vesicle pockets, seam agates developed."[310] When vesicle pockets formed in the matrix rock, they were usually quite regular in shape because the lava was quite fluid—more like molasses than the peanut-butter-like lava that formed rhyolitic thunder egg agates.[311]

Most basalt does not contain much silica. Thus, agates that formed in basalt depended on the chemical weathering (devitrification) of silica from other overlying rocks that were rich in silica, such as ash flow from nearby volcanoes. On Isle Royal in Lake Superior, for example, there is evidence on the surface of over 100 individual basaltic lava flows, but the total number is not known since many more remnants of the lava flows lie beneath Lake Superior.[312] In contrast to the relatively quiet flow of flood basalts, there were at least five violent volcanic eruptions in the Lake Superior region that spread silica-rich rhyolitic lava and ash throughout the area.[313,314] Over geologic time, these different types of igneous material intermixed in layers. Carbonic acid was then able to leach silica from the ash and rhyolite layers, which saturated the aqueous solutions with silica in the intergranular pores of the basaltic host rock.[315] It is believed that the heat and carbon dioxide released from subsequent lava flows and volcanoes may have increased the potential for chemical weathering (devitrification) of the ash and rhyolite, to release even more silica that became available for agate genesis.[316]

Figure 67
This photo shows an amygdaloid Lake Superior agate that is still attached to the basaltic matrix rock in which it formed.

As the basalt continued to cool, it formed a series of cracks, much like mud when it dries out. This crack system and natural porosity of the basalt served as the conduit that delivered silica-rich fluids to the vesicle pockets. When the micro-fractures intersected the vesicle pockets, infiltration channels formed to deliver silica to the pockets. Otherwise, there was diffusion directly from the host rock into the agate pockets through the semi-permeable layers of microcrystalline quartz. Smaller agate pockets, less than the size of a cherry, rarely developed infiltration channels. Larger agates may have developed multiple inflow channels.[317] One of the largest amygdaloid agates ever recorded was a Brazilian geode agate, lined with amethyst, that weighed 35 tons! This agate was exhibited at the Dusseldorf Exhibition of 1902.[318]

Figure 68
This photo shows matrix rock in which there are numerous Lake Superior agate nodules (red circles) as well as some empty pockets from which the agate nodules have been extracted. Notice the crack system that helped facilitate the movement of mineral-rich fluids.

There are a couple of other factors that may have drastically affected the earth during its early years and could have impacted the formation of amygdaloid agates. One is that scientists discovered that at its formation, the Earth rotated at a significantly faster rate. Two billion years ago the Earth rotated on its axis at a 10-hour day rate, compared to the 24 hours that it now takes. This faster rotation speed would have created more centrifugal force to supply dynamic energy for gas bubbles to move efficiently through the viscous lava. The early moon was closer as well. It

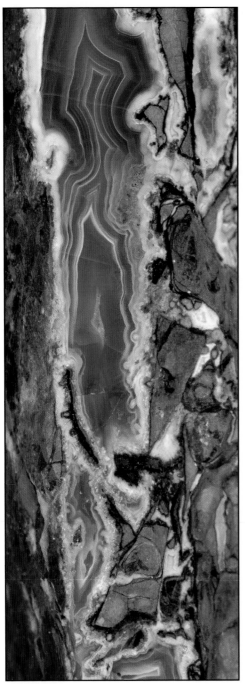

Figure 69
This natural "montage" shows how complex
the relationship sometimes was between
the host rock and the vesicle pockets. This
is a Michipicoten Island agate from Ontario,
Canada.

is estimated that the moon was only 10,000 miles away, compared to the current distance of 240,000 miles. This closeness would have caused its gravitational attraction to be 100 times what it is today. The impact of these forces would have been dramatic. For example, today's 5-foot tide would, in those early days, have been a 500-foot tide.319,320 As the continents developed, it is unclear what these dynamic differences may have had on agate genesis.

RHYOLITIC AGATES

The most common agates found in rhyolitic igneous rock are thunder eggs. They are nodular structures that formed in either this high-silica volcanic rock or in welded tuffs formed from compacted volcanic ash. Generally the silica content in these igneous host rocks ranged from 75 to 80 percent. The thunder egg nodules are usually spherical in shape with an exterior husk made of rhyolite that is more silicified than the host rock. In most cases, thunder eggs have a central cavity that is partly to completely filled with chalcedony, opal, or quartz that typically has a geometric, star-shaped form. The chalcedony can be banded, and it may contain inclusion structures that resemble algae or sea kelp.[321]

Most of the rhyolitic agate areas occur along zones of subduction where one tectonic plate was thrust beneath another.[322] Thunder eggs are the first kind of agate to form in these volcanic settings. The Oregon thunder eggs, for example, are associated with the Baughman Creek volcanic center in northwestern Oregon.[323] This silica-rich rhyolitic flow was nearly 700 feet thick. The area was volcanically active during the Tertiary period (65 to 1.8 million years ago). The oldest rhyolitic thunder eggs formed in the Lake Superior region during the late Precambrian period, around 600 million years ago.[324]

Figure 70
There are more than 80 varieties of agate found in northern Mexico. Although some developed in sedimentary and igneous andesite rock, all were influenced by or formed in rhyolitic rock, which was the source of silica. This is a Mexican Laguna agate.

The rhyolitic host rock formed from igneous material that had large amounts of dissolved gases. As the material was released in a volcanic eruption, it flowed not as a liquid, but more like solid particles suspended in a hot, gaseous medium. Most of the particles in the ash consisted of silica-rich glass shards, but there were also numerous other minerals and trace elements. When the ash settled, it compacted and developed a peanut butter like consistency. Carbon dioxide mixed with percolating water to devitrify and chemically weather the ash, which released silica as well as dissolved gases. As the gas (mostly water vapor steam) was released in the extremely viscous ash, it expanded to form star-shaped irregular cavities. Later, after things cooled down, agate formation commenced when silica-rich fluid infiltrated the cavities through micro-fractures and pores in the thunder egg shell.[325,326] Most of the thunder eggs formed in a single layer near the base of an ash flow, or in a layer where the permeating silica fluids met an impermeable layer of rock.[327]

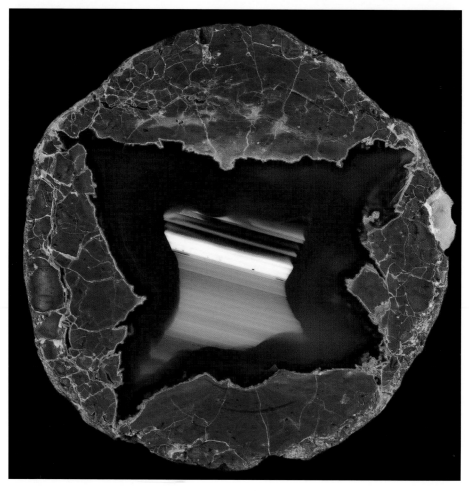

Figure 71
This is a typical star-shaped thunder egg agate from Oregon.

Sedimentary Rock Agates

Although the majority of agates formed in pockets located in igneous host rock, there are worldwide occurrences of agates that formed inside sedimentary rock pockets. A few include:

- Dry head agates, Montana and Wyoming
- Fairburn and Teepee Canyon agates, South Dakota
- Kentucky agates
- Tampa Bay agatized coral, Florida
- Union Road agates, Missouri
- Crazy lace agates, Mexico
- Puma agates, Argentina

Figure 72
This dry head agate from Montana formed in sedimentary rock.

Some sedimentary agates formed in marine limestone that was deposited near shore at the junction of continents and oceans. The ocean levels changed, as a result of continental glacier advances and retreats, which influenced the deposition of sedimentary rocks. This sequence began with the formation of near shore shale. As the sea level rose, dense limestone was deposited. Next, as the water level increased even more, dark colored acidic shale was deposited. As the sea level declined, a different regressive limestone formed. At this point, the cycle began again with the formation of near shore shale. Agate nodules generally formed in the intermediate layers of regressive limestone.[328]

There is not an agreement as to the source of silica for the agates that formed in sedimentary rock pockets. Some feel that air-born volcanic ash was a probable source as it deposited in shallow, near-shore environments. The silica may have been leached from ash or other silica-rich sources into the groundwater, which later percolated through the sedimentary rock to the agate pockets. Others feel that the silica was supplied from organic sources such as radiolarians, sponge, or diatoms.[329] Since fossils are often found in association with sedimentary agates, it is possible that the silica source could have been organic. In fact, some Fairburn agates have been found with identifiable fossil inclusions. Most of the time, though, it appears that agate formed in voids where the fossil or softer organism had been.[330] The Tampa Bay agatized corrals are thought to have silicified from the precipitation of silica in short-term alkaline lakes that formed during periods of low ocean levels. There may have also been weathering and clay-alteration processes. One more possible source could have been upwelling of silica-rich hydrothermal solutions. This latter method has recently been documented as at least a partial contributor to the silica that formed Montana dry head agates.[331]

A hypothesis regarding the formation of Fairburn agates is that limestone carbonate rock pockets were "replaced incrementally" on a volume-for-volume basis by silica (analogous to petrified wood), where silica replaced organic matter with near-perfect preservation.[332,333] Others feel that Fairburns formed from an accumulation of non-crystalline (amorphous) silica into a nodule on the ocean floor during the formation of the sedimentary rock. The silica material later self-organized into agate.[334,335]

Mexican crazy lace agate had a slightly different genesis. These agates are found at an elevation of 6,200 feet above Benito Juarez in the Sierra Santa Lucia Mountains, located in central Mexico. This agate occurs as a vein or seam, with "irregular curved and twisted bands in shapes of zig-zags scallops, bouquets, sunbursts, and eyes."[336] Unlike all other Mexican agates, crazy lace is mined in a silica-rich, dark gray limestone that formed during the Cretaceous period (90 to 65 million years ago). However, the genesis of this agate didn't occur until rhyolitic domes intruded the area between 40 and 50 million years ago during the Tertiary time. The chemical weathering of the rhyolitic rock most probably supplied the silica for the genesis of crazy lace agate.

One interesting thing about some of the sedimentary agates, like the Fairburn agates that formed in limestone host rock, is that some of the structures found in other agates are absent. For an unknown reason, eyes, tubes, horizontal banding, crystal pseudomorph impressions and replacements, sagenite, and other mineral inclusions are not seen in Fairburn agates.[337]

Figure 73
This Mexican crazy lace agate has a nice combination of agate bands that grew around mineral impurities and quartz structures, which formed in the pocket first, prior to the development of banding.

TIMING OF AGATE FORMATION

There are two aspects to timing that will be discussed. First, the relative age of agates will be documented. Second, the possible amount of time that it took agates to form will be reviewed.

Determining the age of rock is conducted by measuring radioactive isotopes such as Potassium 40, Rubidium 87, or Uranium 235. These isotopes are unstable. When the original "parent" isotopes decay, new "daughter" isotopes are spontaneously formed. By measuring the rate of decay, which happens in a predictable manner, age of the original "parent" material can be estimated. A convenient way to express this rate of decay is through the concept of half-life. The half-life of an isotope is the time required for half of a given number of parent isotopes to decay to the daughter isotopes.[338]

The task to accurately date the age of agates is not as straightforward. It is not always certain, for example, if agate genesis is contemporaneous with the formation of the host rock. It appears that in some cases, agates may have formed tens of millions of years after the formation of the host rock.[339] Unfortunately, agates themselves cannot be dated since they usually do not have enough radioactive isotope inclusions. Instead, geologists date the age of the host rock. They must do their best to determine the conditions of agate genesis and decide when the agates formed as compared to the host rock.

Some of these differences in genesis dates have been documented. Agates from North Umbria, England, formed 167 million years ago, over 200 million years after the formation of the host rock. Brazilian agates developed around 80 million years ago in host rock that is 133 million years old. In most of the agate genesis environments throughout the world, however, scientists think that agates formed within a few million years after the formation of the host.[340]

One reason for the delay of agate genesis may have been the climate. In tropical and subtropical regions where there is sufficient rainfall, chemical weathering of silica-rich rocks started immediately after volcanic eruptions. On the other hand, in arid or cool regions, chemical weathering may have been delayed until there was sufficient rainfall. Without enough rain, there would have been less carbonic acid and less fluid to transport silica through the cracks and pores of the host rock.[341]

Agate formation may have also stretched over a long geologic period with interruptions of the genesis process caused by changing environmental and climatic conditions. Agate genesis may have occurred during multiple unrelated periods, each with their own conditions. Since these intervals of genesis may have been separated by great amounts of time, there could have been intermixing of different fluids with varying amounts of silica and trace minerals. These input changes would have changed the appearance of the corresponding agate bands.

Other changes over time could have influenced the banding patterns. The water table may have fluctuated. There could have been uplifting due to plate tectonics, which changed the groundwater flow patterns. Upwelling of lava hot spots could have pushed hydrothermal fluids closer to the surface where agates were forming. Different ratios of the participating fluids could have changed the concentration levels of silica and trace elements that were supplied to the agate pockets. These potentially variable conditions contributed to the genesis of unusual and bizarre agates.[342]

Figure 74
This Mexican agate shows extreme variability of banding that formed either with interruptions in its genesis or with differences in environmental or fluid inflow conditions.

A factor that makes it difficult to determine the age of agates is that they actually change over time. Many studies have shown that these maturation changes happen at known rates. One of the key factors in this discovery was the identification of moganite within agate structures. Moganite is another form of silica that was formally identified in 1984 in rhyolitic rock from Mogan, Canary Islands. It was not accepted as a separate form of silica until 1999.[343] Moganite's crystal structure is different and more random than both chalcedony and macrocrystalline quartz. It also has higher water content (@ 2.7%). These factors allow researchers to measure the precise content of moganite in agates.[344,345]

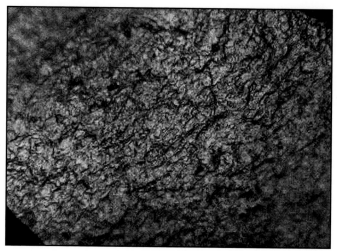

Figure 75
This is a photomicrograph of a small shard of translucent moganite, from the Canary Islands, viewed in transmitted light. The field of view is 1 mm. Note the fine fracturing of the surface. Permission to use this photo was granted by Graham Wilson of Turnstone Geological Services Ltd. Campbelford, Ontario, Canada.

Moganite rarely occurs in nature as a pure mineral. It is instead seen within the structural formation of other silica minerals.[346] Researchers have discovered that the amount of moganite in agates decreases over time. When agate first formed, moganite filled in some of the gaps during the genesis process. During geologic time, moganite transformed into chalcedony.[347] The maximum content of moganite found in agate is 20 percent, although other forms of silica can have as high as 70 percent moganite. Since scientists can estimate the rate of moganite transformation, they can use the measurement of moganite to serve as a general indicator of agate age. They know that agates which are more than 400 million years old have little to no moganite remaining, so they work backwards from there to estimate agate age.[348-350]

Two other indicators of the maturation of agates are the amount of water within agate structure, and the overall crystal size. Research results show that over the last 400 million years, the crystallite size in agates grew by 55 percent, and the amount of water decreased by a similar level. Agates that are older than 420 million years have an internal water content that is constant at around 0.4 percent.[351] The mobilization of water in the agate pocket during geologic time may have dissolved and recrystallized silica into larger crystals. The growth of the crystals resulted in an increase in density of around 2 percent from the youngest to the oldest agates.[352, 353] It is thought that the crystals stopped growing when the transformation of moganite to chalcedony was completed. The moganite transformation process may have also been responsible for using up the internal water content.

Even though agates are hard and resistant to weathering and erosion, there are very few agates from the Precambrian period. One reason may be that the Precambrian atmosphere was composed mostly of ammonia and methane, at least until sometime in the late Precambrian period. This environment was less conducive to agate genesis, which is why most of the world's agates developed after the Earth acquired an oxygen-nitrogen atmosphere.[354]

Some of the estimated ages of agates are listed in Table 3. In cases where multiple sources had slightly different estimates, the range listed was merged. Also when the geologic era was cited, rather than a specific date range, the dates for that era were included. Until recently, it was agreed that Lake Superior agates are the oldest on earth, at around 1.1 billion years old. In the last few years, some of the western Australian agates have been determined to be older, based on radioactive dating of the host rock in which they formed. The estimated agate ages in the table are listed from youngest to oldest.

Table 3: Estimated Age of Agates

Name of Agate	Origin	Estimated Age (millions of years)	Ref. Cite
Yucca Mountain	Nevada, USA	9 – 13	355, 356
Priday agate	Oregon, USA	20	357
Mt. Warning	Australia	23	356
Blue agate	Nebraska, USA	23 – 55.8	356, 358
Creede	Colorado, USA	25.8	359
Cottonwood	Texas, USA	37	356
Coyamito	Chihuahua, Mexico	38	360
Ellensburg	Washington, USA	43	356
Las Choyas	Mexico	45	356
Khur	Khur, Iran	50 – 60	356, 360
British Tertiary Volcanic Province	Scotland	60	360
Gurasada	Romania	60	356
Madagascar	Madagascar	88	361
Lyme Regis	England	65 – 145	356
Puma	Argentina	65 – 145	362
Mt. Somers	New Zealand	89	356
Brazilian	Brazil	100 – 200	363

Name of Agate	Origin	Estimated Age (millions of years)	Ref. Cite
North Umbria	England	167	360
Botswana	Botswana, Africa	140 – 180	356
Nova Scotia	Canada	200	356
Dulcote	Mendips, England	206 – 248	356
Black River	Argentina	220 – 240	364
Fairburn	South Dakota USA	245 – 310	356,365
Montana dry head	Montana USA	248 – 290	366
Rotliegend	Germany	270	367
Teepee Canyon	South Dakota USA	270 – 290	368
Agate Creek	Queensland, Australia	275	360
Thuringia	Germany	285	360
Buxton, Derbyshire	England	311	356,360
Union Road	Missouri, USA	286 – 320	356
Keswick	Iowa, USA	286 – 320	369
Kentucky	Kentucky, USA	325 – 360	370
East Midland Valley	Scotland	412	360
West Midland Valley	Scotland	412	360
Cumbria	England	430 – 452	356
Paint Rock	Tennessee, USA	443 – 448	356
Maydena	Australia	488 – 542	356
Northern Territory	Australia	513	356
Lake Superior	North Central USA	1100	360
Killara Formation	Western Australia	1840	371
Maddina basalt formation	Western Australia	2720	371
Warrawoon, Pibara Craton	Western Australia	3450	372

The length of time it took agates to form is another mystery. Walger, one of the supporters of the inflow theory, estimated how long it would have taken for an agate to form. Using fluid dynamic formulas, he calculated the transport rate as a function of the flow rate. The flow rate, he says, was determined by the silica concentration difference between the intergranular solution in the host rock's pores and that in the agate cavity. He expressed the transport rate as the time needed to deposit 100 grams of silica in the agate cavity, brought into the cavity through a connective channel that was one centimeter in length. He admits that this calculation only provides a crude estimate of the time needed to fill in an agate pocket. He also admits that there are a lot of variables that affected this transport rate. However, by using the range of values for all of the variables, including the size of the agate cavity being filled, he calculated that it would have taken hundreds to some ten thousands of years to complete the genesis process for most agates.[373]

Other researchers suggest that individual, microscopic chalcedony layers would have formed in tens of hours.[374] Since it has been shown with scanning electron microscopes that some agates have up to 100,000 individual bands per inch, if it took 30 hours to form each band in an agate with three inches of banding, the agate would have formed in around 1,027 years:[375]

100,000 bands X 3 inches = 300,000 bands x 30 hours/band = 9,000,000 hours / 8760 hours per year = 1027.4 years

Solutions carrying silica colloid particles have been shown to polymerize and form gelatin layers when the concentration goes over 115 parts per million. In a hot spring area in central Japan, tree trunks that fell into a steam fed by hot springs was completely petrified within 40 years after the trees fell.[376] So given the right conditions, silicification can happen rapidly. Other researchers disagree and estimate that the agate genesis process took much longer, perhaps as much as 25 to 50 million years to complete.[377,378]

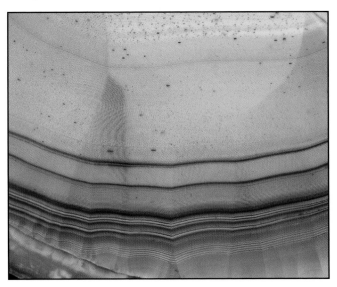

Figure 76
With modern measurement tools, scientists have measured up to 100,000 individual microscopic bands per inch. They are not sure how long it took for each band to form. In this Lake Superior agate there are so many bands in the top section that it would be difficult to count them.

CHAPTER 3   How Do You Find Agates?

This chapter is intended for those of you who have already been bitten by the agate-hunting bug or are about to be. We cannot take responsibility for the change agate hunting may have on your life. Rockhounding is addicting, but is an enjoyable way to spend time that gets you away from the hustle and bustle of daily life. When you are rockhounding, you must focus on the present and not think about your job, bills, or other responsibilities.

The formula for successful agate hunting is:

Focus

+

Patience and Time

+

Confidence

+

Knowledge and Understanding

↓

Successful Agate Hunting

By focus we mean that when you go agate hunting, you must make a commitment to do just that. Most people who look for agates probably like all rocks and suffer from "pretty rock syndrome." What is recommended is that if you want to look for pretty rocks, give yourself a specified amount of time. Allow yourself 15 or 30 minutes to pick up pretty non-agate specimens. Then make a commitment to agate hunt and ONLY pick up agates or agate-want-to-be rocks.

Focus is important because it facilitates the efficient use of your time. Let's say that you are agate hunting on the beach and you pick up one rock a minute. In two hours you can pick up 120 rocks. If you get distracted and pick up pretty rocks that are obviously not agate, over the two hours you may pick up 80 pretty rocks, leaving only 40 specimens that have a chance of being agate. If you focus instead on only agate-looking specimens, you will have 120 rocks that may land you that elusive agate.

Patience is the next key. Other than in designated agate mines, agates in all other locations are few and far between. Patience and time are important. Successful agate hunters commit to the search and spend significant blocks of time. Those who go to a beach, gravel pit, or farm field and look for 20 minutes may get lucky and find an agate or two. Those who designate a half-day or longer will certainly have more success. We recommend making an outing of it. Bring a sack lunch and allow yourself to get totally engrossed in the agate-hunting challenge. In this way each agate expedition is like a treasure hunt.

Confidence is a key variable that many agate hunters overlook. If you start your search with the attitude "I can't find an agate," then you probably will not. An example of how important a positive outlook is occurred a few years ago. A man came into the museum and quickly purchased three $25 agates. He explained that his wife had gone agate hunting with him for 20 years and had never been successful. She threatened that the next day would be her last rock-hunting excursion if she didn't find an agate. Since the man was an avid rockhound who felt that his agate-hunting minutes would be threatened, he decided to take action. The following year he came back to the museum and told the rest of the story. Apparently, that next day he took those three $25 agates and seeded the beach in his wife's path—all day long. She had a negative outlook and was so discouraged that she failed to find them. Finally, after hours of frustrated searching, she threw herself on the sand and claimed that she was never agate hunting again. The man distracted her and re-seeded the beach one last time. His wife found the first one, then the second, and finally the third. She was extremely excited and proclaimed herself a successful agate hunter. Apparently, because of her new found confidence she has been finding agates ever since. He never told her the source of those first three agates.

So when you go out agate hunting, it may be a good idea to beef up your confidence at the beginning of your search. The first thing you should do is look for a little "chipper" or for a seam agate that only has a little bit of agate in it. You may have to get on your knees or sit so that you can see the smaller rocks. There are more tiny agates in the world than there are larger ones; thus, they are easier to find. Once you find one, put that rock in your pocket and declare yourself a successful agate hunter. No matter what happens the rest of the time you agate hunt that day—you have not been shut out. This initial agate may not be one that you would normally keep, but it counts. From a psychological point of view, this confidence can make a difference. The power of positive thinking can go a long way. BELIEVE that you will find agates.

The last part of the formula for success is knowledge and understanding. To be successful, you have to THINK LIKE AN AGATE. You have to think from within an agate nodule and understand the specific characteristics that can help you to pick up rocks that have the highest likelihood of being an agate.

Since the agate genesis process and chemical composition is similar for all agates, there are certain characteristics that are universal. However, there are also nuances that are typical for agates from a particular area. There are also specifics about how, where, and when to look, given the local terrain. You can increase your success rate if you do your homework. If you are interested in information about rockhounding for a particular agate, you may want to complete the following steps:

1. Find out if there is a book that has been published about agates from that location. New agate books are being published all the time that explain the specifics of agates from certain locales.

2. Conduct an internet search. Many web pages have information about how to find agates in specific locations.

3. Look on the internet to find out if there is a rock shop in the area to which you are going. One fairly good list of rock shops in the United States is available at www.osomin.com/SHOP1.HTM. You can visit the local rock shop and ask to see agates found in the area. You can also ask people at the shop for advice about local agate hunting.

4. One of the best sources for information about rockhounding can be obtained from members of local rock clubs. Many clubs organize rock collecting field trips. Clubs are able to secure permission to visit areas that do not grant permission to individuals. Most clubs allow visitors to participate in these field trips. Usually there is a small fee ($5.00 to $10.00). It would be best to attend one of the club meetings so that you can network with members. Most clubs welcome visitors to their meetings. You should also consider joining a club in your area. Many clubs have annual shows that sponsor special field trips to collecting sites. By attending these shows, you get to see what minerals can be found in the local area. A good list of clubs is located at: www.rock-hounds.com/rockshop/clublist.shtml.

Since agates are hard and more resistant to erosion, they usually survive long after their host rock has weathered away. The world's agates are widely distributed and often can be found great distances from the locations of their original genesis. Rivers, glaciers, icebergs, waves, and ocean currents facilitate this transport. Depending on where you live or where you travel to in search of the elusive agate, the prospecting area can vary. Agates can be collected in many locales including:

*   On mountains in areas of snow pack melt and run-off.
*   In and along creek beds and rivers, especially after a heavy rain.
*   In desert gravel beds.
*   In grassland gravel beds.
*   In farm fields that are situated in glacial till areas.

- In piles of rocks next to farm fields.
- In gravel pits, especially those situated in glacial till areas.
- Along old railroad tracks.
- In the root balls of uprooted trees.
- In recently landscaped areas with decorative rock, especially if the rock was supplied from glacial till.
- Along beaches where the rocks have been washed by waves, especially after iceberg melt or storms.
- At construction sites after a heavy rain washes the surface stones.
- On gravel roads after they have been graded, especially after a rain.
- Along hiking trails.
- In areas where the original host rock still exists, allowing access to agates in situ.

It is most important that wherever you look for agates, you make sure the area is available for legal agate hunting. Rockhounding is not allowed, for example, in the national parks in the U.S. and in the provincial parks in Canada. Many gravel pits no longer allow agate hunting because rockhounds have abused the privilege. Some agate hunters have acted in irresponsible and dangerous ways by leaving garbage behind and refusing to stay away from equipment or working operations. This is unfortunate, because gravel pits are ideal places to look since the rocks are washed and mechanically sorted by size. So if you are lucky enough to secure permission to hunt for agates in a quarry or gravel pit, please be respectful. The same is true if you want to hunt on private property. Please secure permission in advance.

Figure 77
The Lake Superior beaches around Grand Marais, Michigan are a pleasant place to look for agates.

Figure 78
This Mexican agate originally belonged to June Culp Zeitner who published one of the first rock hunting books Gem Trails.

Since the Gitche Gumee Museum is located on the south shore of Lake Superior, we can provide tips about hunting for agates on the beach and in rivers. Some of these tips are relevant to hunting in other areas.

1. When you are looking on the beach, go to the water's edge and observe the rock patterns above the high water mark. As the wave heights vary on a day-to-day basis, there are often rows of rocks marking the high water marks for different days. Look at the rock in each row and identify the row that seems to have the most gold chert or red jasper. Since rocks of the same specific gravity tend to fall out of the waves at the same point; agate will be near its first cousins.

2. There are a lot of agate characteristics to think about making the task of finding them more difficult. Concentrate on those agate characteristics that will give you the highest chance for success. The specific characteristics will vary with the agate and the hunting environment. On Lake Superior beaches, rockhounds look for rocks that are "glowing" due to the translucency, shiny due to the waxy luster, and irregular in shape due to the conchoidal fractures.

3. If you are looking for agates that have weathered so the husks have eroded away, these agates will tend to be more translucent than other rocks. It is best to agate hunt on sunny days so that you can take advantage of this characteristic. Orient the angle of your search so the sun is in front of you, shining through the rocks. Agates will tend to "glow."

4. If it is not sunny, bring a small flashlight with you, preferably one with a bright quartz bulb. Many of the new LED flashlights are really not that bright and don't work as well. Use the flashlight to check for translucency. Even agates with a husk can show translucency along the edge of the husk.

5. Bring a magnifying lens or jewelers loop with you. Many rockhounds wear a headband magnifier when they go agate hunting so that they can easily pull down the magnifier as needed.

6. Select agate search locations that are beyond the "umbilical cord" of other rockhounds. Most people only walk a short distance from their vehicle. You can have more success if you are willing to hoof it farther from road access than others are willing to go.

7. If you are looking along a shore, the waves can often make the search more difficult. When the waves are less than a foot in height, sometimes you can construct and use a viewing tube. The museum founder built his out of wood. It was four feet tall with a piece of Plexiglas sealed on the bottom and handles on the side. You can also make a viewing tube out of PVC tubing.

8. There are advantages and disadvantages of looking in wet versus dry rocks. The banding patterns are amplified when the rocks are wet, making them easier to spot. However, you can see the conchoidal fractures and waxy luster better in the dry rocks. We think it is better to look in dry rock, but then use available water or bring a spray bottle to wet down rocks to accentuate any banding.

9. Rock scoops can be very useful. They will save your back by limiting the number of times that you have to bend down to pick up a rock. You can also use them to reach into the water to retrieve a rock as well as dig in sand or in gravel piles.

10. If you are searching near water and don't want to get your feet wet, you may want to think about wearing high boots. You can also designate an old pair of shoes or purchase water shoes.

11. Look in ways that others don't. If you are searching near lakes or the ocean, decide to scuba dive or snorkel. If you are looking on the beach where most agate hunters walk, sit down and dig instead.

12. One idea for river hunting is to take a small collapsible shovel and a bucket. The collapsible camp sink buckets work well. Locate gravel beds in the river and shovel the gravel up on shore. Use the bucket to pour water over the rocks to wash off the silt.

13. If the agates in the area are fluorescent, buy a portable black light and go agate hunting at night. Make sure that the black light has both short and long wavelengths.

The detailed information that follows has been compiled to help you to successfully THINK LIKE AN AGATE. The search can be frustrating, yet rewarding. Luck may help you to be at the right place at the right time, but in the end you will be successful if you commit to the task (focus), spend time, stay positive, and know what agate characteristics to look for. Happy hunting!

A POCKET FILLED IN

Depending on the agate hunting location, you may or may not be able to see actual banding in collected specimens. At the Baker Ranch in southwestern New Mexico, you can dig for nodules that were formed in the rhyolitic ash beds. The nodules are numerous, but not all of them are agates. Most of the specimens you dig you won't bother to cut, and most of what you cut you won't bother to keep or polish. Many of the nodules are "duds." However, the husks of these nodules all look about the same. You cannot see any of the chalcedony banding on the outside since the husks are coated in rhyolite. So you will have to cut them to determine which are keepers.

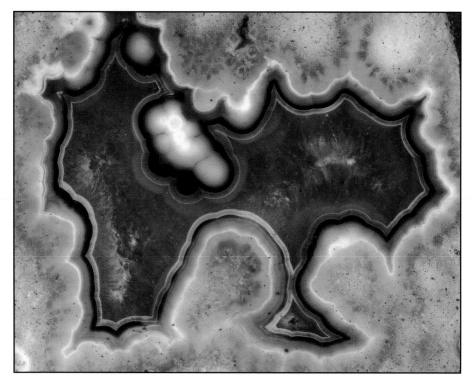

Figure 79
The pocket in which this puma agate from Argentina formed initially filled with other minerals, which were replaced by quartz. Then agate completed the fill. Many puma agates have thick husks and require lapidary work to unveil their hidden beauty.

In other areas, the agate banding is more exposed. When you walk the beaches of Lake Superior, these ancient agates have been subject to the elements for millions of years. They have certainly been rolled by Lake Superior waves for thousands of years. With each new wave, the stones are naturally tumbled up and down the beach. In most cases, this removes some or the entire husk, exposing banding. After several decades of looking for agates on the Lake Superior shoreline, or seeing those found by others, museum staff has been surprised only twice. Both specimens were agate-like nodules that did not show any evidence of banding on the exterior. Backlighting also did not show banding. When the ends were cut off these two specimens, we were quite surprised. Both were high quality grade "A" agates! But most of the time, when you are looking for agates on beaches or in areas where the rocks have been naturally ground down, if you are not sure what you have found are agates—they probably are not.

Sometimes, you may only get a "peek" at what is inside a specimen because maybe only a little part of the husk is fractured off. While agate hunting, always keep your eyes open for any rocks that have fractures showing that there is something different on the inside than what appears on the outside. The photo below shows an agate that is still in matrix, but there is a little corner of the agate fractured off that shows chalcedony and possible agate banding.

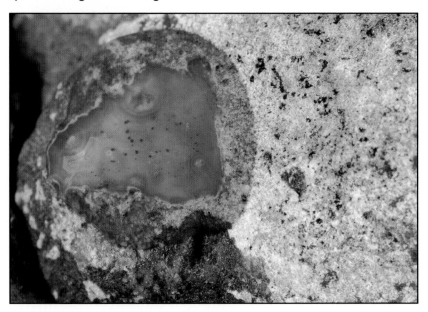

Figure 80
The Lake Superior nodule in this photo has a fracture, which gives you a peak of microcrystalline quartz. There is even some "structure" showing that means there could be more banding on the inside.

BANDING AND OTHER PATTERNS

Essentially, agate is a colored variety of chalcedony, which can exhibit several different types of "self-organized behavior." Most agates exhibit distinctive concentric banding patterns. These concentric bands consist of parallel fibrous crystals that nucleate onto the wall of the host rock cavity and fill in the pocket one band at a time. The elongate fibers orient toward the center of the pocket, perpendicular to the banding pattern.379 Information about how agate bands form is covered in Chapter 2. Other agates form horizontal banding, cloud-like formations, paisley swirls, tubes, eyes or other spherulitic patterns, radiating sagenite rods, and other detailed structures. Further information about the different types of agate structures is included in Chapter 4.

To look for rocks that have the highest likelihood of being agate, you want to keep your eyes open for anything that looks like it may have self-organized into a pattern of some type. Murphy's Law seems to dictate that most of the time, the side of the rock with obvious agate structure will be facing down at the collection site. But even the "rougher" sides of agate nodules sometimes show indications of self-organized banding behavior, as shown below.

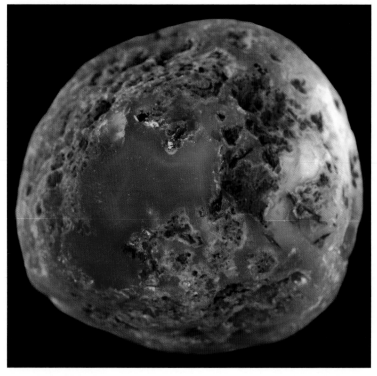

Figure 81
This "back side" of a Lake Superior agate has a hint of self-organized behavior. Faint bands can be seen popping through the chalcedony "window."

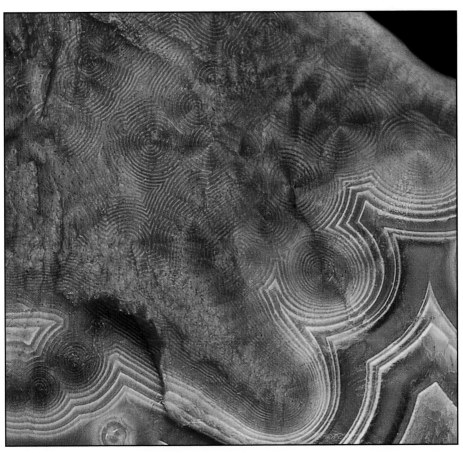

Figure 82
This Lake Superior agate has what look like "crop circles." Although there is obvious banding that shows on the bottom, even if just the "crop circle" section is exposed, it still indicates that there is self-organized banded behavior.

Of course, it is important when you are agate hunting to look at all sides of every specimen. The obvious agate sections may be on the opposite side of a rock you pick up. Even if you have 20-20 vision, it is a good idea to bring some sort of magnifying lens or loupe with you. This can be very helpful since magnification allows you to peak a little closer at any possible agate structure. The photo above is a good example. This photo is a magnification of just a small part of the agate. With magnification, the "crop circles" define interesting self-organizing agate behavior. Without magnification, you may not see this detail when obvious banding is not evident. Another example is shown in Figure 83. The detail in this small "window" popping through the outer husk may be missed without magnification.

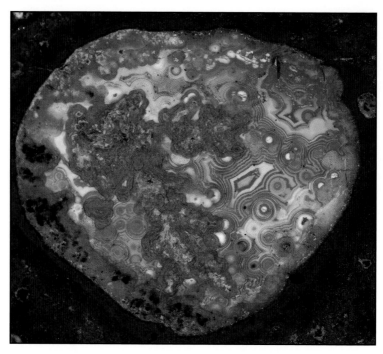

Figure 83
Most of the outer surface of the above Lake Superior agate has a very rough, nondescript rhyolitic husk. There is this small window that pops through showing intricate agate patterns. This was the only "window" that was evident on this nodule, which is why it is important to look at all sides of specimens that you think could be agate.

Figure 84
This Oregon thunder egg has an exterior with part of the original rhyolitic husk, but also with chalcedony sections that display the inner beauty.

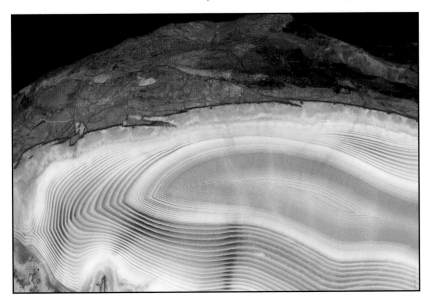

Figure 85
Notice that the husk on top of this Michipicoten agate from Ontario, Canada, has several micro-fractures that later filled in with red jasper. Even if banding doesn't show, a husk with jasper fractures and gray chalcedony is an indication that there may be agate on the inside.

TRANSLUCENCY

Translucency is an optical feature that can be very useful in helping you spot agates, even if they are covered with dust or dirt. Chalcedony microcrystalline quartz allows light to penetrate to varying degrees, depending on the agate's husk, producing a "glow" that distinguishes it from other rocks. Sunny days are the best for observing agate translucency.

While it is true that not all agates are translucent, the vast majority of specimens are. Examples of non-translucent agates would be paint stone agates and some jasper agates (see Chapter 4). With these agates, translucency is inhibited by a higher percentage of mineral impurities, chert or jasper granular microcrystals, or by a non-chalcedony external husk that obscures the transmission of light through the specimen.

Translucency is a key characteristic that will help your agate hunting success. One time when we were agate hunting in a gravel pit in Carlton County, Minnesota, the conditions were muddier than any we had previously experienced. The local area had suffered downpours for about a week, turning everything to mud. After we struggled in the muddy piles of glacial till for around an hour, the sun broke through the clouds. For the next two hours we were able to pull one agate after another out of the pile by focusing only on translucency. The sunlight exposed the translucency causing the agates to "glow" at us.

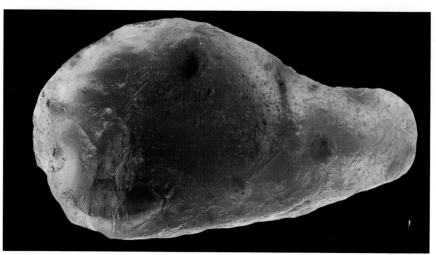

Figure 86
Agates with little or no husks are often very translucent. When looking for agates, focus on rocks that "glow" at you.

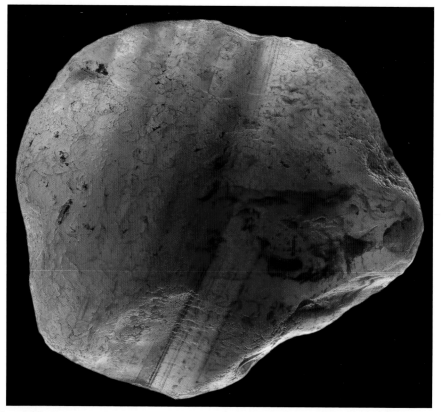

Figure 87
When you look at this Lake Superior agate without back lighting, it appears to be macrocrystalline quartz. However, with back lighting, the banding suddenly appears!

When you are looking for agates without rhyolitic or similar opaque husks, you can increase your success by taking advantage of translucency. In case it is not sunny, we recommend that you bring a flashlight that has a high intensity bulb. Use the flashlight to check for translucency through all angles of the rock. For larger specimens, sometimes the translucency only shows through the outer section of husk. When the sun is out, you can carefully hold up one hand to block the sun and protect your eyes, while using your other hand to hold the rock directly under your "blocking" hand. If the agate nodule is intact with a thick opaque husk, you'll have to cut a slab off the end so that you can get to the interior section and check for translucency.

Now just because a rock is translucent doesn't mean that it is agate. Macrocrystalline quartz can also be translucent, as compared to jasper and chert that usually are not. Many other rocks and minerals are translucent, but in most cases they are not confused with agate because their characteristics are distinctly different. A few that may be confused include feldspar, amazonite, fluorite, calcite, rhodochrosite, dolomite, datolite, and labadorite.

COLOR

There are no two agates alike in the world. Nature formed them in a wide array of colors with an even wider selection of patterns. The colors of agates from a particular locality are often distinctive. So when you decide to agate hunt in a certain area, it is extremely important to do your homework and know what the characteristics are for the agates that are the target of your search. Lake Superior agates, for example, formed in an area that has a lot of iron. Once the hard and resistant agates eroded from the host rock, they were stained by the iron-rich soil. As a result, many "Lakers" have red iron-stained husks. The nodules found at the Baker Ranch in New Mexico all have a husk that is covered with gray volcanic ash. Many of the agates found in Mexico also have this nondescript gray husk.

Agates that tend to have intact husks, may require you to cut them to see the characteristic colors, or for you to find specimens that are fractured by nature. Botswana agates from Africa have a lot of gray, white, and sometimes pink salmon color. Fairburn agates from South Dakota are famous for having a rainbow of color including red, pink, yellow, tan, white, and orange.

The colors in banded agates have been influenced by seven factors:

1. **Chalcedony Layers** The inherent color, clarity, and porosity of the chalcedony layers influences the appearance of a banded agate. The chalcedony fibrous microcrystalline bands themselves develop into three basic types:

a. WHITE BANDS are relatively wide (as much as .20 inches) that consist of very straight and tightly packed fibers. They have very few water-filled spaces and are quite dense with very low porosity and permeability. These apparently opaque bands are not susceptible to the infiltration of post-formation water or dyes.

b. COLORLESS BANDS are transparent bands made up of short, twisted fibers that contain small water filled cavities between the fibers. They can also host large numbers of manganese and iron-bearing mineral inclusions, are moderately porous and permeable, and are susceptible to the infiltration of post-formation ground water as well as dyes. When these narrow bands of colorless chalcedony are sandwiched between bands of opaque white chalcedony, the colorless bands can appear black or dark gray.

c. MILKY-WHITE OR BLUE-GRAY BANDS are translucent bands that are similar to the colorless bands, except that they are less transparent. The reduced clarity of these bands is due to the larger number of small water-filled cavities scattered throughout the crystal matrix. The blue color results when the size of these fluid inclusions is smaller than the wavelength of visible light. When the cavities become larger than the wavelength of light, the chalcedony loses its blue color and appears a translucent milky white. These bands have a relatively high porosity and permeability and are susceptible to the infiltration of post-formation water and dyes.[380]

Figure 88
White chalcedony bands are evident in this Lake Superior shadow agate.

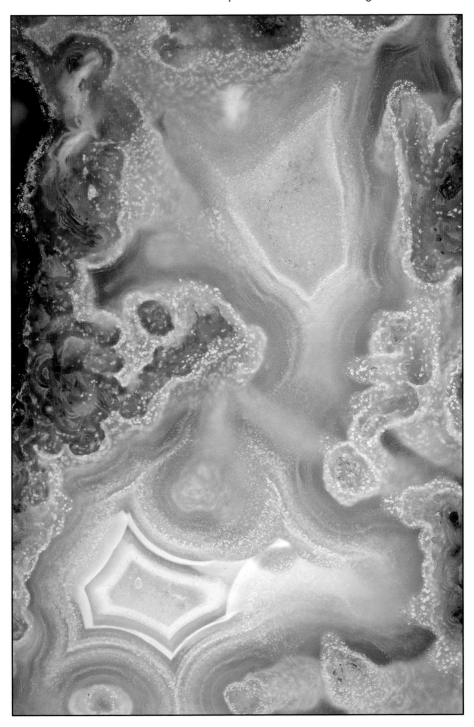

Figure 89
This Oregon thunder egg has interesting translucent layers swirled and intermixed with white bands and mineral inclusions.

Figure 90
Blue-gray chalcedony bands in this Lake Superior agate surround the whiter bands.

2. **Mineral Inclusions** The chemical composition and size of iron and manganese mineral inclusions within or between the chalcedony bands play a key role in the final appearance of the agate. Most of these inclusions gather between rows of chalcedony.[381] Agates that formed in rhyolite and andesite tend to have more manganese inclusions than agates that formed in basalt.[382] There are two different groupings of inclusions.

   a. UNALTERED INCLUSIONS are extremely common in agate banding. The unaltered inclusions usually comprise hematite or goethite. The variety of possible crystal shapes and colors exhibited by these minerals makes it difficult to accurately identify which inclusions are present without the use of sophisticated measurement devices. Sometimes these unaltered mineral inclusions form minute spherulites.

   b. ALTERED INCLUSIONS are responsible for much of the bright red, orange, and yellow coloration exhibited in agates. Since most of the colorless, translucent white, and blue-gray chalcedony is porous and permeable, shallow ground water entered and traveled through these agate layers. When the oxygenated ground water encountered black iron-bearing minerals, they altered them to a more oxidized and hydrous colorful form.[383] This alteration may have happened during or after agate formation.

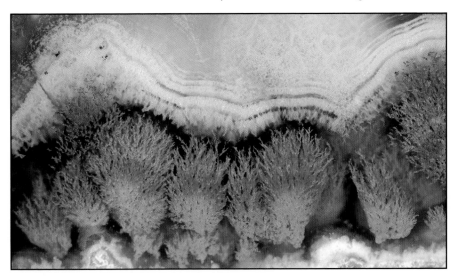

Figure 91
The unaltered mineral inclusions in this Brazilian agate have stood the test of time.

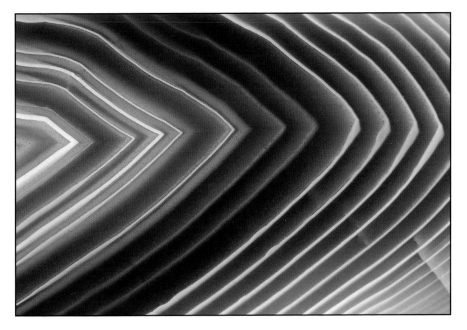

Figure 92
The red iron inclusions in this Botswana agate were altered when they oxidized.

3. **Post-formation alteration of mineral inclusions** The resident mineral inclusions may have been altered by post-formation invading water, resulting in a range of color changes. Water may have invaded the agate from one side and traveled only part-way through it, altering iron-bearing minerals in the invaded part only (See Figure 93.) [384]

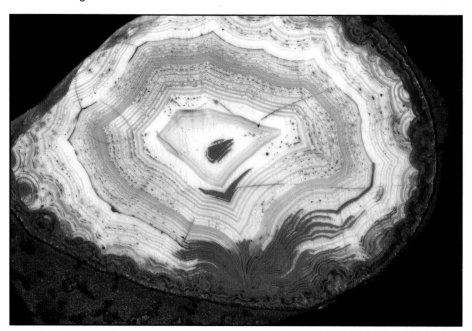

Figure 93
Post-formation alteration of this Lake Superior nodule shows iron-oxide mineral inclusions from ground water that penetrated only the bottom section.

4. **Iron Content** The iron in post-formation invading water may have in-filtrated and deposited new inclusions in the porous and semi-perme-able bands, thus altering the color. Usually, the higher the iron content in the ground water and the less oxygenated the water, the darker the post-formation color change.[385] The various shades of red, orange, yellow, and brown can be attributed to the varying concentrations of iron and the amount of weathering the iron experienced.[386,387]

5. **Macrocrystalline Quartz** The color of macrocrystalline quartz crystal layers between or adjacent to the chalcedony layers can impact the color of the compilation of bands.

6. **Optical Effects** Special optical effects caused by diffraction or re-fraction of light waves travelling through the different agate bands can alter their visible color. This is most dramatically shown with iris agates.

Figure 94
Sometimes the post-formation influences can significantly intensify color as shown in this Kentucky agate.

7. Post-Formation Weathering Over time, agates exposed to the elements can weather or have their appearance altered when they acquire a surface coating.[388] Highly weathered agates often exhibit a chalky white outer layer composed of opal and a small amount of clay. In extreme cases, all banded layers may be altered to a chalky white color.[389] Also, agates with iron inclusions when exposed to sunlight (heat) at the Earth's surface, can turn a dull yellow-orange to bright red color. This is due to dehydration of hydrous iron-bearing mineral inclusions. Sunlight can also fade or bleach the banding. Surface coatings of manganese and iron oxides, sometimes called "desert varnish" have resulted when agates are exposed in arid regions. Agates collected from iron-rich soil may have a thin coating of red iron oxide on their surface, which can also penetrate deep into porous chalcedony layers.[390,391]

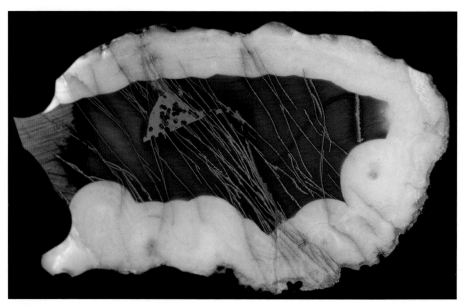

Figure 95
This Lake Superior nodule shows stress fractures that filled in with iron-oxide, supplied by post-formation fluids. The outer chalcedony layers turned a chalky white color from weathering.

If you purchase agate products, one thing you might want to keep in mind is that the colors in many agates sold today have been artificially manipulated. Although there are still incredible natural agates to be found, private companies are expanding their market by dying agates. In fact, most agates sold today have been treated in some way. The art of staining agates has been known for centuries, probably dating from cameo-workers in Italy more than a thousand years ago. In the eighth century, these Italian craftsmen passed on the art of treating agates to the cutting masters in Germany, who further developed the techniques.[392] Agate color is enhanced when chemical compounds are added prior to subjecting the agates to heat. Companies use these techniques on agates that otherwise would not be marketable.

The red color in agate is intensified in a couple of different ways. If the agates naturally have iron oxide compounds, sometimes just subjecting them to heat by baking will intensify the color. In other cases, agates are soaked in ferrous sulfate prior to the baking process. Blue agates were first manipulated to make the stones look like lapis lazuli. These are altered by first soaking them in an iron salt solution, and then in a solution of ferrocanide or ferricanide of potassium. Green agates are dyed to make them look like chrysoprase. This is accomplished by soaking the agates in salts of nickel or chromium. Yellow can be achieved by soaking the agate in hydrochloric acid. To produce a dark brown or black color, the agates are soaked for a few weeks in a saccharine solution at a slightly elevated temperature. Then the agates are washed and soaked for a few minutes in sulfuric acid, which penetrates into the pores and carbonizes the sugar. Since some chalcedony layers are more porous than others, the impact of this dying process can vary across the bands. If the agate bands are darkened too much, they can be lighted by soaking the agate in nitric acid.[393]

Another impact on the color of agate banding is chromatography. This occurred when solutions with trace minerals penetrated to different areas of the agate, based on particle size of the impurities and the porosity of the different agate layers. As groundwater permeated, it moved through certain bands more efficiently than others. The large trace mineral particles were the first to be separated by the porous membrane, followed by the smaller particles. As a result, water-related alteration of an agate was not always uniform and homogeneous throughout the rock. Chromatographs seem to be evident in only geologically young agates, perhaps because the coloring bands in older agates eventually bled into one another, or the trace minerals eventually distributed evenly throughout the agate.[394]

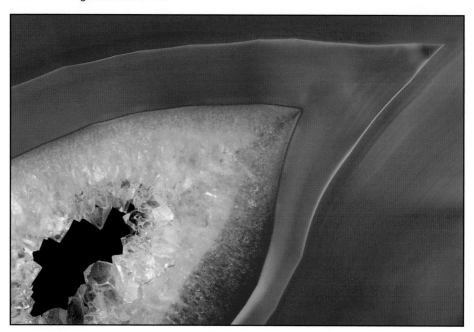

Figure 96
This intricate Brazilian agate shows chromatography color alterations that vary from gold to red.

One more aspect of color in agates involves the use of ultraviolet "black light" to stimulate fluorescence. Fluorescence occurs when non-visible ultraviolet light (either short wave or long wave) excites electrons in molecules of certain impurity compounds. Electrons in these molecules "jump" away from the nucleus. When they are pulled back down to fill the empty electron shell, light of a different visible wavelength is emitted. Most agates do not have these compounds and do not fluoresce. When agates fluoresce the transparent and translucent layers of chalcedony display a bright chalky-green, white, or blue color due to the presence of uranyl or other ions (See Figures 97–99.) [395]

So depending on where you live and whether agates in the area have fluorescence, you may be able to use a portable black light at night to help look for agates. You can check with local rock clubs or rock shops to find out about whether agates in the area have fluorescence. Lake Superior agates, for example, usually do not. However, dry head agates from Montana and many agates from the southwest part of the United States do fluoresce.

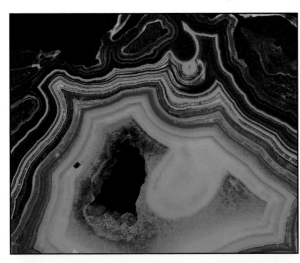

Figure 97
Fluorescence in a Montana dry head agate is shown to the left.

Figure 98
Fluorescence in an Argentina puma agate is shown below.

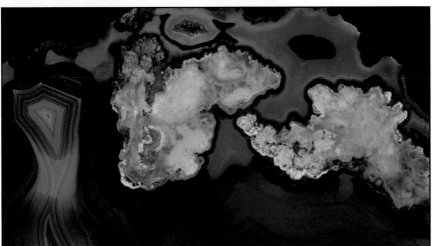

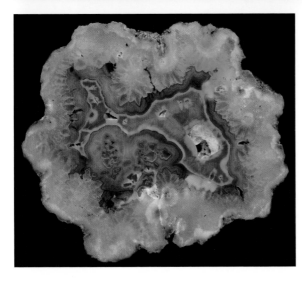

Fig 99
Fluorescence in another Argentina puma agate is shown to the left.

SHAPE, SIZE, AND WEIGHT

The shape of agates can vary, depending on the environmental conditions during formation. Amygdaloidal agates often have an oblong almond shape, due to the movement of gas through the lava or the movement of the lava itself that elongated the gas bubble pocket. Thunder egg agates are a bit more spherical in shape, as are many of the agates formed in sedimentary rock. What is important when agate hunting is to know the typical shape of the agates from the area in which you are searching.

Figure 100
Many amygdaloidal agates that formed in igneous basalt have this oblong almond shape. Notice the post-formation iron oxide staining on the husk of this Lake Superior agate.

Figure 101
Puma agates from Argentina were discovered in 1993. They formed in sedimentary rock and typically have a round shape.

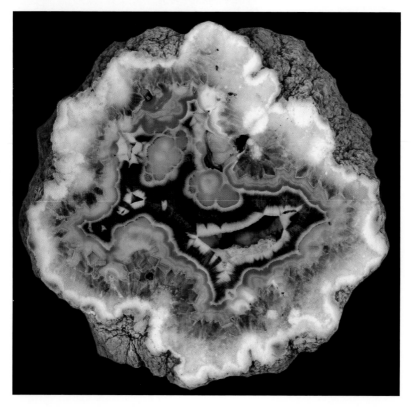

There could also be a difference in shape if you are searching for agates that are in situ (inside original host rock) as compared to those that have eroded free and subsequently have been subjected to weathering, glaciers, or other stresses. Lake Superior agates found on the beach, for example, have endured the ice and waves for millenniums. Since agates fracture in a conchoidal manner, sections break off that do not follow any natural crystal plane. Instead, there is a curved breakage surface that looks like the inside of a mussel shell (conchoid). Since the shape of the broken surface is controlled only by the mechanical stress or force applied, flint knappers take advantage of this tendency when working with flint and other silica minerals to make arrowheads. As a result of conchoidal fracturing, many beach agates will be quite irregular in shape.

Figure 102
Weathered agates that have been subject to mechanical force from glaciers, waves, or icebergs often suffered conchoidal fractures, resulting in an irregular shape. Agates found on Lake Superior beaches are especially known for this tendency.

Another consideration when you are agate hunting is the size of rocks on which you will focus. Since confidence is one of the factors that can influence success, it is recommended that you begin your hunt by looking for small "chippers." When you put that chipper in your pocket you can honestly say that you are a successful agate hunter. In fact, many of the chippers are the most beautiful since they tend to be fracture free.

You can classify the size of agates by using the following scale: small = less than 2 inches; medium = 2 to 4 inches; large = over 4 inches.[396] Of course, these categories offer just a general guideline. In some locations the classification of agate size may differ. Remember that to find a big agate you have to look in the big rocks. Since there are relatively few large agates the likelihood for success will be reduced.

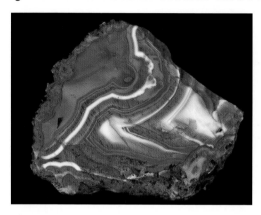

Figures 103 and 104
Pictured above is what we call the "Christmas agate." This amygdaloidal agate was removed from its in situ place of origin in host rock basalt. This Michigan baby nodule was altered significantly by post-formation fluids.

Figure 105
These Lake Superior agates range from a fraction of an inch to softball size.

Because of its high specific gravity agate tends to weigh more than other rocks. Specific gravity refers to how heavy the rock feels. The density of the material affects specific gravity. Because agates comprise densely packed fibrous microcrystals, they tend to have high specific gravities. Some relative specific gravities and weights are listed in Table 4. Although quartz is in the mid-range for weight, it tends to be heavier than the other common rock pebbles. Silica rocks, including agate, will feel a little heavier than other common rocks and even heavier than red brick and cement!

TABLE 4: SPECIFIC GRAVITY OF ROCKS & MINERALS[397,398]

Material	Specific Gravity	Weight (pound per cubic foot)
Feldspar pebbles	1.23	77
Sandstone pebbles	1.51	94
Limestone pebbles	1.55	97
Granite pebbles	1.65	103
Gneiss pebbles	1.86	103
Common red brick	1.92	120
Basalt pebbles	1.96	122
Cement	2.16	135
Agate	2.64	165

LUSTER

Luster is a description of the way light interacts with the surface of a mineral. It has nothing to do with color or shape, but is influenced by the translucency, surface condition, crystal type, specific gravity, and index of refraction (Ratio of the angle light enters the material by the angle the light is bent as it enters.)

The recognized types of luster include the following:

- **Metallic** — opaque and reflective, such as most metals.
- **Sub-metallic** — opaque to nearly opaque and reflective.
- **Vitreous** — glassy. Around 70 percent of minerals have this luster.
- **Adamantine** — transparent to translucent with a high refractive index, which cause these minerals to appear brilliant and shiny, like a diamond.
- **Resinous** — many yellow, dark orange and brown minerals with moderately high refractive indices (degree to which light waves entering the substance are bent) have this luster.

- **Silky** — minerals with a fine fibrous structure have this luster that looks like silk cloth.

- **Pearly** — looks like the inside of a mollusk shell.

- **Greasy** — the surface of the mineral looks like it is coated with oil or grease.

- **Pitchy** — the surface has a tar-like appearance.

- **Waxy** — looks like the mineral is coated with a surface of wax.

- **Dull (earthy)** — has an earthy appearance, much like unglazed porcelain. This includes minerals with poor reflective qualities and those with a rough or porous surface.[399]

Sometimes it is difficult to determine the exact luster of agates. Some have a husk that hides the actual luster. Although it is not true for other minerals, with agates it is best to examine the luster of fractured or husk-free surfaces. These fractured surfaces will expose the actual chalcedony, and thus display the mineral's luster. The waxy look is due to the fact that the chalcedony crystals are extremely tiny, each of which refracts light separately.[400] You can take advantage of this characteristic when looking for agates that are intermixed with other rocks since very few rocks have this waxy luster. When on the beach, for example, the waxy luster will appear to "shine" up at you. Of course, this is only true if you are looking in the dry rocks. When rocks are wet, they all appear to have a similar luster.

Figure 106
The conchoidal fractures on this Lake Superior agate display the waxy luster.

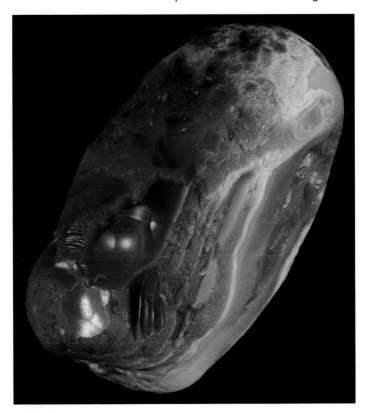

Figure 107
The waxy luster of chalcedony shows on the surface of these conchoidal fractures of this Lake Superior agate.

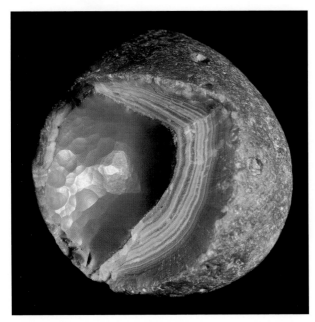

Figure 108
Notice how the center of this Lake Superior agate is pure chalcedony. While it was on the beach, it was subject to waves and ice, which caused part of the banded section to fracture away. There are also small fractures on the chalcedony section that display a waxy luster.

HUSK

Agates from different locations, and even agates from the same location that have been subject to varying amounts of weathering, will have considerably different appearances. Agates, like other minerals, can undergo changes both during and after their initial genesis. Heat and pressure can alter their appearance. Earth movements may cause stress fractures. Ground waters can carry mineral pigments that alter color. Sunlight can oxidize mineral inclusions and intensify color or fade and bleach exposed agates. Erosion and glaciers can abrade and fracture agates. Waves and river currents can serve as a natural type of tumbler to smooth agate exteriors or entirely remove the original husk.[401,402]

Agates that form in rhyolitic rock usually have a light colored, rhyolitic husk.

Figure 109
This is a typical rhyolitic husk on the exterior of an Oregon thunder egg agate. Notice the micro-fracture across the center of the husk that may have been an infiltration pathway to feed fluids into the agate pocket.

Figure 110
Many water-worn Lake Superior agates have no remnant husk. We all want to find agates like this candy stripper while walking down the beach!

The outermost surface of agate husks can be covered with various minerals. One example is a soft green mineral called celedonite (sĕl-ə-don-īte). This mineral forms from the decomposition of lava. It is usually green (See Figure 111.), but can also be light blue, blue, to blue-green. It is transparent to translucent with a heavy specific gravity of around 5.6.[403] Celadonite can be ruptured or torn apart during agate genesis, leaving small greenish filaments trapped within the agate (See Figure 112.) When there are a lot of these filaments, the agate is called moss agate.[404] The outer surface of a celedonite husk is usually smooth, while the inner surface is irregular due to shrinkage. As the chalcedony formed its initial layer over top of the celedonite on the inside of the agate pocket, it actually molded to this inner surface. Therefore, if the celedonite subsequently wore away, which often happened due to its softness, the agate's "new" outer husk became pitted (See Figures 115 and 116.)

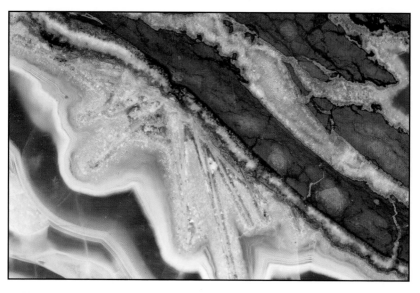

Figure 111
This Michipicoten agate from Ontario, Canada, has matrix with agatized seams on top, then a layer of green celadonite husk, and then chalcedony banding.

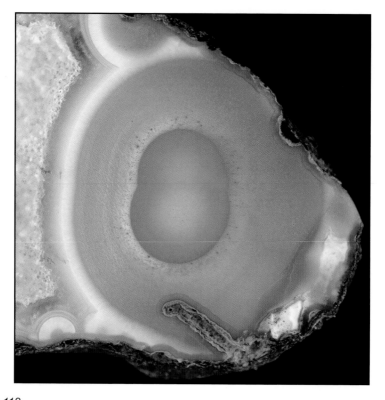

Figure 112
A fragment of the celadonite husk of this Michigan agate broke off and became trapped within the chalcedony. Does it look like a snake, inch worm, or dinosaur to you?

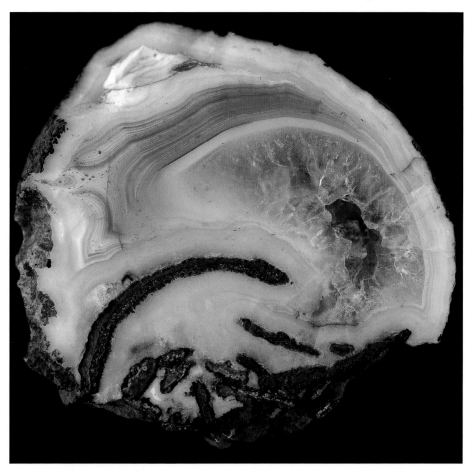

Figure 113
Several fragments of the rhyolitic husk broke off this northern Minnesota thunder egg and became trapped within the chalcedony.

Another material often found on agate husks is limonite (See Figure 114.) This is a brown or golden brown oxide of iron. It is not a true mineral since it is composed of a mixture of various forms of iron oxides.[405] It is not only observed as a coating on agates and other rocks, but it can also serve as a cementing agent in sandstone. When the softer limonite mineral wears away, just as is true with celedonite, the resulting erosion-resistant agate husk can be pitted (See Figures 115 and 116.)[406]

Other minerals that can form outer husks on agates include calcite, siderite, prehnite, epidote, and clay minerals. This original outer husk, which has a different consistency than the interior of most agates, is generally about 1/10 of an inch (1 to 3 mm) but can be up to 50% of the total volume.[407]

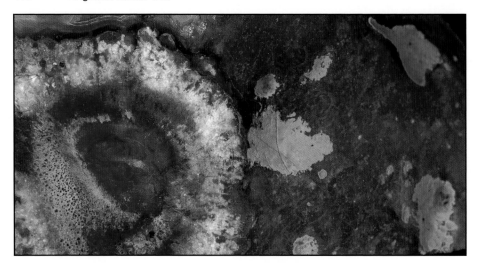

Figure 114
This Lake Superior agate has yellow limonite showing on its husk.

The pit-marked husk with small bubble-like depressions is, with an experienced eye, quite distinctive and helpful to agate hunters. Often, only one side or area of the husk is pitted, such as shown in Figures 115 and 116.[408,409] Because these pits are left over from minerals that accumulated on the inside of the vesicle pocket first, and then eroded away, they appear to have a "molded" appearance. This pattern contrasts with rhyolite and other igneous rocks that have micro-bubbles that may or may not have filled in with minerals (Figures 117 and 118).

Figure 115
This photo shows a typical pit-marked husk on a Lake Superior agate. Most likely these pockets are left over from softer impurity spheroids that have long since worn away, leaving behind the harder chalcedony. Please refer to the "Eye Agate" section of Chapter 4, which begins on page 151, to see photos of agates with the spheroids still intact.

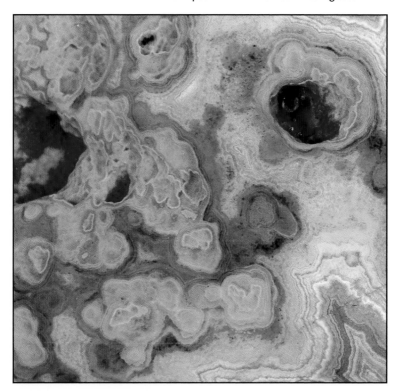

Figure 116
Notice the pits vacated by softer spheroids that have worn away from this Crowley Ridge agate from Arkansas.

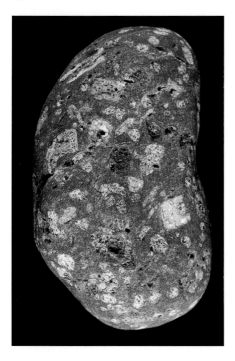

Figure 117
This rhyolite specimen (NOT AN AGATE) has small vesicles that filled in with minerals. Notice how different these vesicle pockets are as compared to the pit-marked surface of agates (see Figures 115 and 116). Also, rhyolite has a dull luster and is opaque.

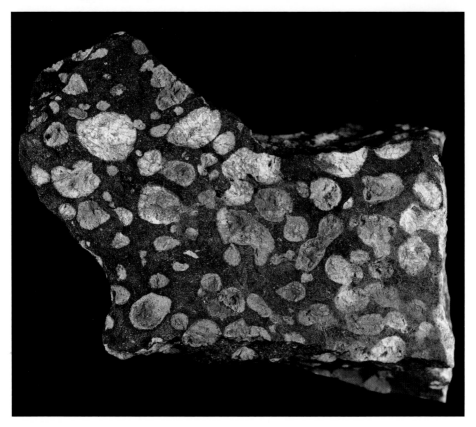

Figure 118
This amygdaloidal basalt (NOT AN AGATE) has individual air pockets that filled in with minerals. Notice how distinctly different these small rounded vesicles look as compared to the pit-marked surface of agates.

CONNECTIVE CHANNELS

Scientists do not agree on whether the channel connections between the interior of agates and the exterior are "entrance" channels that allowed the silica-rich solution to enter the cavity or "escape" channels that allowed the release of pressure built up during agate genesis. For more information about connective channels, refer to Chapter 2.

Either because they are the last section of the agate to fill in during in-flow, or because they are extrusions from pressure release, these connective channels usually have a different appearance. Typically they are more "quartzy" than the rest of the husk. In some cases they fail to fill in at all. While agate hunting you should look for any areas on the outside of rocks that are indicative of connective channels. If agates are fractured, you can occasionally see cross-sections of these channels.

Figure 119
This "raw" Lake Superior agate shows the connective channel which partially filled in with macro-crystalline quartz.

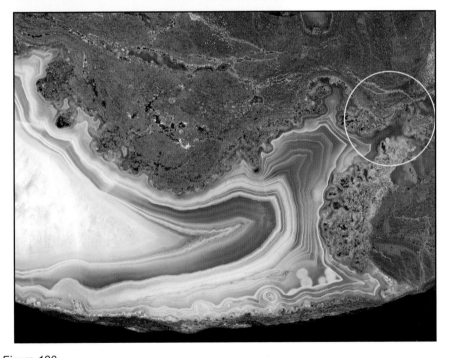

Figure 120
The connective channel in this Lake Superior agate can be seen entering the pocket from the upper right side.

Figure 121
A large connective channel can be seen on the left side of this Lake Superior agate.

PSEUDOBANDS

As you agate hunt and examine specimens, especially if you are look-ing for water-worn or weathered agates wherein the husks have eroded away, you can usually see evidence of banding. In other cases, however, the husk may hide obvious banding, but give you a hint that there is self-organized agate structure inside the nodule. These "pseudobands" can be seen on the surface or sometimes via translucency with backlighting. What is important is to look for evidence on the exterior of the specimen that gives indication that there may be agate structure on the inside (See Figures 122 and 123.)

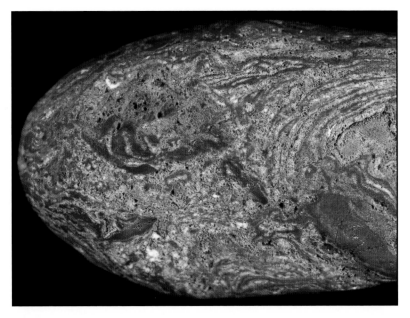

Figure 122
This Lake Superior agate has a thick husk, but you can see the pseudoband structure on the right side. This is indicative of possible banding inside the specimen.

Figure 123
Any time you see structure on the outside of the agate that looks like it could be a result of "self-organized" behavior, then there could possibly be agate banding on the inside of the rock.

AGATE-WANT-TO-BE

In Chapter 1 we reviewed some of the agate first cousins including chert, flint, jasper, petrified wood, and silicified fossils. One of the challenges agate hunters face is differentiating agates from these other silicon dioxide minerals that exhibit similar characteristics. Many of what we classify as "first cousins" can also have conchoidal fractures, waxy luster, and colorful patterns.

Figure 124
Butte Canyon jasper from Oregon has incredible patterns of microcrystalline quartz—but it is jasper and not agate. This does not mean that agates are better than jaspers. We are just suggesting that there are differences in crystal shape and size, as well as translucency. They are chemically the same and both quartz varieties are truly nature's art.

Chert, Flint, and Jasper

As we described in Chapter 1, the difference between chert, flint, and jasper—as compared to agate—is the shape and size of the microcrystals. The microcrystals of quartz in chert, flint, and jasper tend to be smaller and more granular. They are like BBs packed together in a jar so tightly that the specimens are usually opaque. Agate, on the other hand, has microcrystals that are long and fibrous, which results in most agates being translucent.

To make your agate hunting even more confusing, some specimens have a mixture of granular and fibrous microcrystals. It is not always important to be certain about your classification since a nice rock is a nice rock. However, if you want to classify a specimen, you must estimate how much of the rock appears to be more like chert or jasper and how much appears to be more like agate. If it appears that you have a specimen that is 50/50, then you have an agatized chert or a cherty agate. If more than 50 percent of the specimen appears to be agate, then it can be classified as such.

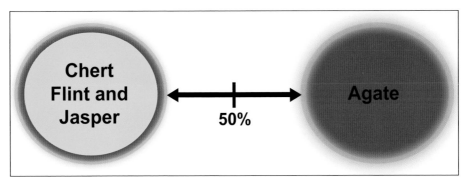

Figure 125
If a specimen has some chert, flint, or jasper AS WELL AS some agate, you must make a determination about the percentage of each and classify the specimen accordingly.

If you examine the specimen pictured below, you might at first think it looks more like jasper or chert. There is some structure showing, but it is not clear where on the continuum that this specimen should be classified. When it was cut, it became clear that it is on the agate half of the continuum. It is a paint stone ruin agate. See Chapter 4 for more information about these types of agates.

Figure 126
Here is the back of a hard to classify Lake Superior stone. There is a hint of structure and some of the right colors, but the exterior doesn't give a good clue as to what is inside. See the next photo for a glimpse of the cut side.

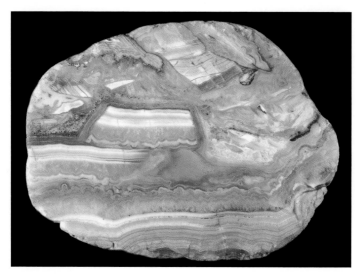

Figure 127
This is the cut side of the specimen in the previous photo. Although we don't recommend cutting most agates, this specimen (which was cut by the museum's founder) clearly shows its "true colors" after the inner beauty was exposed. This is a paint stone agate that is also a ruin agate. Although it does have some chert and jasper, more than half the specimen appears to be agate—thus it can be classified as agate.

Figure 128
These are examples of banded chert. They have a waxy luster, conchoidal fractures, and banding—but their microcrystalline structures are granular, which result in their being opaque and classified as chert. Similarly, you can find banded jasper.

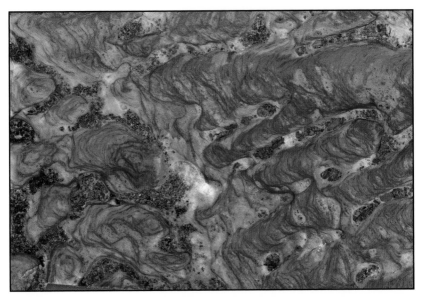

Figure 129
This is Mary Ellen jasper, which is a silicified stromatolite fossil formation. Stromatolites were the first organisms on Earth to photosynthesize. As a result, they were responsible for producing oxygen, which changed the Earth's atmosphere forever. The first stromatolites may have evolved over 3 billion years ago, but they peaked about 1.25 billion years ago. Some species still survive today, so they are one of the oldest organisms on Earth. This specimen is from Minnesota.[410]

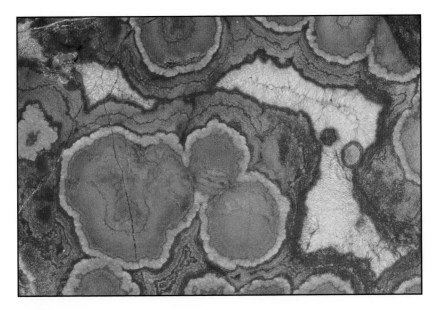

Figure 130
Some jaspers can be as colorful as agate, such as this Morgan Hill poppy jasper from California.

Metamorphic Rocks

Another agate-want-to-be is gneiss, and similar metamorphic rocks. These rocks are formed under extreme heat and/or pressure that caused one type of rock to transform into another. Although gneiss appears to have "bands," these are actually striations, or loose, not well defined groupings of minerals. The segregation of light and dark minerals occurred under high temperature (1112-1292°F, 600-700°C) that caused the different minerals to separate out. Most gneiss was metamorphosed from granite or diorite. The photo below shows "bands" that are actually discontinuous streaks of like-minerals.

Figure 131
This agate-want-to-be is metamorphic gneiss. It has striations of dark and light minerals. Notice how the bands are less distinctive than those in agates.

Figure 132
Banded iron formation, which is a metamorphic rock, contains layers of jasper and hematite. It can be differentiated from agate because it is absolutely opaque and does not have conchoidal fractures.

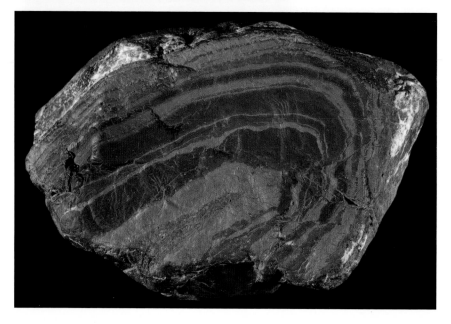

Secondary Fills

When molten igneous rock cooled, it formed a series of cracks, much like mud does when it dries out. In some cases, these cracks or seams agatized when microcrystals of quartz lined and filled in the seams (See the Seam Agate section in Chapter 4.) In other cases, the cracks filled in when molten material was forced through the fractures during subsequent lava flows, or when minerals from ground water precipitated out and filled the cracks. Although agate is also considered a "secondary fill," most secondary fills in basalt seams are not agate.

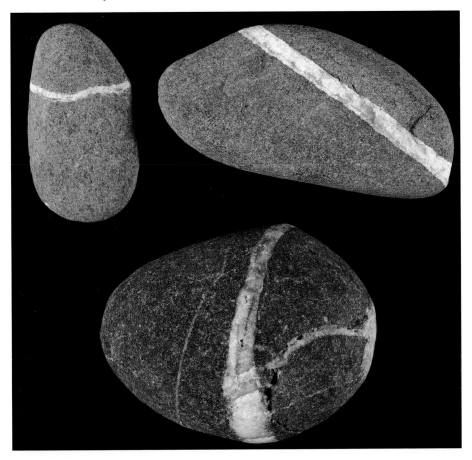

Figure 133
The cracks in this basalt filled in with macrocrystalline quartz instead of microcrystalline agate.

Silicified Fossils

Many fossils formed when silica-rich waters penetrated into deceased organisms and replaced organic structures with silica. In Chapter 1 information is included about petrified wood and other silicified fossils. In some cases, the organism's structure defined the structure and was directly replaced, so the silica did not self-organize to create the fossil. In other specimens, separate miniature pores in the fossil did fill in with miniature agates that self-organized. The pockets also may have filled in with macrocrystalline quartz, jasper, and other forms of silica.

One way to determine whether a silicified fossil may be agate is to examine the structure carefully under a bright light. When you move the specimen back and forth determine whether you can see little sparkles within the supposed banded structure. If you can, then the material is macrocrystalline quartz. Agate quartz crystals would be too small to be seen as "sparkles" by the human eye.

Figure 134
This agate-want-to-be is a silicified fossil. A mixture of chert and macrocrystalline quartz replaced the organic structure. When you hold and move this rock back and forth under a bright light, the individual macro crystals of quartz are clearly visible. This fossil was found on the beach in Grand Marais, Michigan.

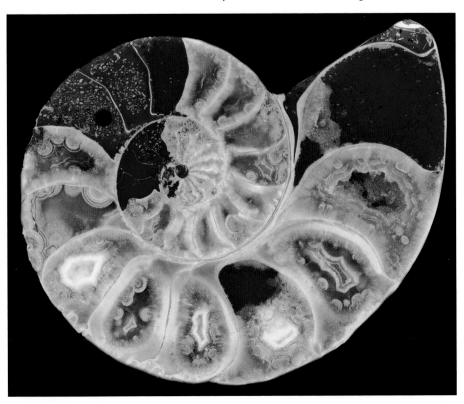

Figure 135
This Madagascar ammonite fossil has some individual chambers that agatized, while others filled in with jasper (red sections), spherulites (yellow and white round structures), and macrocrystalline quartz. Although there are agate chambers, the specimen is still considered a silicified fossil.

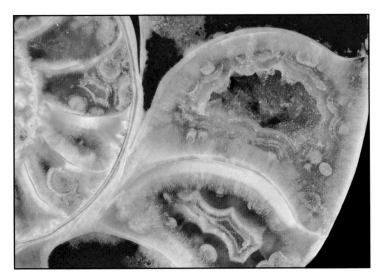

Figure 136
A close up of agatized chambers from the ammonite fossil pictured above.

Figure 137
Some of the indi-
vidual pores in this
Utah red horn coral
filled in with agate,
while others filled in
with jasper or mac-
rocrystalline quartz.
Even though there
are some agatized
pores, it is still a si-
licified fossil.

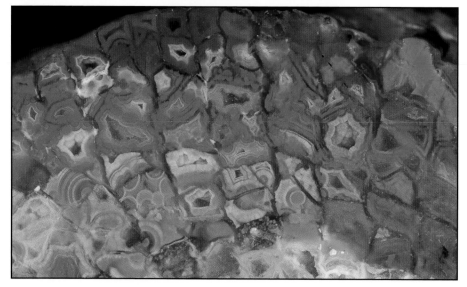

Figure 138
A close up of some of the agatized chambers in the red horn coral pictured above.

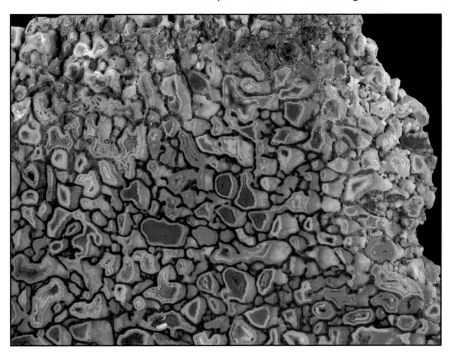

Figure 139
In some cases bone also became silicified. The silica may have formed agate, jasper, or macrocrystalline quartz. This fossilized dinosaur bone is from Utah.

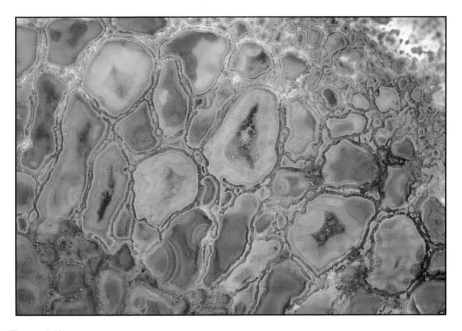

Figure 140
This is a close up of another section of fossilized dinosaur bone. Notice that there are miniature pockets of agate.

Other Agates-Want-To-Be

There are a few other minerals that can be confused with agate. One is binghamite, which is a chatoyant form of chalcedony. Chatoyancy is an optical characteristic exhibited by minerals that have a changing luster or color, like that exhibited in tiger's eye. The chalcedony fibers are dense and random. Occasionally, binghamite contains small agate pockets. When the crystals are parallel in their orientation, specimens are classified as silkstone or cyanite. Binghamite also contains a significant amount of goethite or hematite, which contribute to its colorful patterns. The colors can be gold, white, red, black and brown. This mineral variety was named after Bill Bingham, a lapidarist, who discovered it in 1936 in Crow Wing County, Minnesota in the iron deposits of the Cuyuna North Range.[411,412]

Figure 141
Binghamite from Minnesota is a chatoyant form of chalcedony.

Once in a while you run into someone who tries to pass off "Fordite" as an agate. This "stone" is actually an accumulation of enamel from a paint booth from an automobile factory. It is colorful and agate-like, but it is not even a rock or a mineral.

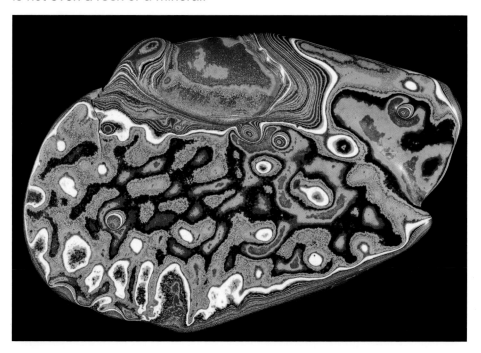

Figure 142
Fordite is actually layered paint enamel from an automobile factory.

Another rock that is can be confused with agate is banded calcite. Mineral dealers should take some blame for this because they sell the material as Mexican Onyx or Pakistani Onyx. Banded calcite is a softer carbonate material often used to carve figurines. Calcium carbonate is the main component of limestone as well as marble, which is metamorphosed limestone. Banded calcite formed in veins and caves when calcium is transported by groundwater. Cave formations include stalactites, stalagmites, columns, and soda straws. These formations are created when rainwater mixes with carbon dioxide to form carbonic acid, which intrudes into the limestone, leaches calcite out of the rock, and then drips from the cave's ceiling depositing calcite. Because the mineral content of the water changes over time, these calcite deposits often form a banded pattern.[413,414]

Figure 143
This Mexican onyx is actually banded calcite, which is significantly softer than quartz.

Still another mineral that can be confused with agate is rhodochrosite. This mineral is a magnesium carbonate that is also softer than quartz. It forms in veins and caves with minerals that are supplied by hydrothermal solutions. Often, it is found near silver deposits. Most of the world's supply comes from Argentina and Colorado.[415]

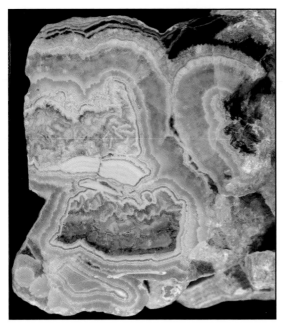

Figure 144
Rhodochrosite is a magnesium carbonate mineral. This specimen is from Argentina.

Figure 145
This is a Lake Superior agate that has intricate banding details.

CARING FOR AND CLEANING AGATES

In the late 1930s, many collectors began cutting large agates (weighing a pound or more) in half to uncover their hidden beauty. A person who had come across a large agate would bring it in to a lapidariest with a diamond saw and have it cut in two, giving the cutter one of the halves. Apparently this practice was commonplace throughout the 1940s and 1950s, until big agates became increasingly scarce. Word soon spread that "sawing for halves" was depleting the number of these treasured finds, and the practice stopped. One exception would be any nodules that have rhyolitic or other very thick husks. Many of the nodules dug out of the Baker Ranch in New Mexico, for example, require cutting to separate the good agates from the duds. Also, since many of the nodules are hollow, it is best to cut these in half to geometrically expose the most banding or macrocrystalline lined pockets.

When people come into the Gitche Gumee Museum and ask for their agates to be cut, we rarely accommodate the request. If the agate has been water worn so that the husk has been removed naturally to expose banding, it may be best to leave the agate in its natural state. If there is only a small section of the agate showing through a thick husk verifying that it is agate, but not exposing any banding detail, it is appropriate to either slice off a small end or to face polish a side.

Some agates look great in their naturally found state, but others need to be "dressed up." Before you perform lapidary on any agate, you might want to think about trying to clean it first.

1. Start by cleaning the rock with soap and warm water. Use a stiff brush or a toothbrush to remove any stubborn dirt. Let the rock dry completely so that you can examine the effectiveness of this initial cleaning.

2. If the rock needs further cleaning, either work outside or place the rock into a plastic container. If you are working inside, make sure you have adequate ventilation. Spray the rock with foaming oven cleaner. Wait around a half hour. Use gloves or tongs to carefully move the rock to a where you can rinse it thoroughly with warm water, being careful not to drip oven cleaner if you are working inside. Let the rock dry completely so that you can examine the effectiveness of this second stage of cleaning.

3. If the rock still needs further cleaning, place it into a small clean and dry plastic container with a tight fitting lid. Pour a measured amount of water over the rock until it is ½ to ¾ submerged. Wearing gloves and eye protection, and working with adequate ventilation, slowly and carefully add the amount of muriatic acid you need to result in a 4 to 1 solution (4 parts water to one part acid). The acid will clean off calcite and other minerals. Seal the container and leave it in a safe place overnight. Examine it the next day and assess whether the acid has been effective in removing the target material. If not, let it sit for another day. Do not let the rock sit in acid for more than three total days. To remove it from the acid, work in an area that you will not drip acid. Wear gloves, eye protection, and use tongs to remove the rock. Thoroughly rinse the rock in warm water. Also carefully dump the acid solution down the toilet taking care not to breathe any fumes. Clean and dry the plastic container and set the rock into it without the lid. Allow the rock to dry completely.

4. Once the rock is dry, sprinkle baking soda over the rock and add water until the rock is completely covered. Wearing rubber gloves, stir the rock and the baking soda solution, mixing well. This step is necessary to make sure that you neutralize any acid that may still be in the pores of the rock. Place the lid on the container and let the rock sit in the solution for fifteen minutes.

5. After the cleaning steps and acid treatment, the agate may have a frosted appearance, caused by light being diffused by tiny surface fractures. Rub mineral oil all over the entire surface. Place the agate in sunlight for an hour or so to heat the stone and allow the oil to seep into the tiny cracks to seal them and minimize or eliminate the frosted appearance. You can also set the rock six inches under a bright quartz lamp instead of placing it in the sun. Use a towel to pick up and clean any excess oil from the agate. Take care since the rock may be hot. Do not soak agates in mineral or any other kind of oil for extended periods as this may alter the banding.[416,417]

Figure 146
This paintstone Lake Superior agate has a wide variety of colorful and intricate bands that alternate between various types of microcrystalline quartz.

ASSESSING THE VALUE OF AGATES

When it comes to agates, there are some guidelines that you can use to assess their value. For the most part, however, beauty is in the eye of the beholder. All agate collectors have their favorite type, so the value of a quality specimen that matches your passion is worth more to you than to others who may prefer a different type of agate.

In a general sense, what makes one agate more desirable than another? The most obvious characteristic is, of course, size. But a large agate that is fractured, has poor banding, or has a large center fill of macrocrystalline quartz may be worth less than a much smaller high-quality agate. Some of the factors influencing value are listed below.

- **Size** It is best if the agate is at least several ounces. Those that are over a pound are rare. We call these large agates "fisters."

- **Color** The value increases if it has bright colors or a variety of color. Any agate from a particular locale with colors rarely seen in that area is also worth more.

- **Number of Bands** The more bands the better.

- **Quality of Banding** Agates with contrasting color in the banding pattern are worth more. Red and white candy striped agates are always a favorite.

- **Agate Structures** Agates that have complex botryoidal, eye, iris, moss, plume, sagenite, shadow, or tube formations are sometimes worth a little more, especially if the agate also has fortification banding. Those with perfectly symmetrical fortification patterns are also desirable.

- **Shape of Pattern** Agates with complex banding patterns or those with holly leaf patterns are highly desired. Collectors also like agates that have banding patterns that run through the center of the agate and appear on the opposite face.

- **Fracture Free Surface** Agates that have no surface fractures are worth more than those with fractures or breaks in the banding pattern. Also, those that exhibit their banding in the natural state have a higher value than those that require lapidary.

- **Artifact** Occasionally an agate is found that has worn spots or has obvious knapped areas indicating that it was used by indigenous people as a tool. If it can be documented that an agate is an artifact, it doubles its value. [418]

<table>
<tr><td>**CHAPTER 4**</td><td># What Are the Different Types of Agate?</td></tr>
</table>

What Are the Different Types of Agate?

CHAPTER 4

For over three billion years agates have formed in empty voids and seams in all types of host rock. They either filled pockets or replaced minerals in sedimentary rock. Cavities in ancient ammonites, corals, and bone may have also filled in with banded chalcedony. Agates range from pea-size to those that weigh thousands of pounds. Although most agates are almond-shaped, they can be round or almost any shape as a result of fracturing, leaving only parts of the agate intact. And just like snowflakes, there are no two agates alike.

There are thousands of different agates, but there is no official scientific method to classify them. They are usually identified by either their structure or by the geographical area in which they are found or both. We do not intend to list all of the world's agates. Instead we will describe the most common types of agate structures. Chapter 5 will list the most common agate structures found in the different states and include photographs of a selection of agates found in the U.S. and around the world.

BOTRYOIDAL (GRAPE) AGATES

Botryoidal means "like grapes." This is one type of "habit" that defines the way minerals form in a free space or in a particular environment. Botryoidal minerals develop globular aggregate masses with interlocking rounded formations. Botryoidal specimens can display their masses on the exterior or occasionally in an interior pocket. In addition to agates, other minerals that display this growth habit include hematite, goethite, smithsonite, fluorite, malachite, and chrysocolla.[419]

Figure 147
This is a botryoidal agate from New Mexico. It also has moss structure.

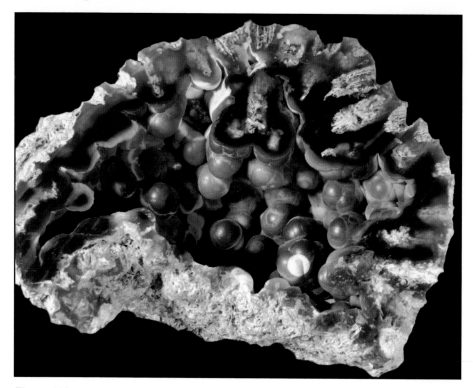

Figure 148
There is not a better representation of "grape agate" than this Tampa Bay coral agate from Florida.

Botryoidal agates can be found throughout the U.S. Some of the locations include Arizona, California, Florida, Michigan, Minnesota, New Mexico, North Carolina, South Dakota, Tennessee, Texas, Wisconsin, and Wyoming.

BRECCIATED (MOSAIC) AGATES

Brecciated rocks are composed of angular fragments of minerals or rocks that are cemented into a matrix of a finer grained material. Rocks with this mosaic pattern can form from landslides, geologic faulting, or explosive igneous eruptions. The fragments are angular because they were cemented together before they could be rounded by erosion. Before the fragments were cemented, they were most likely in a mixture with fine sediment that cushioned inter-particle collisions and inhibited rounding of the angular fragments.[420]

In the case of agate breccias, there can either be pieces of agate fragments that were cemented together, or agate formed in between angular fragments of another material. An example of the latter type of agate breccia formed at the top of some basaltic lava flows when there were numerous cracks in what we call the "frothy" layer. This complex crack system then filled in with agate.[421] Brecciated agates can be found in many locations including Arizona, California, Michigan, Minnesota, Nebraska, Nevada, Washington, Wisconsin, Wyoming, and Germany.

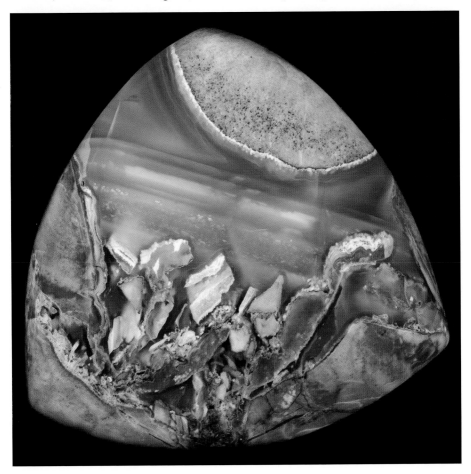

Figure 149
This is a brecciated agate from Lake Superior.

CANDY STRIPED AGATES

This is a descriptive term used to identify agates that have alternating layers of red and white banding, so as to resemble a candy cane. The red bands are colored by iron oxide impurities. In some cases, these red bands formed during the original genesis process. There are some specimens in which alternating bands were more permeable; this allowed post-formation fluids to penetrate and deposit iron oxide.

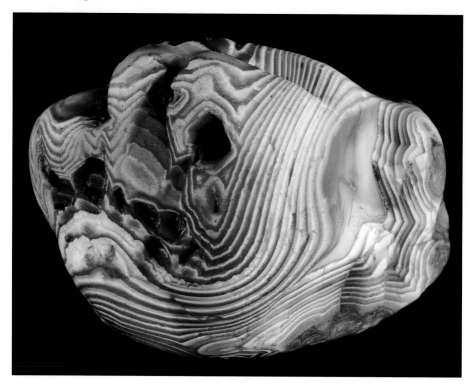

Figure 150
This Lake Superior candy striped agate shows how weathering can expose the beautiful banding. The elements eroded the original husk to expose the banding and display the candy-striped structure. Anyone who saw this rock on a beach would pick it up.

CARNELIAN AGATES

Carnelian is a translucent chalcedony that is stained uniformly throughout with iron oxide. The color can vary greatly, ranging from pale orange to an intense dark reddish brown, depending on the amount of resident iron oxide. Although carnelian does occur in pure form with uniform color, it can also intermix in alternating layers with other forms of chalcedony to form carnelian agates. The word carnelian is derived from the Latin root word *carno* or *carnis*, which means flesh, in reference to the flesh color sometimes exhibited.

Carnelian agates have been used in decorative arts for thousands of years. The Romans used carnelian to make engraved gemstones. Because hot wax does not stick to carnelian, they also used it to make seal rings for imprinting a seal on correspondence or other important documents.[422] Carnelian is especially prized as a semi-precious stone because of its beautiful red translucency. Carnelian agates can be found worldwide. In the U.S. they have been found in Alaska, Idaho, Michigan, Minnesota, New Jersey, Oregon, Texas, Utah, and Wyoming.

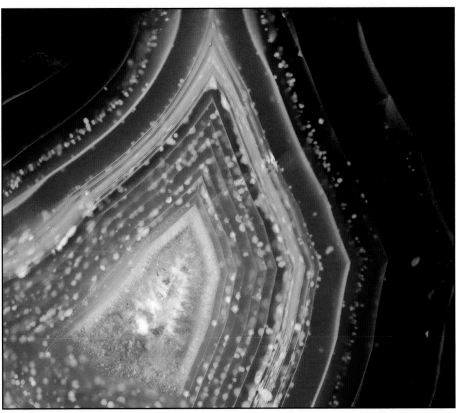

Figure 151
This carnelian agate was found in Grand Marais, Michigan, during the 1930s. It has spheroid inclusions throughout the agate banding.

CLOUD AGATES

This is a descriptive name for agates that have patches of fog or wispy cloud-like formations in a clear or gray chalcedony matrix. They are known to come from Mexico, Brazil, Nebraska (Deuel and Jefferson Counties), and Wyoming.

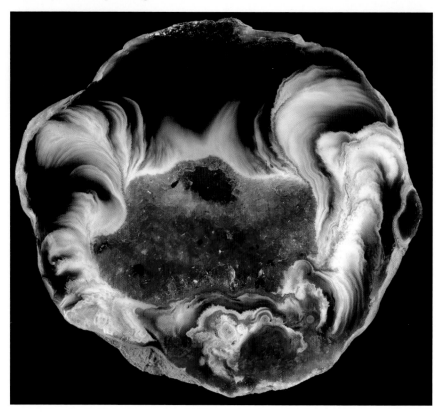

Figure 152
This occo geode from Brazil displays incredible cloud formations.

CRAZY LACE AGATES

When some pockets filled in with chalcedony, the composition of the fluids changed during genesis so that there were periods with less silica and no accessory minerals to serve as catalysts to stimulate banding. When this occurred, quartz crystal tops, or terminations, sometimes formed and protruded into the void space. Many of these pockets remained in this form and never completed their filling process creating geode agates. If, however, additional fluids with the right mixture of silica and accessory minerals subsequently entered the pocket, chalcedony would again develop, but this time laying down new bands over top of the crystal points resulting in an undulating pattern called "lace banding."[423]

Crazy lace agate formed in this manner, with different periods of macrocrystalline and microcrystalline growth. The resulting patterns can be quite bizarre with twisting and turning paisley bands of various colors that are often more random than that in other agates. Some of the sections in crazy lace agate are translucent, but much of it is opaque due to the presence of impurities and other forms of less translucent quartz. The majority of crazy lace agate is from northern Mexico, but it can also be found in Thunder Bay, Ontario, Australia, Texas, Wyoming, and Idaho. In most cases crazy lace agate formed in sedimentary rock with contributions from hydrothermal solutions.[424]

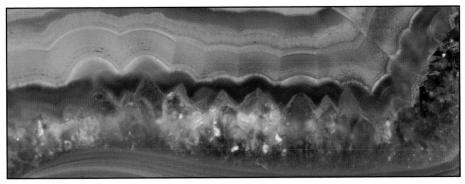

Figure 153
This photo of a Lake Superior agate has a band of macrocrystalline quartz crystals, all with termination points. Chalcedony subsequently added bands on top of the crystal points. It is this type of progression that caused the undulating pattern seen in crazy lace agate.

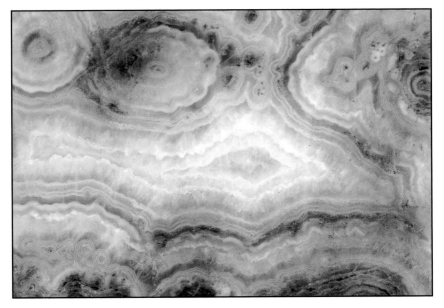

Figure 154
This is a sample of Thunder Bay agate, which includes crazy lace formation.

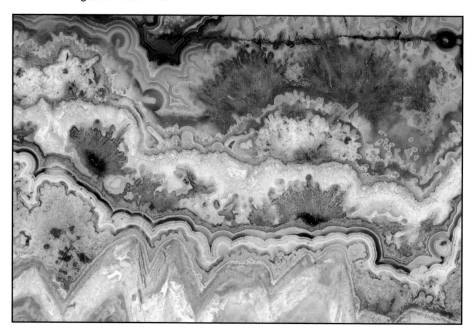

Figure 155
Some of the best crazy lace agate in the world comes from Mexico.

DENDRITIC AGATES

As agates developed, some of the trace impurities acted as catalysts to stimulate banding and were taken up within the fibrous structure (see Chapter 2). Other impurities were forced to the inside of the active crystallization front during the genesis process, only to accumulate and form their own band. Still other impurities grew within the agate pocket to form incredible structures of their own. These "inclusions" developed into many forms including dendrites, moss, plumes, stalk aggregates, and tubes.

One difference between the various "inclusion" structures is the period that they developed relative to agate formation. Dendrites are post-agate-genesis structures, while the other inclusions formed prior to or at the same time as agate banding (The other inclusion structures will be discussed separately in this chapter.) Most inclusions developed closer to the husk because they formed early in the agate genesis process when there were more trace elements available.[425]

Most of the time, dendrites consist of brown or black manganese or iron oxide aggregates or clusters. Dendritic agates can be found in Canada (Manitoba), Iran, Brazil, India, Madagascar, Mexico, and Khazakstan. In the U.S. they are found in Arizona, California, Kansas, Montana, Nebraska, Nevada, New Mexico, Oregon, Tennessee, Texas, and Wyoming.[426,427]

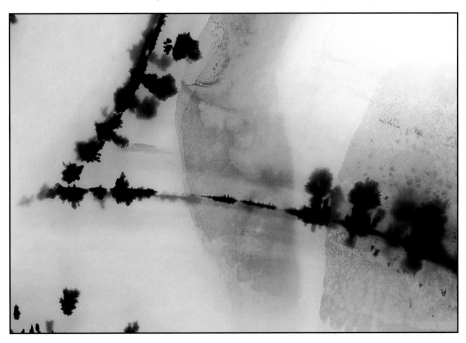

Figure 156
You can see how the dendrites in this Montana moss agate grew along fracture seams. Even though this is called a moss agate, the inclusion structures in this specimen are actually dendrites.

Though dendrites look organic, most are inorganic. A few agates have been found with black, pitchy, organic inclusions, but these are quite rare.[428] Dendrites formed either along micro-fractures within the chalcedony when mineral-rich water seeped into the agate through these fractures or by osmosis with mineral-rich water that seeped through the semi-porous chalcedony layers. At first a few of the impurity molecules precipitated in the agate, and the rest grew around these nuclei. It is thought that dendrites formed in environments with lower temperatures and higher pressures. If the environment had higher temperatures and lower pressures, a sunburst pattern formed instead (See the sagenite agate section in this chapter.) [429,430]

Figure 157
The dendrites in this northern Nevada chalcedony agate formed along micro fractures.

Figure 158
Dendrites grew along a fracture seam in this Brazilian polyhedroid agate, and spread deeper into the chalcedony. Notice the impermeable layer towards the top. A photo of this entire polyhedroid specimen is included as Figure 189 on page 173.

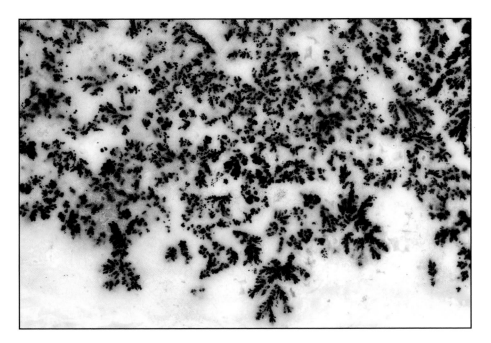

Figure 159
This agate from India shows how dendrites formed when minerals diffused into the chalcedony after agate formation.

ENHYDRO (WATER-FILLED) AGATES

Enhydro agates are nodules that are partly filled with water. Technically, these are "fluid inclusions" that became trapped in the center of the agate by impermeable chalcedony layers. It is interesting to note that this water is quite pure, since it is most likely millions of years old. When polished just right, you can view the internal water moving within the agate. Although it has been reported that Brazil is the only source for enhydro agates, Internet sources suggest that they can also be found in the Beechworth area in Victoria, Australia as well as in Oregon.[431]

Extreme care must be taken when handling enhydro agates. If they are put under stress, they can fracture and release the water. If they are subjected to freezing temperatures, the water can freeze and expand, causing the chamber to break open. Also it is possible that some of the enhydros that have recently been mined from a wet area may dry out once they have been removed from the fluid environment. Thus it may be a good idea to store enhydros in a sealed bag or container.

Most enhydros contain water, but there are cases when yellow petroleum oil became trapped within the agate pocket. These with oil are referred to as "golden enhydros." The contents within the enhydro chamber can be mobile or immobile, depending on the physical characteristics of the chamber. It may be hard to see the fluid inclusion, but with a careful tap you can sometimes dislodge the bubble if it is not too badly trapped inside the agate.[432]

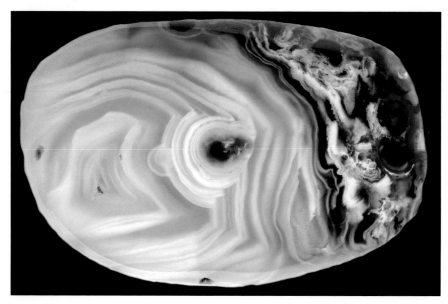

Figure 160
This enhydro agate has water trapped inside the chalcedony bands in this Brazilian agate.

EYE AGATES

The more that we research and examine eye agates, the more we are convinced that there is a relationship between "eyes" that appear on the surface of some husk-free agates and spherulites that appear inside agates. Researchers have multiple explanations for the genesis of these spherical or hemispherical shapes.

One explanation is that spherulitic growths developed in the initial clear chalcedony layer next to the husk. Tiny needle-shaped fibers grew first and served as "nuclei" around which chalcedony or other minerals grew into small spheres. These spheres attached to the outside of the pocket next to the husk.[433] This same process often occurred in rhyolitic rock when spherulites formed in viscous magmas as silica molecules congregated to form spheres. In fact researchers have determined that despite the wide diversity of physical and chemical properties among spherulite-forming environments, the growth process is surprisingly universal.[434]

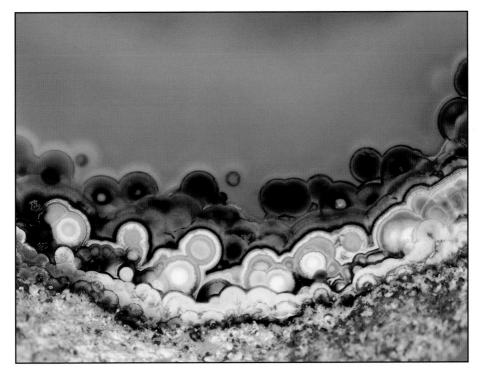

Figure 161
Notice the spheroids attached to the inside of the husk in this Brazilian agate.

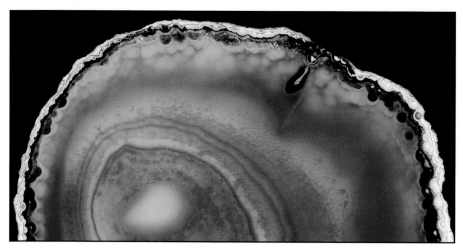

Figure 162
Spheroids are attached to the husk in the first clear chalcedony layer of this Brazilian agate. Although these spheroids did not continue growing in this specimen, perhaps individual spheroids in other agates served as the nucleation starting points for "eyes" to develop when chalcedony either replaced the spheroids, or continued growing around the spheroids to form hemispherical eyes. (See the next photo.)

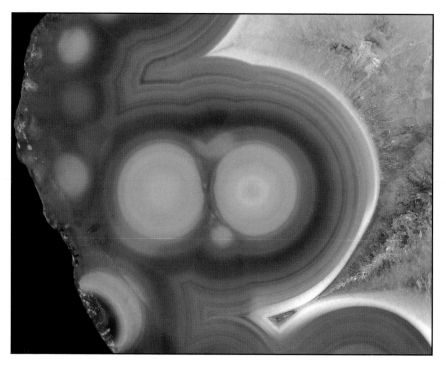

Figure 163
This Brazilian slab has spheroids, one of which developed into a chalcedony hemispherical eye at the husk. There are also some larger spherulites that developed first, after which chalcedony banding formed around the spherical mass.

Another possibility is that before the silica started its precipitation process, pisolite (pis-*uh*-līte) or oolite (ō-ə-līte) concretions formed first when calcium carbonate or limonite precipitated and grew concentrically around nuclei.[435] Both types of spheres developed in the same manner with pisolites being over 2 mm in diameter and oolite spheres less than 2 mm. The concentric layers contain crystals arranged radially, tangentially, or randomly. The nuclei were quartz grains or any other small mineral fragments.[436]

This nucleation process may have been similar to what can be observed after opening a bottle of beer or champagne: carbon dioxide bubbles rapidly nucleate on the glass surface.[437] Over geologic time, these orbicular concretion structures may have remained just as they were when they formed. In other cases, they may have been replaced by chalcedony and served as nucleation sites for larger "eyes" to develop."[438]

Another hypothesis is that "eyes" may have formed when chalcedony replaced zeolite minerals such as thomsonite.[439] Eye agates are characterized by concentrically arranged bands that form a hemisphere with its flat surface showing on the exterior of the agate nodule. Others believe that they formed in localized Belousov-Zhabotinskii reactions (see Chapter 2). Eyes are usually only found in amygdaloidal agates with very few, if any, seen in thunder eggs and none in continental sedimentary agates or marine sedimentary agates. If eye agates are a manifestation of the Belousov-Zhabotinskii reaction, then they are a phenomenon associated with the banding process. If they are agate replacements of zeolite minerals, then they are a pre-banding formation.[440]

One more hypothesis about eye agate formation is that when vesicle pockets were still empty, a small amount of silica-rich fluid seeped in and "beaded up" on the inside of the vesicle wall. Subsequently, the silica bead crystallized into the first ring of a solid chalcedony "eye." Later, more fluid seeped into the pocket, allowing additional concentric fortification bands to form around the bead that now served as a nuclei. Some believe that individual eyes may have continued developing until they formed clustered botryoidal formations.[441]

There are other agates that instead of having spherulites, pisolites, or oolites, have small white discs or egg-like ovids formed between the layers. These structures have been shown to be a mixture of chalcedony and opal.[442]

Eye agates can be found in many places including California, Kentucky, Michigan, Minnesota, Mississippi, Nebraska, Nevada, Tennessee, Texas, West Virginia, Wisconsin, and Wyoming. They can also be found in Australia, Canada, Germany, Panama, and Scotland.

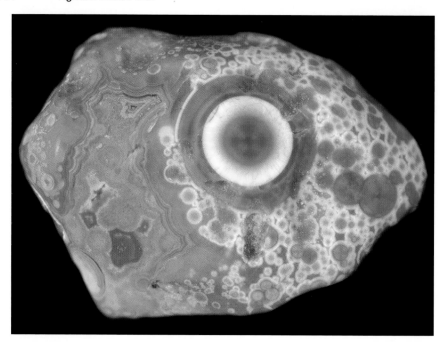

Figure 164
This Lake Superior agate has a well defined eye.

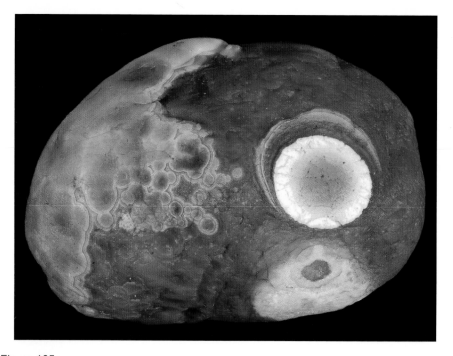

Figure 165
Here is another Lake Superior eye agate. Notice the "peeler" section on husk at the top of the photo.

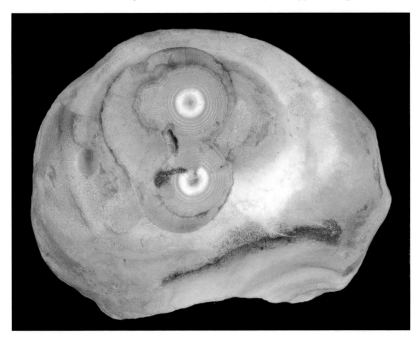

Figure 166
This Lake Superior agate has a pair of eyes.

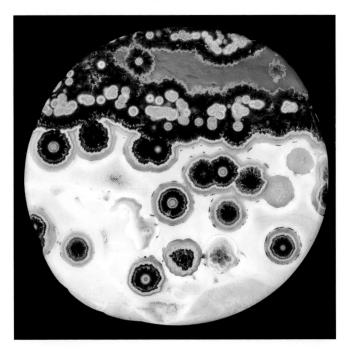

Figure 167
Although this specimen is ocean jasper from Madagascar, it is very translucent and appears to be agate. It is also called orbicular jasper because of the orbs that formed throughout. The green band is chrysoprase.

FIRE AGATES

Fire agate is a variety of microcrystalline chalcedony that contains inclusions of goethite or limonite that produces an iridescent effect. Iridescence happens when a material shows shifting changes in color or rainbow-like colors when the material or viewing perspective is shifted. This "schiller" effect is like looking deep into a burning ember. Fire agates are found in Mexico as well as U.S. locations including Arizona (Graham, Greenle, La Paz, Maricopa, Mohave, and Yuma Counties), and California (Riverside and Imperial Counties).[443]

Colors in fire agate may appear as tiny pinpoints, bubbles, bull's eyes, flashes, specks, or swirls. Iridescent colors range from orange to red, yellow, green, purple, and blue. If fire agates are cut and polished correctly, most or all of the colors can be displayed. Although both fire agate and opal flash color, they are quite different in their composition. Fire agates are comprised of microcrystalline quartz crystals; opal is formed from non-crystalline silica. As a result, fire agate has a hardness of 7 and opal only around 5½. Because it is softer, opal can crack, fade, and scratch; fire agate will not.

Fire agate formed when thin layers of iron oxide deposited on botryoidal chalcedony and then were covered with more chalcedony.[444] The components were delivered to host rock cavities by hydrothermal water saturated with silica and iron oxide. The color results from the layers of iron oxide that cause light beams to interfere with each other, resulting in the display of color. As the iron oxide in the solution was depleted, chalcedony continued to grow, producing the typical brown and white husk color of rough fire agates.[4450]

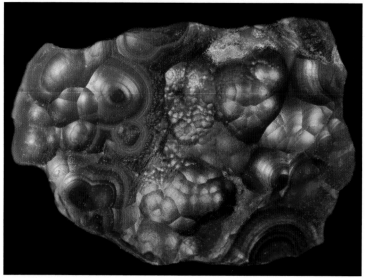

Figure 168
This fire agate from Mexico has a colorful botryoidal array.

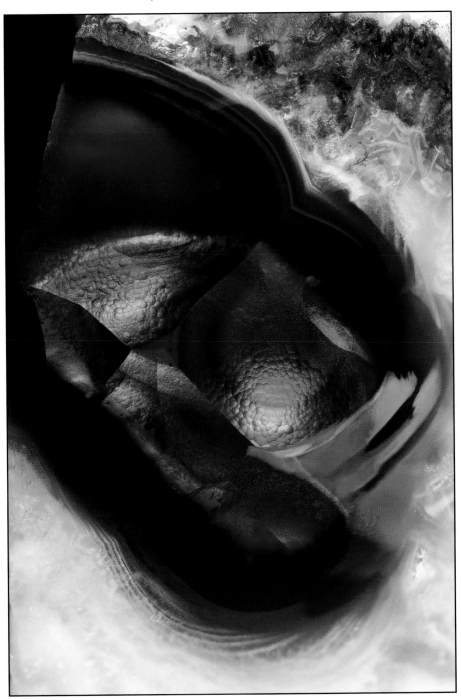

Figure 169
This specimen is a Mexican fire agate.

FLAME AGATES

There are two different agates that have been labeled as having a "flame" appearance. Some identify these as *any* agate that has a pattern resembling a candle flame. Also, flame agates have been described as highly translucent, colorless agates that have long streaks of bright red color.[446,447]

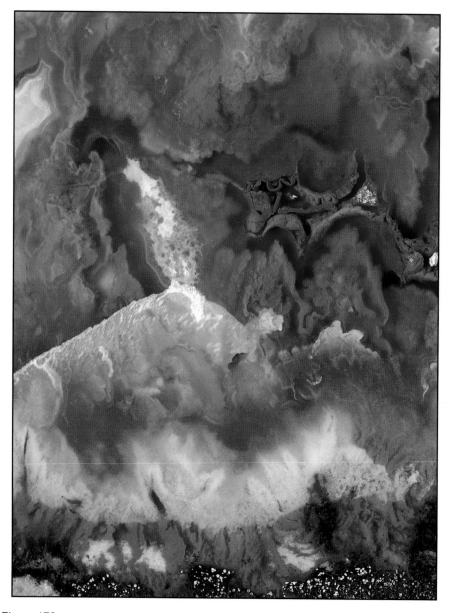

Figure 170
This is a Mexican flame agate that looks as though it has a volcano with a burning landscape.

FLOATER BAND AGATES

Floater band agates are those with layers of contrasting color that are sandwiched between either clear quartz or translucent chalcedony.[448,449] An individual specimen can have one or more "floating bands." The existence of floater bands is a nuance of individual agates. This structure can be found in agates from Arizona, Louisiana, Michigan, Minnesota, Missouri, Montana, Nevada, South Dakota, and Wisconsin.

Figure 171
The dark floater bands are sandwiched between the colorful bands of this Montana dry head agate.

FORTIFICATION AGATES

The majority of the world's agates can be classified as "fortification agates." The term fortification describes the concentric bands of the agate's interior that have the appearance of the walls of an old-time fort, if observed from a bird's eye view. This typical agate banding results from the adhesion of silica to the walls of a vesicle cavity, creating multiple thin bands. Trace mineral impurities serve as a catalyst to facilitate banding but also add contrast between different banded layers.

In addition to fortification banding, other names used to describe this pattern include adhesional banding, zonally concentric banding, common banding, and wallpaper banding.[450] Other people describe this banding pattern as being similar to the rings of a tree or the layers of an onion. Additional information about this and other banding patterns is included in Chapter 2. Fortification agates can be found almost anywhere that agates are found.

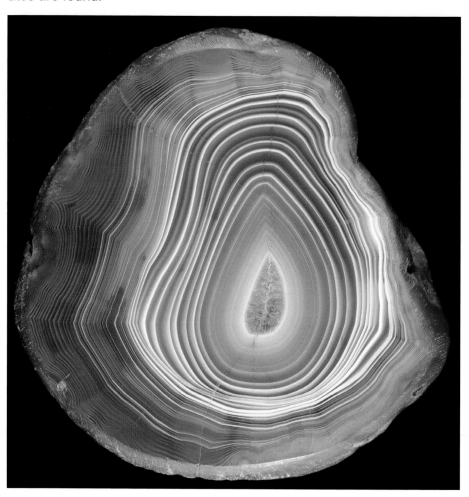

Figure 172
This Lake Superior agate shows fortification bands. Also notice the shadow bands (See the Shadow Agate section that begins on page 180.)

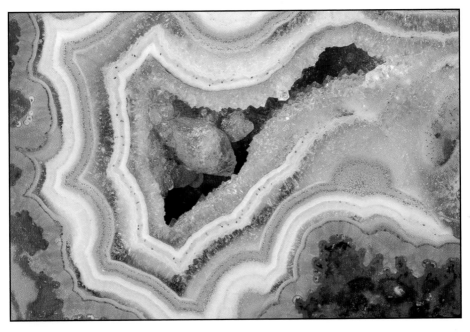

Figure 173
Agates that developed in igneous, sedimentary, and metamorphic rock pockets all formed fortification bands. This is a Teepee Canyon agate that formed in sedimentary rock in South Dakota. This specimen is also a geode agate.

GEODE AGATES

Geodes are hollow nodules with internal chambers that are usually lined with macro crystals. They formed in rock cavities or vugs in sedimentary rock, or occasionally in igneous vesicles. Many geode husks are made of limestone and usually have a round or slightly oblong shape.[451] The interiors filled with silica and/or carbonates when mineral rich groundwater or hydrothermal solutions seeped into the host rock pockets. Some, but not all, geodes contain agate. When there is agate in a geode, the chalcedony adhered to the husk first. As the silica concentration of the penetrating fluids decreased below the threshold needed to form microcrystalline quartz, larger quartz crystals began to form. When no further crystal quartz or banded chalcedony growth took place, quartz crystal tops, or terminations, developed and protruded into the void space. Some geodes consist entirely of macrocrystalline quartz crystals and do not contain agate.[452]

Geodes are commonly found in Brazil, Nambia, and Mexico, as well as in several states, including Indiana, Iowa, Missouri, Kentucky, New Mexico, Arizona, Utah, and Wyoming.[453] Most commercially available geodes come from Mexico. These "coconut" geodes developed in ash-flow volcanic rock (tuff) and still have the white ash on their husk exterior.

Only 20 percent of Mexican geodes are hollow, and those that are usually have an outer wall of variable thickness consisting of blue-gray banded agate. The remaining 80 percent of the nodules are solid agate.[454]

Figure 174
This Brazilian agate has a geode center pocket lined with macrocrystaline quartz crystals.

IRIS (RAINBOW) AGATES

Iris agates are truly a treasure trove, although they may not seem that way at first. When you first look at these agate slices without a bright light transmitted at the right angle, they appear uniform and boring. When held, rotated, and observed in transmitted bright light, the band structure causes the light to break up into its spectral rainbow colors.

This optical property has been known for more than a hundred years. Although it seems that most iris agates have incredibly tight bands, this is not the only characteristic that causes the iris effect. Scientists have determined that an agate will iris in a range of a hundred to more than 15,000 bands per inch. Instead, the key factor is that the alternating layers must have higher and lower refractive indices. When light travels from air into a substance, its velocity is reduced. This change of speed at the surface interface causes light passing between the substances to be bent, or refracted. When white light is refracted, as when passing through a prism, waves of different frequencies (i.e., the various colors) are bent at different angles. The result is that light is dispersed and spread out into its component colors. When droplets of water in the air form the refracting interface, the result is a rainbow. When this happens between agate bands, the result is an iris effect.[455-458]

It appears that all agates have some zones that exhibit iris banding.[459] The oscillating nature of the agate bands is caused by differences in silica structure. Some of the bands have long complex, polymeric chains of silica molecules, while the alternating bands have simpler, monomeric chains.[460] This difference in complexity changes the refractive index of the alternating bands. Iris agates can be found in Arizona, California (Alameda and Kern Counties), Idaho (Custer County), Michigan, Minnesota, Montana, New Mexico (Catron County), Oregon (Wasco County), Tennessee (Bedford County), Texas (Brewster County), and Wisconsin.[461]

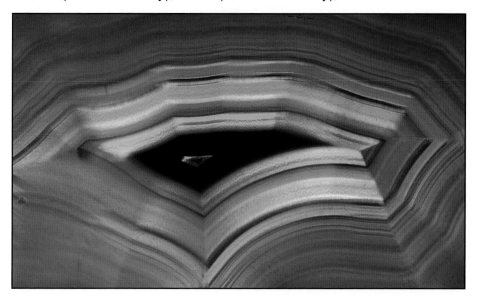

Figure 175
Only some of the bands of this Brazilian agate display the iris effect.

Figure 176
This Horse Mountain, Tennessee, agate irises in an out-of-this-world manner.

Figure 177
Here is another Brazilian agate that has iris in just some of the bands, but it offers its own delicate beauty.

JASPER AGATES

When vesicle pockets fill in with silica, the conditions over geologic time may have varied. Not only may the temperature and pressure in and around the pocket have changed, but the chemical makeup of the fluid entering the pocket may have also varied. As a result, the type of silica crystals from band to band or within sections of the agate could have varied. Jasper agates, or agatized jasper, have alternating bands of translucent chalcedony agate and opaque jasper. Jasper agates can be found in Arizona (La Paz County), California (Imperial, Kern, San Bernadino, and Santa Barbara Counties), Georgia (Crisp County), New Mexico (Sierra County), Oklahoma (Dewey County), Rhode Island (Providence County), South Dakota (Washabaugh County), Utah (Garfield County), and Wyoming. They can also be found throughout the upper Midwest states including Michigan, Wisconsin, Minnesota, Nebraska, and Iowa.[462]

Figure 178
This Lake Superior jasper agate has alternating layers of chalcedony, jasper, and carnelian.

MOSS AGATES

Although some classify dendritic and moss agate as being the same, they actually have a different genesis. Dendrite structures formed AFTER agate banding when mineral-rich solutions osmotically seeped into the agate, or entered through small fractures. Minerals from these solutions precipitated out and attached between bands or along fractures.

Additional minerals formed around these nuclei. Moss structures formed BEFORE agate banding. Moss-like aggregates of randomly branching material either crystallized inside the vesicle before silica started to precipitate, or the minerals entered and precipitated at the same time as the silica. Like dendrites, moss material is composed primarily of iron-oxide or manganese-oxide.[463] When these mineral impurities were present before agate bands began to form, the moss structure inhibited or at least impacted the formation of chalcedony bands that subsequently developed. If there were a lot of moss inclusions, the pockets filled in and solidified with non-banded chalcedony trapping the moss structures in a quartz tomb.[464]

Moss agate may have also formed from inclusions of hornblende.[465] Hornblende is a complex natural composite of calcium, iron, magnesium, silica, aluminum, manganese, titanium, sodium, and fluorine.[466] Sections of green celadonite husk may have also broke off and became incorporated as moss-like structures within the chalcedony banding.[467] Still other moss structures may have formed when fine inclusions of calcite were subsequently covered with black manganese dioxide.[468] Moss agate can be found world wide in too many locations to list here.

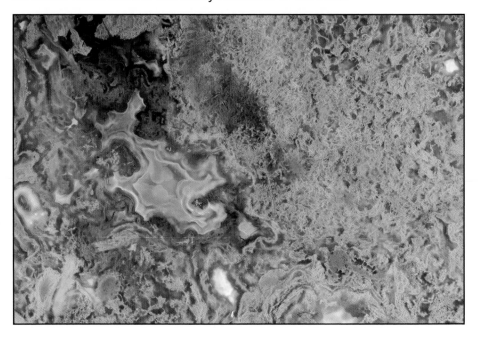

Figure 179
This moss agate is from Texas.

Figure 180
This interesting moss agate from Brazil has fortification bands that developed after the moss structure.

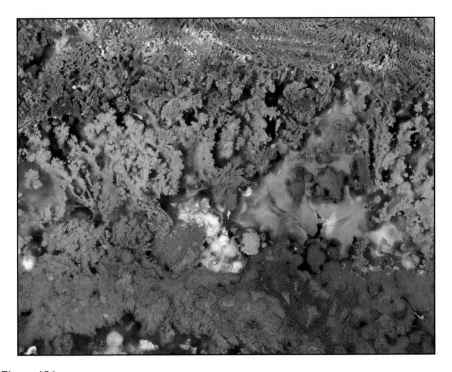

Figure 181
Moss agate originally was given its name because of green inclusions, such as in this specimen from Laredo, Texas. Notice the gray chalcedony sections between the moss inclusions.

PAINTSTONE AGATES

The banding on painted agates, or paintstone agates, appears as a series of deep colored zones that look as though they were painted with a brush. The colors are primarily red, orange, and pink with white banding. Sometimes blue, green, and yellow colors are also seen. The painted appearance is caused by high concentrations of mineral impurities within the agate structure, combined with subsequent chemical weathering and oxidation. Most paintstone agates are opaque because of the high level of impurities.[469]

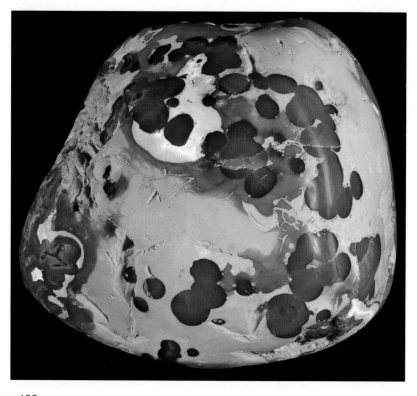

Figure 182
This specimen was found on Paradise Beach along the Lake Superior shore in northern Minnesota. Although there are some translucent agates found on this beach, most are opaque paintstone agates. They have chert and jasper mixed in with the chalcedony.

PEELER AGATES

Because agates are extremely hard, most eroded out of the softer host rock matrix. During the millenniums of time that they have been "free," they have been rolled by waves, tumbled by rivers, blasted by grit-carrying winds, suffered through alternating freeze-thaw temperatures, and dragged by glaciers. The violent abrasions suffered from these transporting and erosional forces sometimes fractured agates along banding planes between well-developed agate layers. As a result of repeated fracturing, a "peeled" texture was naturally carved. The result is a smooth, undulating banded surface that seems to step down from layer to layer. The erosion of the layers may have exposed and oxidized iron inclusions, which resulted in many peelers having colorful surfaces.[470,471]

Figure 183
This dramatic Lake Superior agate made the most of the wear and tear it suffered over the last billion years. The peeler bands were artistically carved by nature. Notice the waxy luster on the fractured surfaces of the peeler bands.

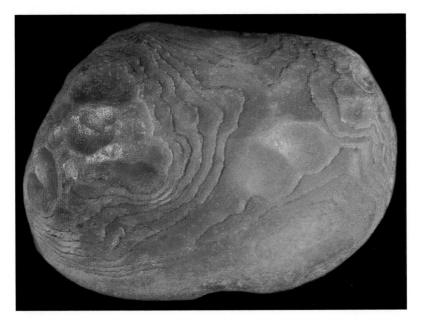

Figure 184
This is another Lake Superior peeler agate. Notice the waxy luster on the fractures.

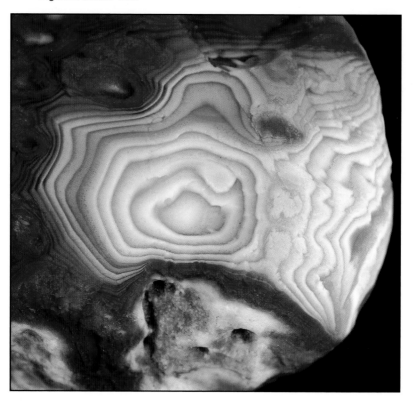

Figure 185
This Lake Superior peeler agate exposed candy striped coloration.

PLUME AGATES

Like dendritic and moss agates, plume agates are known for their inclusions. Plumes appear in translucent chalcedony as large fluffy inclusions that resemble feathers, plants, or flowers.[472] Most are one to two inches long, but can be up to five inches in length. They formed from iron oxide or manganese oxide crystals. As fluids first entered the vesicle pockets before agate genesis began, there was often a chemical reaction between alkaline minerals and silica because both had like electrical charges. This caused minerals to form plumes or other inclusion structures.[473] Unlike dendritic and moss agate, plumes formed in a variety of colors including black, brown, red, yellow, and orange. Realgar or orpiment minerals sometimes contributed to the coloring. These are yellow, gold, and orange arsenic sulfide minerals that are used to manufacture pigments, arsenic, and fireworks, as well as in the tanning of hides.[474]

Plumes are most common in geologically young agates but have been seen in 1.1 billion-year old Lake Superior agates. In some of the older agates, the plume structures may have been destroyed by weathering or abrasion or replaced by subsequent chalcedony.[475]

Plume agates are found in Arizona (Maricopa, and Yavapai Counties), California (San Bernadino County), Colorado (Saguache County), New Mexico (Hidalgo County), Oregon (Malheur County), South Dakota (Pennngton County), Texas (Brewster County), and Virginia (Warren and Wise Counties).[476]

Figure 186
This plume agate looks like it may have come from Texas or Mexico, but it is actually from a Lake Superior agate found in Grand Marais, Michigan.

Figure 187
This is a Tapado Canyon plume agate from Texas.

Figure 188
Plume agates can be found in Argentina, too.

POLYHEDROID AGATES

The unique polyhedroids are strange looking agates with geometric shapes that have smooth flat sides. Their shape appears more angular than the typical almond-shaped agate, but there is no consistency to the angles of formation. Most are either triangular or trapezoid and hollow, with the bands running parallel to their shape. Although no one knows for sure how these agates formed, there are at least two theories. Some believe that polyhedroid agates are pseudomorph replacements of other, more angular crystals. Another hypothesis is that they formed in spaces between other crystals, perhaps calcite. Unlike the rest of the Brazilian agates found in the southern part of the country, these unusual agates are found at a single site in the northern state of Paraiba. There has been no mining of polyhedroids in recent years. Most were mined during the 1970s.[477] Believe it or not, a few polyhedroids have also been found in the Lake Superior region and in Wyoming.

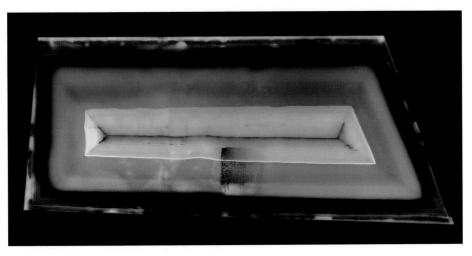

Figure 189
This polyhedroid agate from northern Brazil has an angular shape that resulted when it formed in a hollow space between calcite crystals. A close-up of the dendrites in the bottom center of this specimen can be seen in Figure 158 on page 149.

PSEUDOMORPH AGATES

Pseudomorph means "false form."[478] The same process that allows agates to form in empty voids also contributes to their replacing other, less durable minerals. As water moved through the pores of the original material, acids in the water dissolved it away, leaving behind a "crystal mold" which later filled with silica. Pseudomorphs usually have an atypical shape resulting from the substitution process in which the silica molecules took on the shapes of the original material. Some of the best examples of pseudomorph agates are the Coyamito agates from Chihuahua, Mexico. In this case, agate replaced aragonite. These pseudomorphs formed when aragonite crystals grew in vesicle pockets within andesite host rock. Chalcedony then started to coat the crystals and continued filling in the pocket. Later, the aragonite dissolved away leaving voids that either remained empty or were also filled with chalcedony.

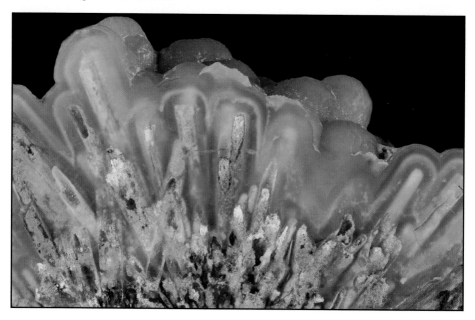

Figure 190
This Mexican coyamito agate has pseudomorph rods, as well as botryoidal formation. Researchers think that coyamito agates have structures that are pseudomorphs from aragonite.

RUIN AGATES

There are many different opinions about what constitutes a ruin agate. Some believe that they are the same as brecciated agate. Others feel that they look like ancient ruins or ruined buildings. Still others claim that they are agates with significant fractures that have subsequently healed with infilling of additional silica or other minerals. In this case, the original banding pattern is fairly intact but intersected by large healed fractures.[479] We classify ruin agates as those which have been subjected to geological pressure, causing the original banding to fracture apart and be re-cemented so that the bands are displaced or offset. The ruin process occurred when the agate pockets were still within the host rock. Tremors from earthquakes or other geologic forces caused the agates to fracture. The now disfigured and disorganized banding was subsequently re-cemented by additional silica. The intensity of the geologic forces can be seen by the amount of displacement of the banding pattern.[480,481]

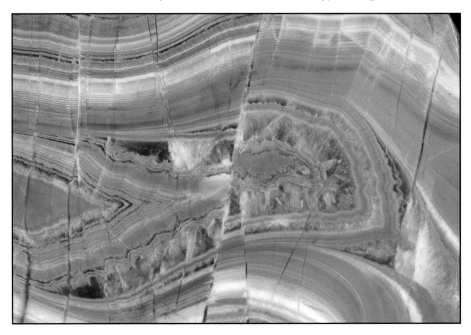

Figure 191
Due to post-formation stresses, the bands of this agate faulted and shifted, before being re-cemented back together. Although it is technically a "ruin" agate, it has its own mystery and beauty.

SAGENITE AGATES

Sagenite refers to clusters of needle-like mineral inclusions within an agate. These radiating mineral inclusions may have formed from several different minerals including rutile, natrolite, mordenite, anhydrite, aragonite, goethite, and tourmaline. In most cases, the original mineral dissolved away and was replaced by silica, resulting in pseudomorph formations.[482,483]

Sagenite inclusions can consist of needle-like formations arranged in a random pattern, but the "needles" usually radiate in a sunburst, fan-like spray from a central point. Sagenite clusters can vary in color from jet black to yellow, white and golden copper.[484] Some believe that the solution in the pocket in which these sagenite patterns developed may have been rich in titanium. Others feel that they formed under higher pressures. Most sagenite agates contain typical banding patterns, in addition to the clusters, while other sagenite sprays are encased in pure, non-banded chalcedony.[485] Sagenite agates are found in many places including Arizona, California, Colorado, Idaho, Michigan, Minnesota, Oregon, Texas, Washington, Wisconsin, and Wyoming.

Figure 192
This is an extremely colorful display of sagenite formation! The source location is unknown since this slab was purchased out of a bargain bin.

Figure 193
This Lake Superior sagenite agate has an intricate spray.

Figure 194
This extreme close up lets you see the structure in these sagenite sprays. This is a Brazilian agate.

SARDONYX

This is a banded form of microcrystaline quartz that is known for having red bands, but the colors can also include white, gray, brown, and black. Usually, there are alternating light and dark colored bands, which can either be translucent or opaque. The word "sardonyx" is derived from the Greek word "sard", which means reddish brown.[486]

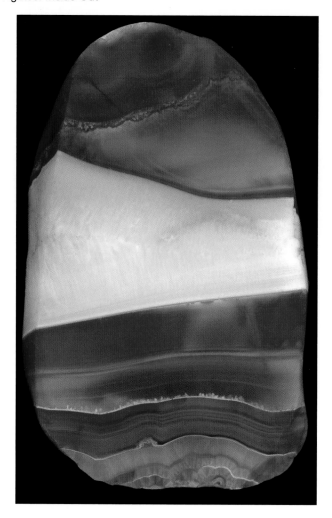

Figure 195
This Sardonyx agate was purchased from a box with other Minnesota agates at a gem show in Two Harbors, Minnesota.

SEAM AGATES

Not only did agates form inside hollow vesicle pockets, but some of the cracks or seams in host rock also agatized. In this case, instead of the chalcedony adhering to form concentric rings, it adhered to both sides of the seam and filled in toward the middle. Some seam agates also formed in sedimentary rock along bedded planes or in open spaces on top of bedrock. In Thunder Bay, Ontario, for example, they have partially excavated a seam agate that is over 20 feet long! Blue lace agate from Nambia in Africa also developed in a seam. A prospector who found it with dolomite vein deposits discovered the African seam agate during the early 1960s.[487]

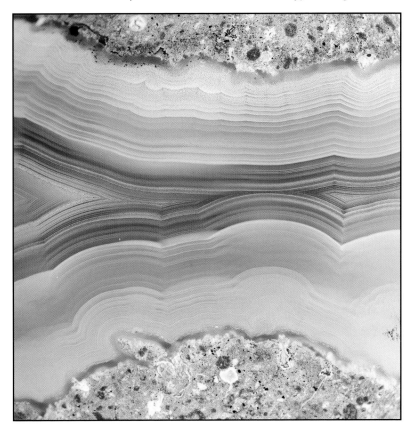

Figure 196
This Mexican seam agate is sandwiched in a crack within rhyolitic host rock.

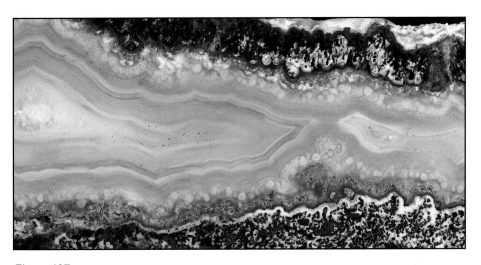

Figure 197
Not only did vesicle pockets fill in with agate, but the cracks and seams in host rock did as well.

SHADOW AGATES

People have been mystified about shadow agates for hundreds if not thousands of years. Moving these agates back and forth under a bright light causes a "shadow" to race across the surface. At first scientists thought that the shadow resulted from light diffraction. Diffraction is an optical effect that occurs when light waves are bent or deflected. If this optical property defines what occurs with a shadow agate, then the light would be displayed in its spectral colors, similar to what occurs with iris agates. Others thought that the shadow is due to a chatoyant effect. Chatoyancy is an optical effect that occurs when light reflects off a surface with closely packed fibers (resembling a cat's eye).[488] As it turns out, neither of these hypotheses explains the shadow effect.

Although this optical property is called a "shadow," it is actually more like a "black hole." Because of the physical properties of the alternating bands, light goes into the agate and doesn't come out. Many factors contribute to the shadow phenomenon including the density of the bands, the regularity between bands, alternating opaque and exceptionally clear chalcedony bands, and even the depth of the agate layers. Basically, light goes into the agate, bounces off the opaque layer, is refracted by the translucent layer, and relative to your line of sight into the agate—the light gets lost.[489]

A similar optical effect can be seen when driving past a farmer's field. If the crop rows are planted perpendicular to the road, a dark area or shadow is seen in the field as you drive by.[490] Little or no light is reflected back to the eye from the field; this lack of reflection is interpreted as a shadow.[491]

The eye perceiving depth in the agate causes the shadow effect. Depth is observed because the opaque bands are sandwiched between clear chalcedony bands. The effect is further enhanced because the bands are not perfectly parallel to each other or to the line of sight. As the bands undulate and turn within the agate, so does the shadow. When the agate is rotated, the shadow races along the banding and turns at corners, creating an enjoyable visual display. It was once thought that up to 10,000 bands per inch were needed to produce this effect, but using a binocular microscope to count the bands in agates displaying shadow gives an actual range between 50 and 500 bands per inch.[492] Shadow agates can be found in many locations including Arizona, Michigan, Minnesota, Mississippi, Nevada, New Mexico, Wisconsin, and Wyoming.

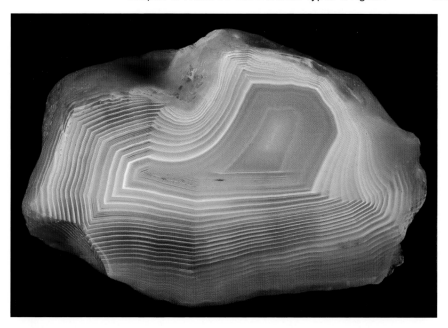

Figure 198
Although it is hard to show a shadow effect in a two-dimensional photo, you can actually see the shadow in this picture of a Lake Superior agate.

Figure 199
This is a shadow agate from Queensland, Australia.

STALK AGGREGATE AGATES

These unusual agates look like they have cave stalagmites grow-ing in them. They formed when a mineral impurity of lower density rose upward through a viscous silica solution of greater density. Since the ag-gregates formed early in the agate genesis process, they often deformed the agate bands that subsequently developed and grew around the ag-gregate columns.[493]

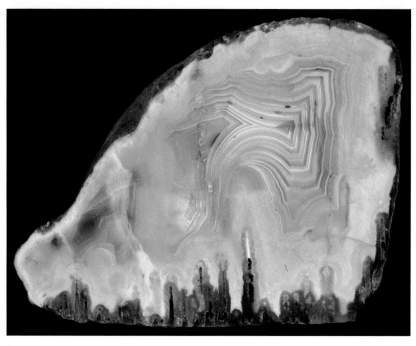

Figure 200
Notice the stalk aggregate growths in the bottom of this Lake Superior agate. Doesn't it look like a city sky line?

THUNDER EGG AGATES

Thunder eggs are irregular, star-shaped agates that developed in ex-tremely viscous rhyolitic lavas soon after volcanic eruptions.[494] The rhyo-litic magma had significant amounts of dissolved gases such as carbon dioxide and steam. Because of its composition, the ash was plastic and flowing, with solid particles suspended in the very hot, gaseous medium. The particles that made up the ash were mostly silica-rich glass shards (75 to 80 percent), but there was also biotite, feldspars, rutile, hornblende, augite, magnetite, etc. When the ash settled, compaction took place and silica and dissolved gases were released that formed irregular cavities in which the thunder eggs formed. The ash flow cooled and chemical weath-ering broke down the silica and released it into the groundwater.[495]

Agate formation occurred by infiltration of fluids supersaturated in silica, followed by crystallization under comparatively low temperature and pressure conditions. Infiltration of fluids was through cracks and microscopic pores in the thunder-egg husk. The silica came from late-stage hydrothermal fluids that were derived from the host rock and local groundwater.[496]

Thunder egg nodules are spherical in shape with an exterior husk of rhyolite that is more silicified than the host rock. The agate cavities inside the thick husk are often star-shaped, due to the rapid expansion of the gases that initially formed the pockets. The central cavities are partly to completely filled with chalcedony, opal, or quartz. The chalcedony may have either concentric or water-level bands, or it may contain algae-like mineral inclusions.[497,498]

Thunder eggs are most common in Tertiary or even geologically younger rocks. An exception are the world's oldest thunder eggs from the late Precambrian age, which are found along the north shore of Lake Superior (Minnesota).[499] Thunder eggs are also found in Oregon, Washington, New Mexico, Colorado, Wyoming, Australia, Germany, Poland, Africa, Romania, Turkey, Argentina, Canada, France, and Mexico.[500]

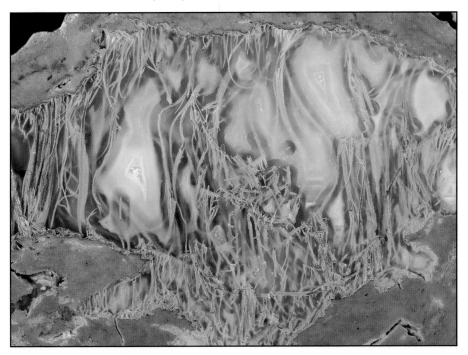

Figure 201
This is a priday thunder egg from the Richardson Mine in Oregon. It certainly has bizarre mineral inclusions that resemble sea kelp.

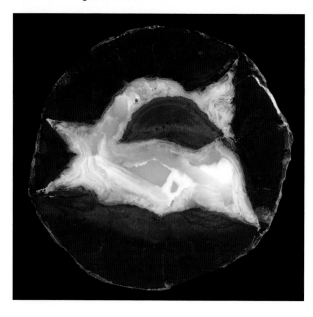

Figure 202
This thunder egg from
Oregon has the typical
star-shaped center.

TUBE AGATES

Tube agates are a rare and beautiful variety of agate. They developed when rod-like minerals such as goethite or rutile provided the template around which the chalcedony fibers grew.[501] In many cases, the rod-like minerals were oriented parallel to one another. The chalcedony crystallized around these obstructions, causing the banding to also follow the contours of the projections.[502] Sometimes tubes are confused with eyes. The difference is that tubes are elongated rods whereas eyes are hemispherical or spherical in shape.[503]

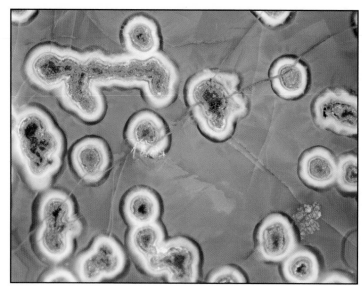

Figure 203
Tube formations
can be seen in
this very unusual
Michipicoten ag-
ate from Ontario,
Canada.

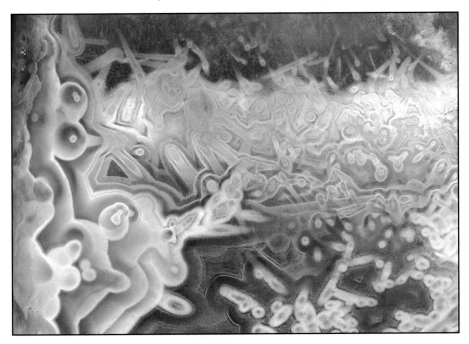

Figure 204
An amazing collection of tubes can be seen in this Lake Superior agate.

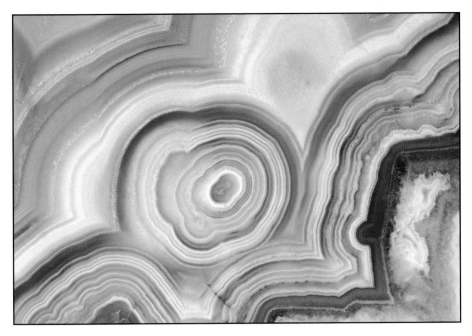

Figure 205
This Mexican crazy lace agate has a double-tube that formed first, and then chalcedony agate bands formed around the tubes.

WATER-LEVEL AGATES

While most agates have concentric fortification banding patterns, many also have horizontally deposited bands. The formation of this banding pattern is discussed in Chapter 2. The horizontal bands in water-level agates differ from concentric bands because they tend to be thicker and less regular. The silica crystals in horizontal bands are more granular, compared to the fibrous structures that formed in concentric bands. Horizontal bands usually developed in the lower sections of agates when coagulated particles of silica settled under the influence of gravity. Their bands, therefore, precipitated like sediments into a horizontal plane, which defines the initial orientation of the vesicle pocket in the host rock.[504] This banding structure supports the fact that at least these agates formed in a fluid environment since the deposition planes most likely would not have developed in a silica gel environment.[505,506]

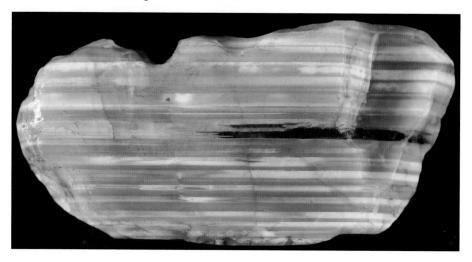

Figure 206
This Lake Superior water-level agate with parallel bands formed under the influence of gravity.

A SELECTION OF UNITED STATES AGATES

It is difficult to compile a comprehensive list of all the agate finding locations. The classification of silica minerals makes this task complex. For example, some claim that there is chalcedony in every state.[507] If there is chalcedony, you might think there would be agate, but this does not appear to be the case. It is also difficult to be "technical" about exactly what constitutes an agate when the definition you employ may not match up with common practice. For example, there is some question whether chalcedony with mineral inclusions, such as Montana moss agate, is in fact agate at all. If you define an agate as microcrystalline quartz with self-organized banding, then at least some of the Montana specimens have chalcedony with no pattern other than the post-formation development of dendritic inclusions. We are certainly not going to settle this debate here.

Our original intent was to compile a comprehensive list of agates found in the United States and provide information about geographical locations, type of matrix host rock, search environments, color, types of agate structures, and husk descriptions. Despite a massive effort, the data base is not yet complete enough to publish. Even if we were able to fill in all the blanks, it may be too long to publish in this book. Instead, we have listed the information on the www.agatelady.com web page. Please feel free to review the data base and make suggestions by sending an email to Karen@agatelady.com

During our internet research, we identified two web sites that are already available. We refer you to the University of Nebraska site listed below. This web page lists some, but not all, of the world's agates and includes photos in most cases.

www.snr.unl.edu/data/geologysoils/agates/agatedatabase.asp

We also refer you to the Mineral Data Site www.mindat.org. Jolyon Raoph from England compiled this site. He started the project in 1993 and should be commended for list's comprehensiveness, which includes the majority of the world's agates and thousands of collecting locations.

While the more comprehensive list will be on the agatelady web page, we have compiled a chart listing the types of agate structures found in the different states (See Table 5.) The accuracy of this list is equal to the accuracy of what has been reported by others. If there are errors or omissions, please send an email with your suggestions to Karen@agatelady.com.

Table 5: Agate Formations Found in the States

STATE	Agates	Agate Fossils	Botryoidal	Brecciated	Candy Striped	Carnelian	Cloud	Crazy Lace	Enhydro	Eye	Fire	Floater Band	Fortification	Geode	Inclusions *
Alabama	•												•		•
Alaska	•					•							•		
Arizona	•		•	•		•				•	•		•	•	•
Arkansas	•												•		
California	•		•	•				•		•	•		•	•	•
Colorado	•	•											•	•	•
Connecticut	•														
Delaware															
Florida	•	•	•										•		
Georgia	•														
Hawaii	•														
Idaho	•	•				•		•					•		•
Illinois**	•												•		
Indiana**	•												•	•	
Iowa**	•												•	•	
Kansas	•												•		•
Kentucky	•	•		•		•		•		•		•	•	•	•
Louisiana	•										•	•	•		
Maine	•												•		•
Maryland															
Massachusetts	•														
Michigan	•	•	•	•	•	•		•		•		•	•		•
Minnesota	•	•	•	•	•	•				•		•	•	•	•
Mississippi	•									•			•		
Missouri**	•							•			•	•	•	•	
Montana	•	•										•	•	•	•
Nebraska**	•			•		•				•			•		•
Nevada	•			•						•		•		•	•
New Hampshire															
New Jersey	•	•				•									
New Mexico	•		•									•	•	•	•
New York	•														
North Carolina	•		•												
North Dakota	•														
Ohio	•														
Oklahoma	•														
Oregon	•	•				•			•				•	•	•
Pennsylvania	•	•													
Rhode Island	•														
South Carolina	•														
South Dakota	•		•									•	•	•	•
Tennessee	•	•	•							•			•		•
Texas	•	•	•			•				•			•	•	•
Utah	•	•				•							•	•	•
Vermont	•														
Virginia	•														•
Washington	•	•		•									•		•
West Virginia	•	•								•			•		
Wisconsin**	•		•	•	•					•		•	•		•
Wyoming	•	•	•	•	•	•	•	•		•	•	•	•	•	•

* Agates with inclusions include dendritic, moss, and plume agates.

STATE	Iris	Jasper Agate	Paintstone	Peeler	Polyhedroid	Pseudomorph	Ruin	Sagenite	Sardonyx	Seam	Shadow	Stalk Aggregate	Thunder Egg	Tube	Water Level
Alabama			•						•						
Alaska						•									
Arizona	•	•				•		•		•	•		•	•	
Arkansas															
California	•	•				•		•					•		•
Colorado								•	•	•			•		•
Connecticut															
Delaware															
Florida						•			•						
Georgia		•													
Hawaii															
Idaho	•							•							•
Illinois**															
Indiana**															
Iowa**					•										
Kansas															
Kentucky		•	•			•	•						•	•	
Louisiana															
Maine															
Maryland															
Massachusetts															
Michigan	•	•	•	•			•	•		•	•			•	•
Minnesota	•	•	•	•	•	•	•	•		•	•	•	•	•	•
Mississippi															
Missouri**						•						•			•
Montana	•		•											•	•
Nebraska**															•
Nevada						•					•		•		•
New Hampshire															
New Jersey									•						
New Mexico	•	•										•	•		
New York															
North Carolina															
North Dakota		•													
Ohio															
Oklahoma		•													
Oregon	•					•		•					•		•
Pennsylvania															
Rhode Island		•							•						•
South Carolina															
South Dakota		•	•												•
Tennessee	•		•			•									
Texas	•							•							
Utah													•		•
Vermont															
Virginia															
Washington			•					•							
West Virginia															
Wisconsin**	•	•	•	•			•	•		•	•			•	•
Wyoming		•	•	•		•	•	•	•	•	•		•		•

** The states with glacially delivered Lake Superior agates may have agates with other structures similar to those listed under Minnesota.

A few of the hundreds if not thousands of agate that can be found in the United States are featured in the following pages. If you live in a state, or have a favorite agate that we are not including, please don't feel slighted. We, like you, adore all agates (and other rocks for that matter). The purpose of this chapter is to provide a sampling of some of the beautiful agates that can be found in the U.S. and around the world.

California

There are numerous agates from California, especially from the southern part of the state. Some of the named agates include Berkeley thunder egg, Bicycle Lake agate, Cady Mountain agate, China Lake plume agate, Death Valley plume agate, Horse Canyon agate, Kramer Hills sagenite agate, California blue agate, nine mile dendritic agate, Nipoma sagenite agate, paisley lace agate, Paul Bunyon agate and Windgate Pass agate. Agates can also be found on the Pacific Ocean beaches, although most of the time these are small and not very banded. It is not surprising that there would be a lot of agate in California, given the plate tectonic influences.

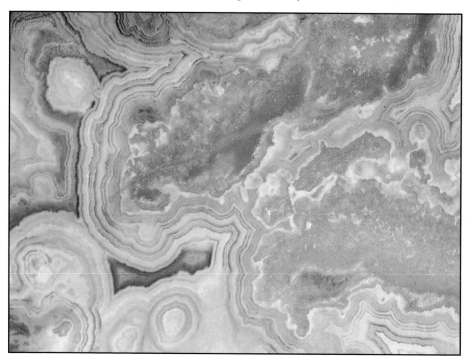

Figure 207
California lace agate.

Florida

One of the few agates found in Florida is the Tampa Bay agatized coral. Originally, it was easily accessible near the shore in the Tampa Bay area. Collecting started in the 1940s and continued until the 1960s. Due to the easy accessibility, as well as to development in the area, these agates have become scarce.[508]

Most of this agatized coral was formed when a thin layer of agate replaced the coral near the outer husk of the coral formation, leaving the majority of the interior either completely hollow, or sometimes partially filled with botryoidal formations.

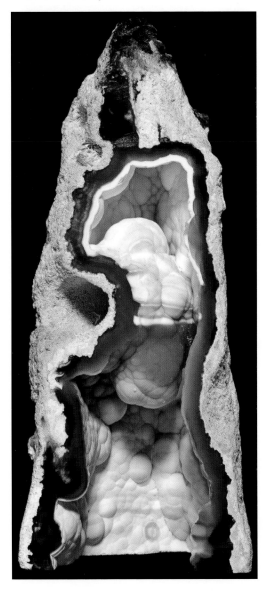

Figure 208
Tampa Bay agatized coral from Florida is a pseudomorph of coral that formed when agate replaced the original coral material.

Figure 209
Is this a bunch of grapes, or a botryoidal formation from Tampa Bay agatized coral?

Idaho

Many fortification nodules are found in Idaho from the Carey area. You can find carnelian and crazy lace agates in Bennett Mountain (Elmore County). Plume and sagenite agate are found near the Graveyard Point, Challis, and Snake River areas. Other agate names from Idaho include Muldoon agate, Regency Ross agate, and Beacon Hill agate (Washington County). In fact, the rough agate nodules found in Beacon Hill truly look like Idaho potatoes!

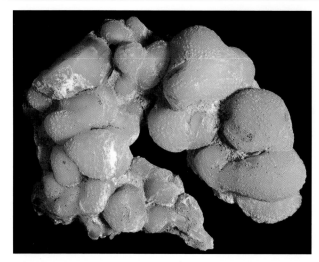

Figure 210
This Idaho botryoidal agate was in the museum collection. It is probably one that someone traded to the museum founder many years ago, during their travels through Grand Marais, Michigan.

Iowa

This state is at the southern boundary of the range in which Lake Superior agates, which were dragged and pushed by a series of 11 glaciers, can be found. In this state, you can also find coldwater agates near Vinton, rice agates in Winterset and Atlantic, and the Keswick agate in Keokuk County, which is in the southeastern area of the state. This latter agate was formed in sedimentary host rock.

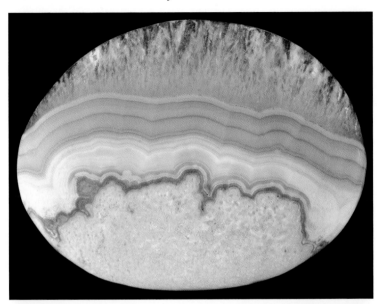

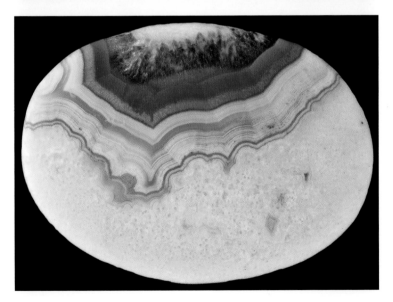

Figures 211 and 212
Keswick agates from Iowa that were formed in sedimentary rock pockets.

Kentucky

In 2000 the Kentucky agate became the official state rock. The language in the legislative bill stated that the agate is "characterized by delicate bands of blue, red, orange, black, yellow, or gray shades, is often displayed at local rock shows and used as an ornamental material and in semiprecious jewelry." The bill also said that "designation of a state rock will promote interest in geology, the hobby of mineral collecting, and the lapidary arts." 509 This designation was somewhat of a surprise since these agates have always had a secretive stigma, most likely because they are usually found on private land.

This distinctive agate was formed in shale and siltstone in the Borden layer of the Mississippian geologic period between 225 and 375 million years ago. These agates can be found in Estill, Jackson, Lee and Powell Counties, especially in the Buck, White Oak, and Middle Fork Creeks.

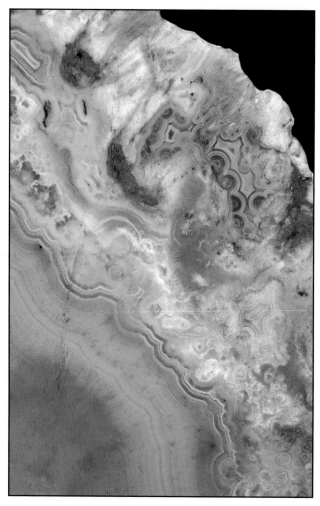

Figure 213
Notice the eye-like spheroid formation in this close up of a Kentucky agate.

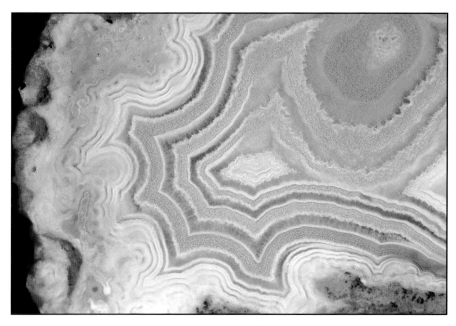

Figure 214
Kentucky agates can have a multitude of colors and formation patterns.

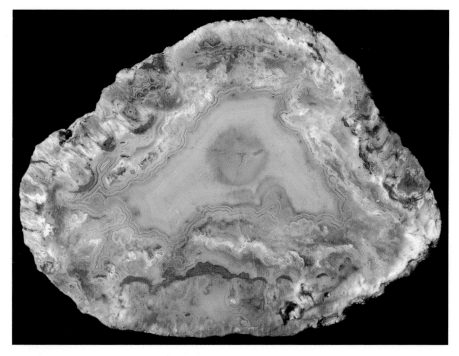

Figure 215
Many Kentucky agates seem to have this bright yellow color.

Michigan

Since the Gitche Gumee Museum is located in Michigan, we of course have to include Michigan in our limited list of states. The majority of agates found in Michigan are Lake Superior agates that formed 1.1 billion years ago in basaltic lava flow pockets. A geologist named A.C. Lane recorded these agates in a Michigan Geological Survey Bulletin in 1911 and used the name Lake Superior agate.[510] You can find them anywhere in the state, but the only place that is worth your time to search for them is on the shore of Lake Superior where the rocks are water-washed and available.

The surface area of Lake Superior is larger than that of any lake on Earth. Once around its entire shore is a journey of 2,725 miles. That is a lot of potential agate hunting territory![511] There are a few gravel pits and quarries in the west side of the Upper Peninsula that are worthwhile, plus you can search in some of the ancient host-rock lava flow outcroppings. Keep in mind that there are a lot of vesicular lava flows, but only a few that are agate-bearing. During the summer of 2004, one of these was discovered offshore near the tip of the Keweenaw Peninsula in about 30 feet of water. Many agates have since been recovered from an oxidized section of this original matrix rock. Specimens generally portray a beautiful fortification of white, green, red, brown, and other earth-tone colorations. Because of the size, quality, and number of specimens, this is considered one of the most significant agate finds in many decades from this region.[512]

In addition to the amygdaloidal Lake Superior agates, you can also find seam (vein) agates and iron lace agates in Marquette County and copper replacement agates in the Keweenaw Peninsula.

Figures 216 and 217
The founder of the museum, Axel Niemi, in Grand Marais, Michigan, discovered this beautiful amethyst-filled carnelian agate.

The first published description of Lake Superior agates was made by Henry Schoolcraft in 1820. He made his observations during his tenure as chief geologist of two expeditions into the Lake Superior region, in 1820 and 1832.[513] Lake Superior agates have been prized among collectors ever since. Schoolcraft described the Lake Superior shoreline:

The rocky and elevated nature of the country, leads us to look for those treasures in the mineral kingdom which nature has denied in soil and climate. In various places have lead, iron, and copper already been discovered, and the beauty of the carnelian, the agates, and the chalcedonies, picked up along the shores of Lake Superior, prove that the hardy regions of the north are not unfavourable to the production of mineral gems.[514]

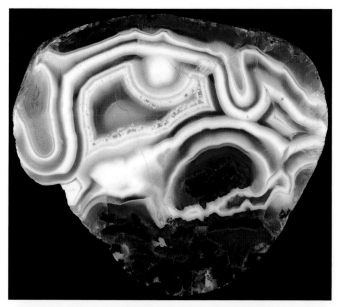

*Figure 218
This is another one of the museum founder's agates from Grand Marais, Michigan. The mineral inclusions complicated the banding during this agate's genesis process.*

*Figure 219
Some of the agates found in the Keweenaw Peninsula have copper that has replaced agate banding.*

Minnesota

If you want to find Lake Superior agates, your best bet is to go to Minnesota. In the summer of 1969, the Lake Superior agate received its highest honor when it was named the official state gemstone in Minnesota.[515] It is also where most of the Lake Superior agates were formed. As reported in Chapter 2, there was a rift zone 1.1 billion years ago out of which lava flowed and piled up over 65,000 feet tall. That is a lot of lava with a lot of vesicle pockets, some of which filled in with agate. During geologic time, the basaltic rock weathered and eroded, reducing the mound. Sedimentary rock was subsequently deposited from these eroded fragments. The hard and erosion-resistant Lake Superior agates were "freed" from their lava rock captor and have been spread throughout the upper Midwest by the glaciers, as well as by the waves and ice of Lake Superior and its predecessor lakes.

Lake Superior agates have one of the widest array of formations including: botryoidal, brecciated, candy striped, dendritic, eye, floater band, fortification, iris, jasper, moss, paintstone, peeler, plume, pseudomorph, ruin, sagenite, seam, shadow, thunder eggs, tube, and water-level agates. Lake Superior agates are especially known for having red Iron-oxide staining.[516,517] Some of this staining happened during the time of agate genesis. In most cases the agates were stained after their formation by iron-rich solutions that penetrated the semi-permeable chalcedony when they were dragged by glaciers through iron-rich soil.

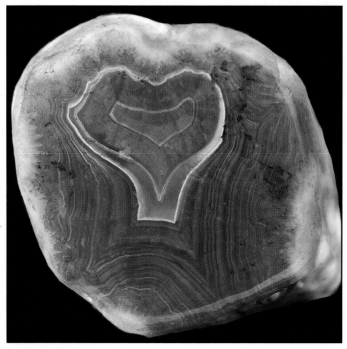

Figure 220
This Minnesota Lake Superior agate is showing some love back to all you rockhound fanatics!

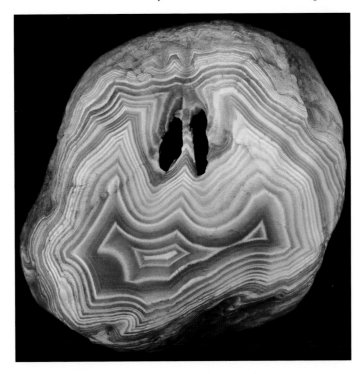

Figure 221
What, me worry? Of course not! This is one of those agates that the museum founder, Axel, would have made up an entire short story, with this Lake Superior agate as the main character.

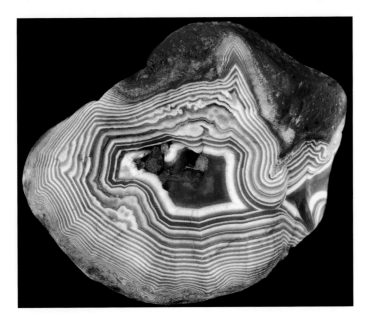

Figure 222
This Lake Superior agate is a terrific example of a candy striped agate.

Missouri

There are four main types of agate found in Missouri. Occasionally, a Lake Superior agate deposited by the glaciers can be found in the northeastern part of the state or along the Mississippi River. Coldwater agates, which are psudomorphic replacements from coral, can also be found in the northeastern part of the state. Near the Arkansas border, Crowley Ridge agates have been successfully located. Probably the most well known indigenous agate in Missouri is the Union Road agate found in St. Louis County within a few miles of the intersection between interstates 270 and 55. They were originally discovered when the I55 interstate was under construction in south St. Louis County. This area is now built up with shopping centers and housing developments, making this a rare agate to find. The Union Road agate was formed during the Mississippian period 286 to 320 million years ago.[518]

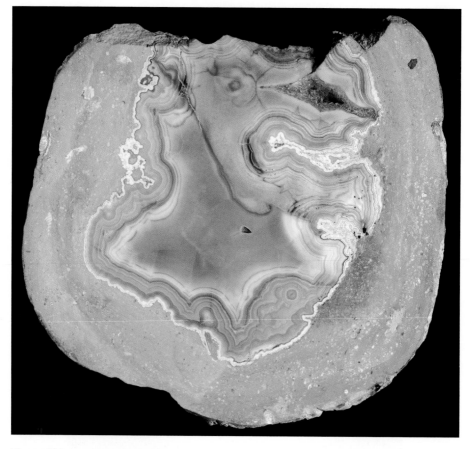

Figure 223
This is a Union Road agate from Missouri. Notice how its coloration is similar to the Keswick Agate from Iowa, which was formed during the same time period. Also note the infiltration channel on the top right section of this specimen.

Montana

The most famous agate from Montana is the dry head agate. It is primarily found in Big Horn and Carbon Counties, Dead Indian Hill, East Pryor Mountains, and Big Ice Cave Quadrangles. This is a marine sedimentary agate formed during the Permian time, from 251 to 299 million years ago. It is an extremely colorful agate known for its swirls and eyes. Specimens tend to be round nodules that usually don't reveal their beauty until cut.[519] This agate received its name because the area where it is found, Native Americans hunted by driving bison toward steep cliffs, where the animals fell and died. The animals were butchered on the spot and the heads were piled up. As a result, the area received its name of "dry head."[520]

One of the more well known moss agates also comes from Montana. Some of these moss agates appear to be chalcedony with mineral inclusions, while others clearly have banded chalcedony. They can be found in the Yellowstone and Elk Rivers, as well as in gravel deposits scattered over hundreds of square miles. Like the Lake Superior agate, there is no one central site that can be dominated by a small number of individuals who stake out mining claims.

When the Montana moss agate formed around 50 million years ago, the eastern part of the state was an inland ocean that resembled a large shallow swamp. There were forests lining the shores, as well as volcanoes throughout the area. The lava from these volcanoes engulfed the trees, which left open cavities in the rock that later filled in with chalcedony.[521] After formation, mineral-rich water seeped into the chalcedony and formed dendritic patterns that look like mountains, rivers, trees, and other objects.

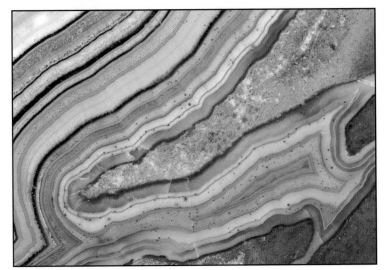

*Figure 224
This is a close up of a Montana dry head agate. Don't you just love the colored swirls?*

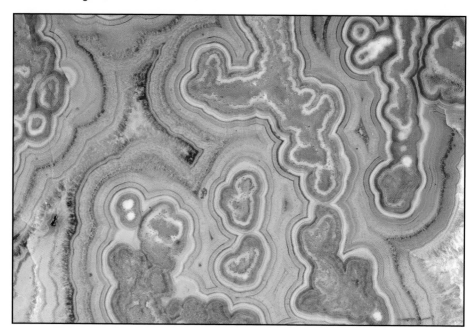

Figure 225
Another close up of a colorful Montana dry head agate.

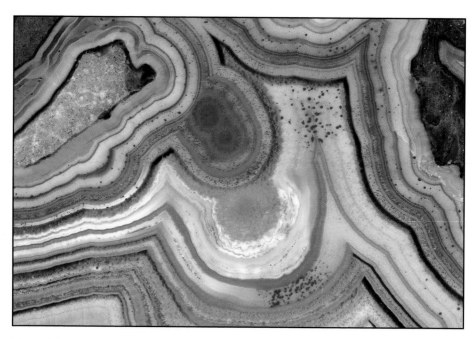

Figure 226
Many Montana dry head agates have spherical shapes, intricate patterns, and colorful bands.

Even though it is called "moss" agate, the inclusions are actually dendrites that formed along fractures when mineral-rich solutions seeped into the agates after they were formed, developing the dendrites between chalcedony layers or along fracture seams.[522]

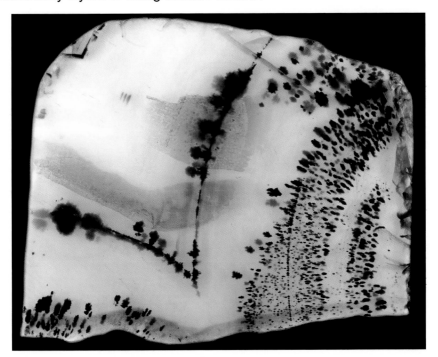

Figure 227
This is an excellent example of Montana moss agate.

New Mexico

There is a considerable amount of chalcedony and agate throughout the state of New Mexico. This is likely due to the influence of the Jemez Volcanoes and other tectonic activity during the geologic past. Much of the agate, like that around the Abiquiu area, does not have gem-quality banding. Although it doesn't have spectacular banding, the agate from the Luna area in the western part of the state does exhibit a good iris. There is also agate in the Rio Puerco Valley.

Two exceptions regarding quality banding are the big diggins agate from Demming, New Mexico, and the Baker Ranch thunder eggs located in the "boot heel" of New Mexico. Both of these agates can have excellent banding as well as hollow geode pockets lined with macrocrystalline quartz. Most of the coloration in the southern New Mexico agates is thought to have been from iron-bearing waters that penetrated the chalcedony layers.[523]

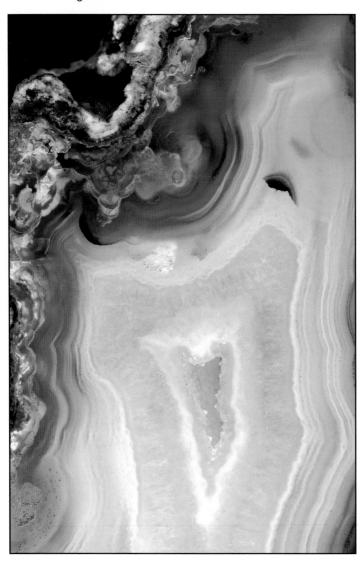

Figure 228
An example of
big diggins agate
from Demming,
New Mexico.

Oregon

The state of Oregon has a tremendous number of agates. There are both a wide variety of agate structures and hunting locations. The types found include agatized fossils, carnelian, dendritic, enhydro, fortification, geode, iris, moss, plume, sagenite, sardonyx, and thunder eggs. They can be found in Antelope, Crooke County, Florence, Graveyard Point, Hornbrook, Mill Creek, Newport, Paiute Reservoir, and Succor Creek, as well as along the Pacific coastline. The reason for the vast array of agates is probably due to the volcanic activity in the area, which supplied silica-rich ash and rhyolite. New agates, which are buried under sandstone, are continuously eroded out of their originating deposits off the coast.[524]

The thunder egg is Oregon's most famous agate. A prime location to look is the Richardson Ranch in Madras, Oregon. There are so many different types of agates on this ranch that they have divided the area into different beds or search areas. The Oregon agates are thought to be quite young, having formed in the early Miocene around 20 million years ago.[525]

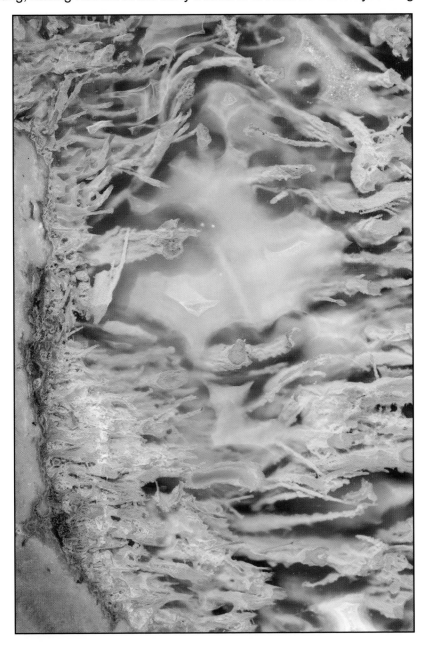

Figure 229
This is a Priday agate from the Richardson Ranch in Oregon.

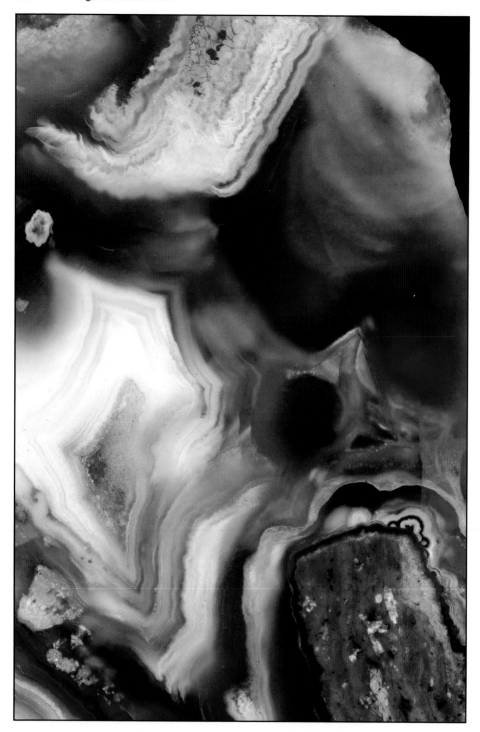

Figure 230
This is a close up of some of the structure in an unusual Oregon agate.

South Dakota

Like the Montana dry head agate, many of the agates indigenous to South Dakota formed in sedimentary rock pockets. They formed between 245 and 310 million years ago in limestone when silica became concentrated. The source could have been either biologic or air-born volcanic ash.

It is interesting that the genesis of Fairburn agates does not seem to have involved preexisting pockets. Silicic acid dissolved away limestone, leaving behind silica which may have first developed into chert. Over time, spherulites formed which further developed into agate banding. In some cases, the banding formed around larger, adjoining spherulites, which caused the bands to twist and turn into the typical holly leaf pattern.[526] Because they appear to have formed on the ocean floor during compaction of the sedimentary limestone layer, there were no open spaces within which impurity crystals or inclusions could develop before agate genesis began. Crystal molds and pseudomorphs seen in agates from other areas are rarely, if ever, seen in Fairburn agates. Similarly, Fairburns do not appear to have eyes, tubes, water-level banding, or sagenite.[527] Like other agates, Fairburns can have macrocrystalline centers or quartz alternating between chalcedony bands. This is because of varying conditions during the formation process when there were periods of silica under saturation.[528]

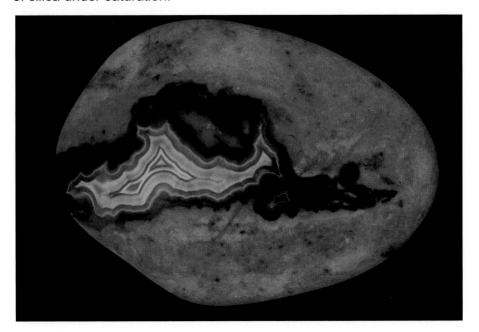

Figure 231
This Fairburn agate shows how matrix rock can comprise over half the specimen.

The sedimentary rock in which the South Dakota agates formed eventually eroded away, freeing the agates to be distributed by the glaciers.[529] Many Fairburns still have matrix attached. The first Fairburn was found in 1876. They have been a favorite of agate collectors ever since. In 1966, the Fairburn agate was officially recognized as the state gemstone. Throughout the southwestern part of the state, Fairburn agates can be found in the prairies, badlands, and Black Hills.[530] They were also spread by the glaciers into Wyoming and Nebraska.

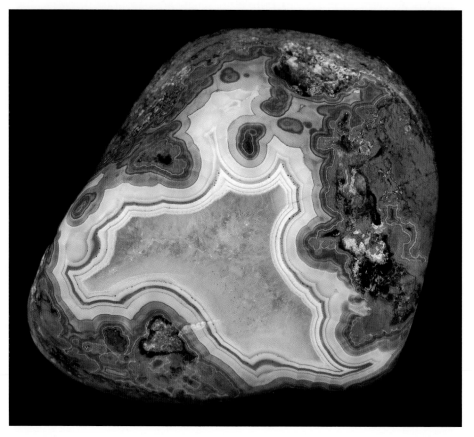

Figure 232
This is a South Dakota Fairburn agate with some holly leaf banding and a quartz center fill.

The Fairburn, because of its rarity combined with its brilliant colors and patterns, is one of the most valued agates in the world. A few years ago, a Fairburn agate sold on eBay for around $13,000! But rockhounds and buyers should beware because there are a couple of other South Dakota agates often confused with Fairburns. Prairie agates are more plentiful. They can be distinguished from Fairburns because they do not have distinct holly-leaf banding patterns, and they are not as colorful. Prairie agates have more concentric and less dramatic banding.[531]

Teepee Canyon agates from Custer County, can be very colorful and can have the holly-leaf pattern. They are usually bright red and yellow and often have a limestone husk, which is different from Fairburns that have a waxier, microcrystalline husk. Teepee Canyon agates are thought to be mostly "mined" out, and are now difficult to come by.

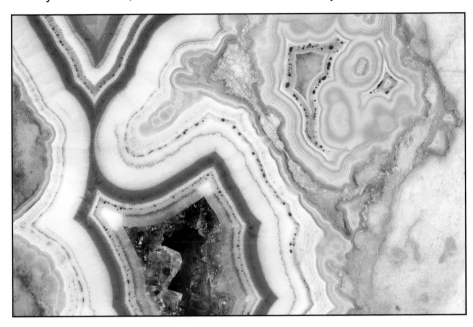

Figure 233
This is a polished slab of Teepee Canyon agate from South Dakota.

Figure 234
This is an unpolished piece of Teepee Canyon agate from South Dakota.

Texas

Many "snowbirds" like to go to Texas during the winter months to rockhound. Those that do can enjoy finding several types of agate including: Marfa plume, Morion, fossilized palm wood agate, Rio Grande agate, thistle agate, Toyah agate, pompom agate, Balmorhea blue agate and cathedral agate. The latter type derived its name because the patterns look like spires of a Gothic cathedral. It comes from the Cathedral Mountains in Brewster County Texas.[532] Some of the moss agate from Texas can be out of this world, such as the example below.

Figure 235 This is an incredible moss agate from Texas.

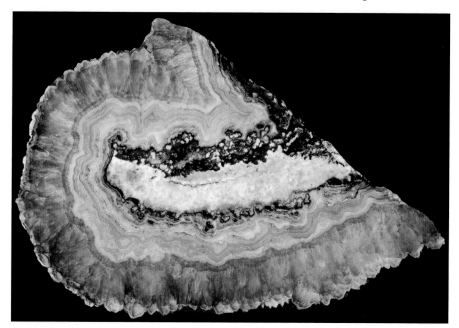

Figure 236
This is a Texas cathedral agate.

Wyoming

Several agates are found in Wyoming including algae agates, Eden Valley agatized wood, Guemsey Lake agates, Lysite agates, Medicine Bow plume agates, Shirley Basin agates, Spanish Point and Wiggins Fork dendritic agates, Sweetwater agates, sagebrush agates, and turitella agates. Also, Fairburn and dry head agates were distributed by the glaciers from adjoining states. The turitella agate formed when chalcedony completely replaced the original snail species that lived in a shallow sea between 40 and 60 million years ago. The agatized fossil is now found on the Delaney Rim and Beaver Rim in south central Wyoming.

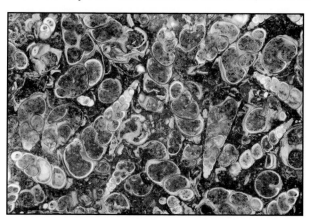

Figure 237
This is a turitella agate from Wyoming. Although it is called agate, it is silicified fossil wherein various forms of quartz filled in the snail shells.

Figure 238
This is close up of the agate replacement in a turitella agate. Scientists now agree that these fossilized agates did not replace the turitella snail, but instead the Elimia tenera species.

A SELECTION OF INTERNATIONAL AGATES

Just as we did for the agates found in the United States, we will offer just a sampling of agates found in other countries. Again our purpose is to present photographs and information to help promote understanding and appreciation for agates from around the world. Our selection was based more on the specimens we had available than on any judgment of agate quality.

Argentina

During the past several years Argentina has become one of the new hot beds for agate prospecting. The condor agate was introduced to the U.S. market in 1992 by the former Argentinean actor, Luis de los Santos. Since then he discovered the puma agate in 1993, the crater agate in 1997, and more recently the Black River agate. Prospecting and mining these agates is difficult. Not only are the locations extremely remote, but the work must be done at elevation where the weather is often not cooperative. The puma agate, which was a pseudomorph after coral that formed in sedimentary rock matrix, is mined at around 4,000 feet. It was named after cougar tracks that are often seen in the caves near the prospecting area. The newer crater agate is mined at 6,000 to 7,000 feet. It was named after the ancient volcano where the agate is collected.[533]

Figure 239
This is a close up of an Argentina Black River agate.

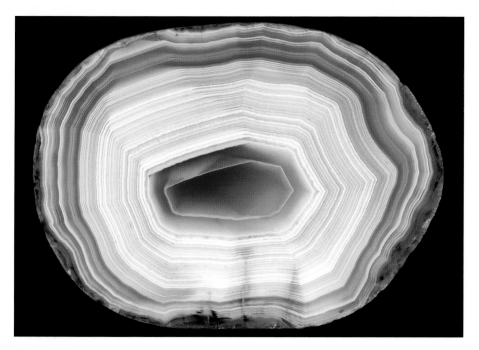

Figure 240
This is a Black River agate from Argentina. It has a floater band in the center pocket.

Figure 241
This is a splendid condor agate from Argentina.

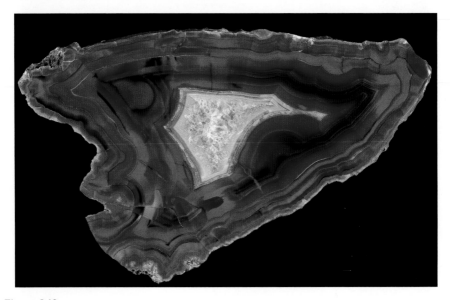

Figure 242
Many of the condor agates recently mined in Argentina have this deep red carnelian color.

Australia

One of the most famous agate hunting locals in the world is Agate Creek in Queensland, Australia, located in the northeast part of the country. In the mid 1890s, prospectors scoured the area looking for gold. While walking the riverbeds, they came across the brilliantly colored agates lying everywhere. Because of their find, they called the river Agate Creek. Later, after World War II, a conflict in the area developed between individual rockhounds and those who wanted to develop commercial mining claims. The rockhounds won, and the use of big equipment to mine agates was prohibited.[534]

Queensland agates formed after a large inland sea covered ancient basaltic rock. Over geologic time a thick layer of sandstone was deposited. Silica leached from the sandstone provided the silica source for agate genesis.[535] Most of the Queensland agates are thought to have formed during the Permian period between 250 and 300 million years ago. More scientists are beginning to agree that they have discovered what may be the world's oldest agates in Western Australia. Until recently it was thought that the Lake Superior agate is the oldest having formed 1.1 billion years ago. However, dating of host rock in Western Australia has determined that there may be three older agates including Kilara, Maddina, and Warrawoona agates that are thought to be 1.84 billion, 2.72 billion, and 3.45 billion years old, respectively.[536] It has yet to be verified that the agates formed at the same time as the host rock. Three indications of aging have been observed in these Western Australia agates that may verify their age. Scientists agree there is usually a reduction in water content, an increase in crystal size, and a decrease in moganite content. The Western Australia agates exhibit all three of these characteristics. Also it appears that these Western Australian agates suffered post-formation changes apparently as a result of heat generated from regional metamorphism.[537]

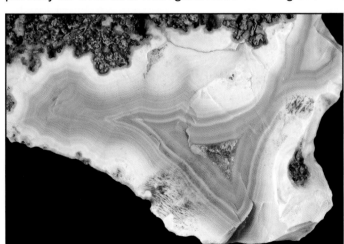

Figure 243
This is a salmon colored Agate Creek agate from Queensland, Australia.

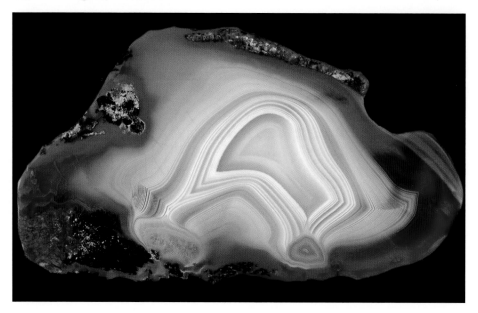

Figure 244
This is a Queensland agate with a shadow evident on the right side of this specimen.

Botswana, Africa

Botswana agate is very characteristic with alternating purplish-gray and white banding that sometimes has ovoid spherical inclusions. Bands can also be black, brown, red, and pink, and very rarely green, lavender, reddish or golden. Mineral impurities as well as post-formation changes due to natural heating from the sun and oxidation appear to have impacted the color of these agates. They have nice fortification bands, although the agates are usually fairly small in size ranging from an ounce to a half pound. These agates were first introduced on the world's market in 1971, although they had been known for at least a century before that. They have less red due to smaller amounts of iron oxide in the area Botswana agates, but otherwise are very similar in structure and appearance to Lake Superior agates. They formed in basalt vesicle pockets between 140 and 180 million years old. Originally a lot of the material was shipped in the raw to enthusiasts and lapidariests world wide, but that practice was discontinued decades ago. Now the availability of Botswana agates has significantly diminished. Apparently, the mining and processing of agates, which was under government control, has now ceased.[538,539]

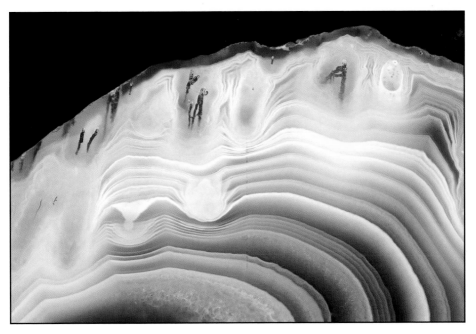

Figure 245
This Botswana agate has interesting stalk aggregate mineral inclusions as well as the typical delicate banding.

Figure 246
This photo shows more delicate banding from a Botswana agate.

Brazil

Agates were discovered in Brazil and Uruguay in 1827.[540] The agate supplies in Germany had been exhausted so they were in search of a new supply. For an unknown reason, the supply of agates in Brazil exceeds anywhere else in the world. Single agates have been found in excess of 1,000 pounds![541,542]

Brazilian agates have been dated between 100 and 200 million years old.[543] However, the basalt flows in which the agates formed occurred much before that. The volcanic eruptions took place when South America separated from Africa. The separation created the southern Atlantic Ocean and caused a hot spot to form under the east coast of South America. The hot spot uplifted to create a "dome" that was over 600 miles wide. The uplifted dome fractured, causing lava to flow out onto the Earth's surface. These lava flows were the largest in Earth's history, even larger than the ones in the Lake Superior region. During an 11 million year time period, the lava spread over 386,000 square miles to an average depth of 6,000 feet![544,545]

During the time of these lava flows, the area that is now Brazil was around 50°F warmer and the carbon dioxide in the atmosphere was much higher. These conditions would have supported the development of carbonic acid, which would have intensified the chemical weathering of the basalt.[546]

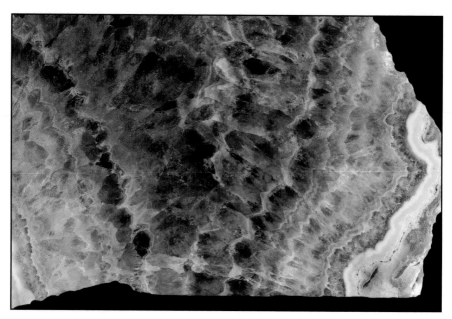

Figure 247
This specimen has a mixture of micro- and macro-crystals of amethyst, chalcedony, and quartz.

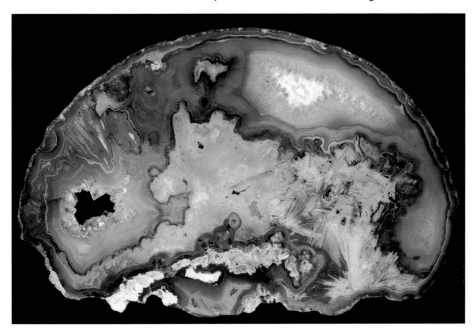

Figure 248
There is a lot going on in this slab of Brazilian agate! Do you see the unicorn?

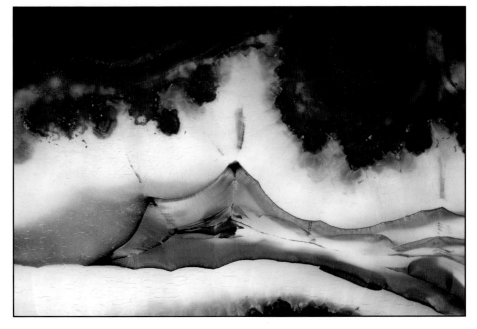

Figure 249
This Brazilian slab has a landscape scene.

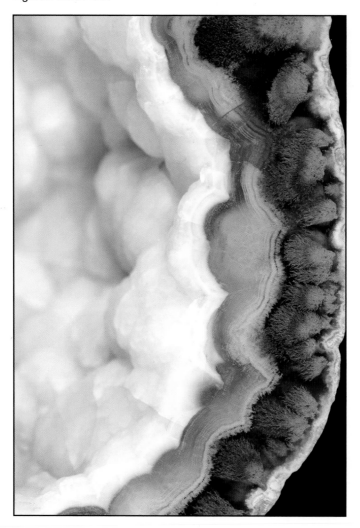

Figure 250
This Brazilian agate has unusual plume inclusions as well as botryoidal formations.

Canada

There are agates in several sections of Canada including the Bay of Fundy, Cape Blomidon, Rier Island, Manitoba, British Columbia, Thunder Bay and Michipicoten Island in Ontario. The first few photos below are Michipicoten Island agates. This is not an easy place to get to since the island sits in the northeastern part of Lake Superior. There are no ferries or airplanes to take tourists to the island, even though most of the island is a provincial park. If you want to go there, you have to find someone with a big enough boat or a plane and make the arrangements yourself. Since it is illegal to keep the rocks you find in the park, you may want to think twice before trying to arrange the logistics.

The island itself is around 6 miles by 18 miles. People have known about agates from this island since at least the mid-1800s. The agates are mostly found encased in the matrix host rock. Like the Lake Superior agates, they were also formed during the middle to late Precambrian period.[547]

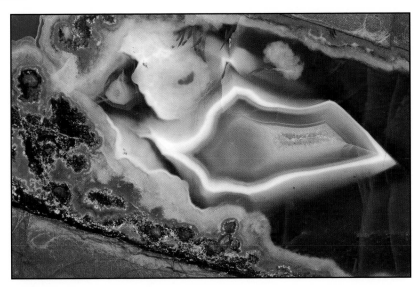

Figure 251
Although many Michipicoten Island agates have a rugged exterior, their agate banding can have delicate detail.

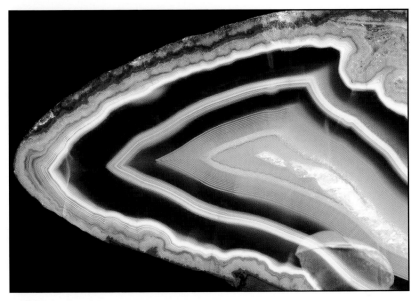

Figure 252
Many of the Michipicoten agates have very fine banding that oftentimes exhibit a shadow effect.

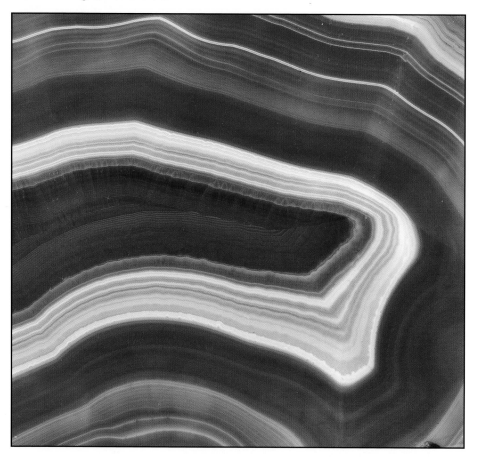

Figure 253
Although this looks like a Brazilian agate, the museum founder acquired this Michipicoten agate from a Canadian woman. See the story below.

In 1958, the museum founder, Axel Niemi, found the largest agate of his life: a 5.5 pound Lake Superior agate. An article was published in the *Detroit News*. Soon thereafter, Axel received a letter from a Mrs. J. Oldenkamp, who at the time lived in St. Clair Shores, Michigan. She said her father's friend had found a ten pound agate on Michipicoten Island, and sent it to Germany to be cut in half and polished sometime before the first World War. Mrs. Oldenkamp's father then purchased it from his friend for $5.00, after which it sat on the family's fireplace mantel. Her father passed away in 1929, and she ended up with the agate. After reading the article about Axel's 5.5 pounder, she offered to sell the Michipicoten agate to him. For the next seven years, they squabbled over the price until Axel finally purchased the agate in 1965. Unfortunately, in the final correspondence, Axel cut the price out of the letter. We would love to know what he paid for it. A detailed section of this agate is pictured above.

Another interesting Canadian story has to do with the Thunder Bay Agate Mine, located northwest of Lake Superior. It opened up in the 1990s but then was closed for a number of years. Ads have recently appeared on the internet, so hopefully the mine has re-opened. Mine owners boast of having the largest seam agate in the world, which they are in the process of excavating. Although you cannot dig near their excavating site, there are several other areas where visitors are allowed to dig. In addition to seam agates, there are also some very different looking agatized stalactites and stalagmites. To find out more about this mine, search the internet for Thunder Bay, Ontario, tourism web pages.

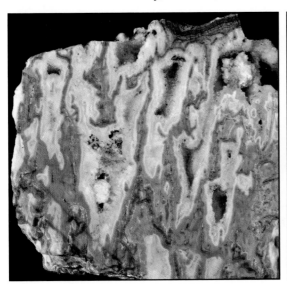 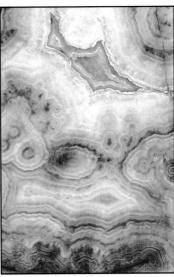

Figures 254 and 255
These specimens are unusual seam agates from Thunder Bay, Ontario. Do you see the shark in the agate on the right?

Caribbean

The specimen in the following photo was sold as having come from the Caribbean, but no additional information was provided. The "agate" appears to be a pseudomorph of coral. Johann Zenz in his first book *Agates* on page 16 has a somewhat similar agate that he called "parrot wing agate." His description is "Agatized material of green and yellow minerals with blue chrysocolla." The specimen has blue and green colors instead of yellow and green, but is quite similar.

Figure 256
This unknown agate or agate-want-to-be is from somewhere in the Caribbean. It appears to have malachite and maybe chrysocolla as well as some microcrystalline quartz—all formed with agate-like banding.

When you rockhounds see the next photo, you will bet that it is African blue lace agate. This specimen requires a personal story. During my (Karen's) corporate career, I travelled over a million and a half miles. Wherever I went, I always looked in the phone book to find out if there was a rock shop in the area. If there was one, I ventured over to buy at least one specimen. Back in the early 1990s, I had to go to St. Thomas on business. I wasn't even going to look in the phone book since most material in the Caribbean is coral. However, I decided to stay true to my practice and was surprised when the phone book had one rock shop listed. I hurried over and was blown away by a sales display of amazing blue lace agate specimens. I picked out the best one and told the owner that I wanted to buy the "African blue lace agate." He said that he would be glad to sell it, but that it wasn't from Africa. He claimed that he and a friend were fishing somewhere in the Caribbean from a boat next to a deserted island. When he looked up on the cliff, he saw the agate. Later, he went back with dynamite, blew up the cliff, snorkeled for the rocks, and threw them in his boat. Then, while finishing the story, the guy grabbed my arm and said "Come back here. I want to show you something." I was a little scared but my curiosity made me follow. In the alley behind his shop, he had a huge cement mixer that he had fashioned into a rock tumbler. Once I saw the polishing equipment, as well as the piles of rough rock, I was convinced that he was telling the truth. It appears that there is nearly identical blue lace agate on both sides of the Atlantic Ocean.

Figure 257
This blue lace agate is from a secret location in the Caribbean.

China

Minerals from China have been flooding the market during this past decade, but they include very few agates. The only exception is the Chinese Rain Flower agate. These are nodular in form and have been water washed by the Yangtze River. In many cases, they appear to be almost polished. For those of you who frequent eBay, sometimes you will see these listed as "Lake Superior-like." Many have similar coloration with rich banding patterns. They are found near the ancient site of the Gaozuo Temple. In fact, they are so admired that they were taken by the Chinese delegation to the 24th Seoul Olympic Games to represent "Peace Lucky Stone." A legend says that during the Liang of Southern Dynasties (502-557 A.D.), Master Monk Yunguang placed a table on top of the local terrace and expounded the texts of Buddhism. Apparently, this so moved the God that the heaven rained flowers, which later became these beautiful and colorful agate stones.[548]

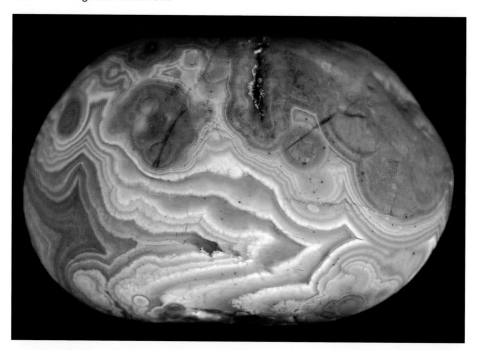

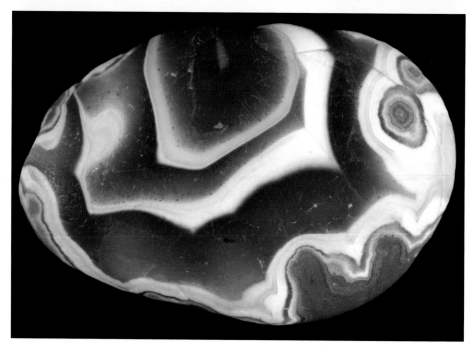

Figures 258 and 259
These Chinese rain flower agates were river washed to a natural weathered polish.

Mexico

For decades, some of the best agates in the world have come from northern Mexico. There are more types of agate and more locations than can be listed here. In fact, there are more than 80 varieties of agate that have been found in Mexico![549] They first became known in 1913, but mining did not ramp up until after 1945 when a highway was constructed to access the area. During the early prospecting period new agate finds were discovered every few years. Even now, additional agate locations are still being found.

One of the most unusual Mexican agates is crazy lace agate. It is mined at 6,200 feet above the desert in the Sierra Santa Lucia area. It occurs as a vein agate and is known for its paisley patterns with a vast array of curves, twists, scallops, zigzags, sagenite, tubes, and eyes. It is mined in limestone that is of Cretaceous age (65 to 145 million years ago). The agate, however, is much younger. It is thought that the agate did not form until silica-rich rhyolitic domes intruded the area between 40 and 50 million years ago. The rhyolite apparently supplied the silica that eventually accumulated in the ground water or hydrothermal fluids that later flowed through the pores and seams in the limestone to contribute the silica needed for agate genesis.[550]

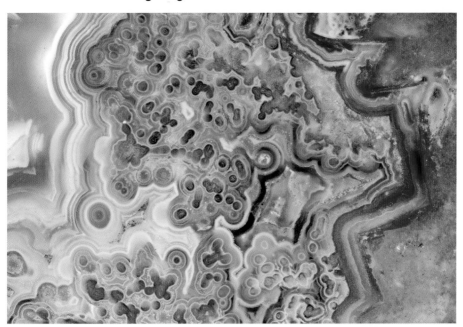

Figure 260
The crazy lace agate from Mexico can be incredibly complex.

*Figure 261
This Mexican
crazy   lace
agate resem-
bles   an   ice
cream cone.*

One of the most prized of the nodular Mexican agates is the Laguna. It is from the Estacion Ojo Laguna area in the state of Chihuahua. Not only do these agates have nice crisp fortification bands, but they also have some of the best color of any agate in the world. This agate formed in volcanic andesite approximately 38 million years ago. The original deposit was discovered in the late 1940s and has continued to produce agate ever since. Once the surface deposit was depleted in the 1990s, heavy machinery was used to continue the mining operation. Although the original Laguna deposit is now exhausted, additional digging sites have been discovered in the area.

Figure 262
This Mexican Laguna agate displays a nice shadow, along with its iron inclusions and brilliant colors.

Figure 263
This Laguna agate has an interesting sagenite formation.

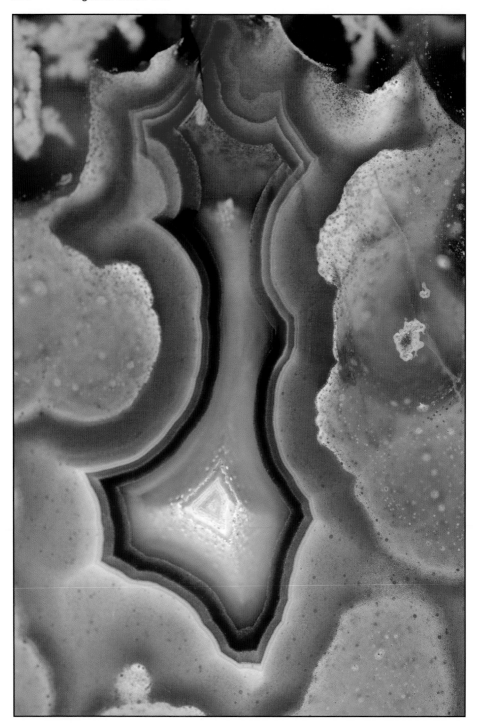

Figure 264
This Laguna is delicate, beautiful, mysterious, and calming to look at.

REFERENCES

1. Tolle, Eckhart. *A New Earth: Awakening to Your Life's Purpose.* New York: Plume—Penguin Group, 2006.
2. Brodrick, Harold J. *Agatized Rainbows: A story of the Petrified Forest.* Petrified Forest Museum Association, Popular Series No. 3, 1951:13.
3. Kile, Daniel. "The Nomenclature of Crystalline, Cryptocrystalline, and Non-Crystalline Phases of Silica." *Symposium on Agate and Cryptocrystalline Quartz.* Golden, CO:, Sept 10-13, 2005: 11.
4. Lee, David R. *Characterisation and the Diagenetic Transformation of Non- and Microcrystalline Silica Minerals.* Liverpool U.K.: University of Liverpool, Dept. of Earth and Ocean Sciences: 2.
5. Beaster, Timothy J. *Agates: A Literature Review and Electron Backscatter Diffraction Study of Lake Superior Agates.* Northfield, MN, Carleton College Senior Integrative Exercise, March 9, 2005: 4.
6. Conway, W. Rick. *Origin of Rocks and Minerals.* New Albany, IN: Earth Exploration Co., 2003: 13.
7. Carlson, Michael. *The Beauty of Banded Agates: An Exploration of Agates from Eight Major Worldwide Sites.* Edina, MN: Fortification Press, 2002: 3.
8. Weinberger, Sheri. "A Superior Collection: His Treasures are Lake Superior Agates." *Rock and Gem*, July 1999: 40.
9. Pabian, Roger with Prian Jackson, Peter Tandy, and John Cromartie. *Agates: Treasures of the Earth.* London: Firefly Books, Natural History Museum: 7.
10. Weinberger: 43. See Cite 8.
11. Brown, Nancy Marie. "The Agateer." *Penn State Online Research.* 22: Sept 2001:1.
12. Weinberger:.43. See Cite 8.
13. www.gujaratplus.com/news/archiv/arc37: 3.
14. Pabian et al, p. 5. See Cite 9.
15. Pabian et al , p. 159. See Cite 9.
16. Pabian, Roger K and Andrejs Zarins. *Banded Agates: Origins and Inclusions.* Lincoln, NB, University of Nebraska, Ed Circular No. 12, June 1994, p. 1.
17. www.cst.cmichi.edu/users/dietr1rv/agate.
18. Pabian and Zarins,: 1. See Cite 16.
19. www.gemstone.org/gem-by-gem/English/agate: 1.
20. Pabian & Zarins: 3. See Cite 16.
21. www.jewelinfo4u.com.
22. Schumacher, Renate. "Idar-Oberstein and its Agate History." *Symposium on Agate and Cryptocrystalline Quartz.* Golden, Co., Sept. 10-13, 2005: 73.
23. Pabian and Zarins:. 3. See Cite 16.
24. Wolter, Scott F. *The Lake Superior Agate.* Edina, MN: Burgess Publishing, 1996: 2.
25. American Toy Marble Museum, www.americantoymarbles.com/akronhist.htm
26. Brodrick: 11. See Cite 2.
27. Clark, Roger. *Fairburn Agate: Gem of South Dakota.* Appleton, Wi: Silverwind Agates, 2002:. 85.
28. American Geological Institute. *Dictionary of Geological Terms.* Garden City, NY: Dolphin Books, 1962.
29. www.quartzpage.de/print/intro.html.
30. Brodrick: 13. See Cite 2.
31. www.quartzpage.de/print/bergkristall.html.
32. www.quartzpage.de/print/intro.html.
33. www.quartzpage.de/print/gen_types.html.
34. www.quartzpage.de/print/intro.html
35. Moxon, Terry. *Agate: Microstructure and Possible Origin.* Chippenham, Witshire: Terra Publications, 1996: 39.
36. Wolter: 101. See Cite 8.
37. www.en.wikipedia.org/wiki/Piezoelectricity.
38. www.quartzpage.de/print/intro.html.
39. www.quartzpage.de/print/eyes.html.
40. www.quartzpage.de/print/milky.html.
41. Moxon, T, D.R. Nelson and M. Zhang. "Agate Recrystallisation: Evidence from Samples Found in Archean and Proterozoic Host Rocks, Western Australia." *Australian Journal of Earth Science.* 53: 2006: 235.
42. Moxon: 1. See Cite 35.
43. Moxon: 22. See Cite 35.
44. www.quartzpage.de/print/carnelian.html.
45. www.quartzpage.de/print/chalcedony.html.
46. www.quartzpage.de/chrysoprase.html
47. Moxon: 1. See Cite 35.
48. www.quartzpage.de/print/flint.html.
49. Moxon: 81. See Cite 35.
50. www.fossilmuseum.net/Tree_of_Life/Stromatolites.htm#Warrawoona
51. www.fossilmuseum.net/fossilrecord/fossilization/fossilization.htm.
52. Brodrick: 10. See Cite 2.
53. Brodrick: 11. See Cite 2.
54. Brodrick: 12. See Cite 2.
55. Brodrick: 11-12. See Cite 2.
56. www.scienceviews.com/parks/treestostone.html.
57. Wolter: 56. See Cite 24.
58. www.quartzpage.de/print/gen_types.html.
59. www.quartzpage.de/print/gen_min.html.

60. Wolter: 55. See Cite 24.
61. www.quartzpage.de/print/gen_types.html.
62. Wolter: 55. See Cite 24.
63. Conway: 6. See Cite 6.
64. www.en.wikipedia.org/wiki/Timetable_of_ the_Precambrian.
65. Conway: 8. See Cite 6.
66. Conway: 10. See Cite 6.
67. www.en.wikipedia.org/wiki/Age_of_the_ Earth.
68. LaBerge, Gene L. *Geology of the Lake Superior Region.* Tucson, AZ: Geoscience Press, Inc., 1994: 2.
69. Erickson, Jon. *Plate Tectonics: Unraveling the Mysteries of the Earth.* New York: Checkmark Books, 2001: 28.
70. Erickson: 28. See Cite 69.
71. Erickson: 27. See Cite 69.
72. Erickson: 27. See Cite 69.
73. Erickson: 28. See Cite 69.
74. LaBerge: 2. See Cite 68.
75. Pivko, Daniel. *Natural Stones in Earth's History.* Barislava: 58, ACTA Geological Universitatis Comenianae Nr, 2003: 74.
76. www.astrobio.net/exclusive/421/earths-old-est-fossils-reverse-course.
77. Erickson: 32. See Cite 69.
78. www.en.wikipedia.org/wiki/Barberton_ Greenstone_Belt.
79. Erickson:33. See Cite 69.
80. Erickson: 31. See Cite 69.
81. Erickson: 34. See cite 69.
82. Erickson: 35. See Cite 69.
83. www.starofthenorth.org/minnesota.html.
84. LaBerge: 148. See Cite 68.
85. Wolter: 10. See Cite 24.
86. Erickson: 48. See Cite 69.
87. Erickson: 46. See Cite 69.
88. Erickson: 41. See Cite 69.
89. LaBerge: 145. See Cite 68.
90. Petranek, Jan. "Gravitational Banded ("Uruguay-type") Agates in Basaltic Rocks – Where and When?" *Bulletin of Geosciences.* 79: 4: 2004: 198.
91. www.en.wikipedia.org/wiki/Plate_tectonics
92. Erickson: xi-xiii. See Cite 69.
93. Erickson: 78. See Cite 69.
94. Erickson: 82. See Cite 69.
95. www.empb.net/en/agate.php.
96. Beaster: 4. See Cite 5.
97. Moxon et al: 235. See Cite 41.
98. www.en.wikipedia.org/wiki/Gemstone.
99. Beaster: 4. See Cite 5.
100. Owen, L.B. "Precipitation of Amorphous Silica from High-Temperature Hypersaline Geothermal Brines." Livermore, CA, Lawrence Livermore Laboratory, University of California, June 1975: 1.
101. Wolter: 16. See Cite 24.
102. Perry, Carole C. and Tracey Keeling-Tucker. "Crystalline Silica Prepared at Room Temperature from Aqueous solution in the Presence of Intrasilica Bioextracts." *Chem.. Communication.*1998: 2587.
103. www.en.wikipedia.org/wiki/Biomineralisation.
104. Lyklema, J. "fundamentals of Interface and Colloid Science, Volume IV." *Particulate Colloids.* Oxford, UK, 2005: 239.
105. www.de.wikipedia.org/wiki/Eckart_Walger
106. Walger, Eckart. Compiled by Georg Matteb, Volker von Seckndorff and Friedrich Liebau. "The Formation of Agate Structures: Models for Silica Transport, Agate Layer Accretion, and for Flow Patterns and Flow Regimes in Infiltration Channels." *Neves Jahrbuch Fur Mineralogie Abhandlungen.* 186: 2: August 2009: 113.
107. Walger: 114. See Cite 106.
108. Moxon, Terry. "Agate: A Study of Ageing." *European Journal of Mineralogy.* 14: 6: Nov/Dec 2002: 1109.
109. Pabian and Zarins: 3. See Cite16.
110. Gotze, J, M. Tichomirowa, H. Fuchs, J. Pilot, Z.D. Sharp. "Geochemistry of Agates: A Trace Element and Stable Isotope Study." *Chemical Geology.* 175: 2001: 526.
111. Petranek: 199. See Cite 90.
112. Petranek: 199. See Cite 90.
113. Kasting, James F. "Methane and climate During the Precambrian Era." *Precambrian Research.* 137: 2005: 119.
114. Petranek: 203. See Cite 90.
115. Petranek: 199. See Cite 90.
116. Petranek: 201. See Cite 90.
117. Moxon: 26. See Cite 35.
118. Owen: 8. See Cite 100.
119. Petranek: 200. See Cite 90.
120. Zarins, Andy. "Stratigraphic Distribution, Environments of Deposition and Formation of Agate in the Buck Hill Volcanic Series, Brewster County, Texas." *Symposium on Agate and Cryptocrystalline Quartz.* Golden, CO, Sept 10-13, 2005: 71.
121. Petranek: 200. See Cite 90.
122. Owen: 1. See Cite 100.
123. Lee, David R. "Characterisation of Silica Minerals in a Banded Agate: Implications for Agate Genesis and Growth Mechanisms." University of Liverpool: 1.
124. Pabian and Zarins: 1. See Cite 16.
125. Owen: 13. See Cite 100.
126. Petranek: 198. See Cite 90.
127. Petranek: 200. See Cite 90.
128. Pabian and Zairns: 6. See Cite 16.
129. Pabian et al: 118. See Cite 9.

130. Baxter, P.J., C. Bonadonna, R. Dupres, V.L. Hards, S.C. Kohn, M.D. Murphy, A. Nichols, R.A. Nicholson, G. Norton, A. Searl, R.S.J. Sparks, B.P. Vickers. "Cristobalite in Volcanic Ash of the Soufriere Hills Volcano, Montserrat, British West Indies." *Science.* 283: 5405: Feb 1, 1999: 1142.
131. Erickson: 46. See Cite 69.
132. Nazari, Maziar. "The Khur Agate Field, Central Iran." *Symposium on Agate and Cryptocrystalline Quartz.* Golden, CO: Sept 10-13, 2005: 43.
133. Pabian, Roger K. "Chalcedony Occurrences in the Central Great Plains." *Symposium on Agate and Cryptocrystalline Quartz.* Golden, CO: Sept 10-13, 2005: 30.
134. Simons, Frank S. "Devitrification Dikes and Giant Spherulites from Klondyke, Arizona." *The American Mineralogist.* 47: July-Aug 1962: 875.
135. Rodewald, Peter. "Lake Superior Copper Agates." *The Wonderful World of Agates Conference Program.* Menasha, WI: July 10-13, 2008: 24.
136. Pabian and Zarins: 6. See Cite 16.
137. Dumariska-Stowik, Magdalena, Lucyna Natkaniec-Nowak, Maciej J. Kotarba, Magdalena Sikorska, Jan A. Rzymetka, Agata Koboda and Adam Gawel. "Mineralogical and geochemical charterization of the "bituminous" agates from Nowy Kosciot (Lower Silesia, Poland)." *Neves Jahrbuch Fur Mineralogie Abandlungen.* 184: 3: 2008: 256.
138. Howard, Paul. "Agate Creek Agate." *The Gemological Association of Australia.* 2005: www.gem.org.au/agate.htm: 4.
139. LaBerge: 153. See Cite 68.
140. Clark: 67. See Cite 27.
141. Clark: 87. See Cite 27.
142. Moxon: 77. See Cite 35.
143. Saunders, James A. "Oxygen-Isotope Zonation of Agates from Karoo Volcanics of the Skelton Coast, Nambia: Discussion." *American Mineralogist.* 75: 1990: 1206.
144. Owen: 1. See Cite 100.
145. Nazari: 43. See Cite 132.
146. Hattori, Isamu, Myuki Umeda, Tomio Nakagawa, and Hirofumi Yamamoto. "From Chalcedonic Chert to Quartz Chert: Diagenesis of Chert Hosted in a Miocene Volcanic-Sedimentary Succession, Central Japan." *Journal of Sedimentary Research.* 66: 1: January 1966: 172.
147. www.bwsmigel.info/Lesson10/De.Gem.Formation.html.
148. Petranek: 199. See Cite 90.
149. www.chromatography-online.org/topics/silicic/acid.html.
150. www.en.wikipedia.org/wiki/Silicic_acid.
151. Owen: 1. See Cite 100.
152. Owen: 6. See Cite 100.
153. Owen: 8. See Cite 100.
154. Lyklema: 2.8. See Cite 104.
155. Pabian et al: 118. See Cite 9.
156. Wolter: 16. See Cite 24.
157. Walger et al: 126. See Cite 106.
158. Walger et al: 126. See Cite 106.
159. Adapted from Walger et al: 121. See Cite 106.
160. Walger et al: 130. See Cite 106.
161. Walger et al: 130. See Cite 106.
162. Walger et al: 130. See Cite 106.
163. Petranek: 200. See Cite 90.
164. Walger et al: 127. See Cite 106.
165. From private notes of K. Brzys.
166. www.britannica.com/EBchecked/topic/331528/lateral-secretion.
167. Walger et al: 126. See Cite 106.
168. Walger et al: 132. See Cite 106.
169. Walger et al: 129. See Cite 106.
170. Slastnikov, V.V., Yu O. Punin, and A.R. Nesterov. "Microzoning of Agates as a Reflection of their Formation Dynamics." *Geology of Ore Deposits.* 50: 8: 2008: 787.
171. Walger et al: 114. See Cite 106.
172. Nazari: 48. See Cite 132.
173. Clark: 61. See Cite 27.
174. Pabian and Zarins: 20. See Cite 16.
175. Wolter: 26. See Cite 24.
176. Jackson, Brian. "A History of Scottish Agates." *Symposium on Agate and Cryptocrystalline Quartz.* Golden, CO: Sept 10-13, 2005: 79.
177. Pabian et al: 17. See Cite 9.
178. Clark: 61. See Cite 27.
179. Walger et al: 114. See Cite 106.
180. Adapted from Walger et al: 119. See Cite 106.
181. Walger et al: 125. See Cite 106.
182. Walger et al: 139, 142. See Cite 106.
183. www.ma.water.usgs.gov/publications/ofr/scour.htm
184. Walger et al: 132. See Cite 106.
185. Walger et al: 132. See Cite 106.
186. Walger et al: 139, 142. See Cite 106.
187. Wolter: 101. See Cite 24.
188. Walger et al: 116. See Cite 106.
189. Walger et al: 123. See Cite 106.
190. Walger et al: 148. See Cite 106.
191. Walger et al: 122. See Cite 106.
192. Walger et al: 128. See Cite 106.
193. Walger et al: 148. See Cite 106.
194. Walger et al: 125. See Cite 106.
195. Walger et al: 148. See Cite 106.
196. Slastnikov: 787. See Cite 170.
197. Beaster: 10. See Cite 5.
198. Lee: 17. See Cite 123.
199. Walger et al: 115. See Cite 106.
200. Walger et al: 131. See Cite 106.
201. Petranek: 195. See Cite 90.

202. Cordua, Bill. "Agates—Rich in Fiber." River Falls, WI, University of Wisconsin, unpublished paper: 1.
203. Pabian et al: 13. See Cite 9.
204. Taijing, Lu and Ichiro Sunagawa. "Texture Formation of Agate in Geode." *Mineralogical Journal.* 17: 2: 1994: 54.
205. Walger et al: 116. See Cite 106.
206. Cordua: 1. See Cite 202.
207. Beaster: 6. See Cite 5.
208. Kis, Viktoria Kovacs and Istvan Dodony. "Mineralogical and Microstructural, Features of Chalcedony from Matra Mountains, Northern Hungary – A TEM Study." *Axia Mineralogica-Petrographica.* Szeged: 45: 1: 2004: 102.
209. Heaney,Peter. www.rps.psu.edu/0109/form.html: 2.
210. Owen: 13. See Cite 100.
211. Lyklema: 2.21. See Cite 104.
212. Taijing, Lu, X Xhang, Ichiro Sunagawa, G.W. Groves. "Nanometre Scale Textures in Agate and Beltane Opal." *Mineralogical Magazine.* 59: March 1995: 08.
213. Heaney: 2. See Cite 209.
214. Petranek: 200. See Cite 90.
215. Owen: 13. See Cite 100.
216. Heaney: 2. See Cite 209.
217. Walger et al: 145. See Cite 106.
218. Walger et al: 127. See Cite 106.
219. Walger et al: 129. See Cite 106.
220. Lee: 16. See Cite 123.
221. Pabian, Roger K. "Agates: Banding and Beyond." *Symposium on Agate and Cryptocrystalline Quartz.* Golden, CO: Sept 10-13, 2005: 14.
222. Pabian et al: 13. See Cite 9.
223. Beaster: 9. See Cite 5.
224. Cordua: 1. See Cite 202.
225. Gotze: 528. See Cite 110.
226. Walger et al: 130. See Cite 106.
227. Pabian et al: 13. See Cite 9.
228. A) Permission for use granted by Stephen W. Morris, University of Toronto Physics. www.flickr.com/photos/nonlin/
    B) Permission for use granted by DR. ANDRÁS BÜKI, www.insilico.hu/liesegang/index.html
229. Lyklema: xvi. See Cite 104.
230. Beaster: 9. See Cite 5.
231. Beaster: 15. See Cite 5.
232. Wang, Yifeng and Enrique Merino. "Self-Organizational Origin of Agates: banding, Fiber Twisting, Composition, and Dynamic Crystallization Model." *Geochimica et Cosmochimica Acta.* Pergamoe Press, 54: 1990:1627.
233. Wang, Yifeng and Enrique Merino. "Origin of Fibrosity and Banding in Agates from Flood Basalts." *American Journal of Science.* 295: January 1995: 49.
234. Wang and Merino: 1627. See Cite 232.
235. Corner, J. and P. Ortholeva. "Coexistence of Twisted and Untwisted Crystals: An Impurity/Structural Order Model with Implications for Agate Patterns." *American Mineralogist.* 92: 2007: 1952.
236. Pabian and Zarins: 3. See Cite 16.
237. Wang and Merino: 1629. See Cite 232.
238. Wang and Merino: 1629. See Cite 232.
239. Adapted from Wang and Merino: 1629. Used with permission. See Cite 232.
240. Adapted from Wang and Merino: 1633. Used with permission. See Cite 232.
241. Wang and Merino: 1628. See Cite 232.
242. Kis: 103. See Cite 208.
243. Taijing: 08. See Cite 211.
244. www.djmcadam.com/agate.html
245. Wang and Merino: 1628. See Cite 232.
246. Personal notes of Karen Brzys.
247. Pabian et al: 17. See Cite 9.
248. Lee: 16. See Cite 123.
249. Lee: 13. See Cite 123.
250. Lee: 10. See Cite 123.
251. A) Kis: 102. See Cite 208.
    B) Lee: 10. See Cite 4.
252. Lee: 15. See Cite 123.
253. Kis: 102. See Cite 208.
254. Walger et al: 127. See Cite 106.
255. Walger et al: 132. See Cite 106.
256. Petranek: 195. See Cite 90.
257. Petranek: 195. See Cite 90.
258. Petranek: 201. See Cite 90.
259. Petranek: 203. See Cite 90.
260. Petranek: 196. See Cite 90.
261. Petranek: 196. See Cite 90.
262. Taijing: 66. See Cite 204.
263. Taijing: 71. See cite 204.
264. www.geology.about.com/od/geoprocesses/ig/sedstrucs/geopetal.htm.
265. Walger et al: 122. See Cite 106.
266. Petranek: 202. See Cite 90.
267. Walger et al: 114. See Cite 106.
268. Walger et al: 114. See Cite 106.
269. Walger et al: 114. See Cite 106.
270. Walger et al: 121. See Cite 106.
271. Petranek: 203. See Cite 90.
272. Petranek: 201. See Cite 90.
273. Wolter: 25. See Cite 24.
274. Pabian and Zarins: 3. See Cite 16.
275. Lee: 2. See Cite 123.
276. Gotze: 67. See Cite 110.
277. Wang and Merino: 1627. See Cite 232.
278. Enrique Merino. "Very-High-Temperature, Closed-System Origin of agates in Basalts: A New Model, New and Old Evidence." Symposium on Agate and Cryptocrystalline Quartz." *Symposium on Agate and Cryptocrystalline Quartz.* Golden, CO: Sept 10-13, 2005: 67.
279. Wang and Merino: 1634. See Cite 232.

280. Wang and Merino: 1627. See Cite 232.
281. Wang and Merino: 1637. See Cite 232.
282. Pabian and Zairns: 20. See Cite 16.
283. Wang and Merino: 1637. See Cite 232.
284. Hoffmann-Rothe, Rainer. "Reflections on the Formation of Agates." *The Wonderful World of Agates Conference Program*. Menasha, WI: July 10-13, 2008: 11.
285. Beaster: 13. See Cite 5.
286. Wang and Merino: 1628. See Cite 232.
287. Pabian, Roger K. "Developing More Effective Research Methods for the Study of Agates and Other Microcrystalline Forms of Silicon Dioxide." *The Wonderful World of Agates Conference Program*. Menasha, WI: July 10-13, 2008: 17.
288. Pabian and Zarins: 22. See Cite 16.
289. Erickson: 28. See Cite 69.
290. Lee: 1. See Cite 4.
291. Ichikuni, Masami and Ryozo Nakagawa. "Direct Formation of Crystalline silica from Acid Thermal Spring Water." *Bulletin of the Chemical Society of Japan*. #10: 1967: 2439.
292. Proust, Dominique and Claude Fontaine. "Amethyst Geodes in the Basaltic Flow from Triz Quarry at Ametista do Sul (Rio Grande do Sul, Brazil): Magmatic Source of Silica for Amethyst Crystallization." *Geological Magazine*. 144:4: July 2007: 1.
293. Moxon: 84. See Cite 35.
294. www.en.wikipedia.org/wiki/Isotope_ratio_mass_spectrometry.
295. Fallick, A.E., J. Jocelyn, Donnelly, M. Guy, and c. Behan. "Origin of Agates in Volcanic Rocks From Scotland." *Nature*. 313: February 21, 1985: 672.
296. Walger et al: 124. See Cite 106.
297. Beaster: 12. See Cite 5.
298. Moxon, T. S.J.B. Reed, and M. Zhang. "Metamorphic Effects on Agate Found Near the Shap Granite, Cumbria, England: As Demonstrated by Petrography, X-ray Diffraction and Spectroscopic Methods." *Mineralogical Magazine*. 71:4: August 2007:461.
299. Moxon et al: 473. See Cite 298.
300. Moxon et al:461. See Cite 298.
301. Pabian and Zarins: 7. See Cite 16.
302. www.starofthenorth.org/minnesota.html.
303. Cordua, Bill. "How Amethyst Cathedrals Form." River Falls, WI, University of Wisconsin, unpublished paper: 1.
304. Jones, Thomas D, Larry A Lebofsky, John S Lewis, Mark S. Marley. "The Composition and Origin of the C,P, and D Asteroids: Water as a Tracer of Thermal Evolution in the Outer Belt." Elsevier Science, *Science Direct:* Nov 1990: 172.
305. Conway: 1. See Cite 6.
306. Moxon: 83. See Cite 35.
307. Moxon: 1. See Cite 35.
308. www.agateworld.co.uk/worldagates.html.
309. Petranek: 196. See Cite 90.
310. LaBerge: 149. See Cite 68.
311. Pabian and Zarins: 11. See Cite 16.
312. Huber, Norman King. "The Geologic Story of Isle Royal National Park." *U.S. Geologic Survey Bulletin*. 1309: 1975: 2.
313. Hudak, G.J., R.L. Morton, J.M. Franklin, D.M. Peterson. "Morphology, Distribution, and Estimated Eruption Volumes for Intracaldera Felsic Tuff Deposits in the Archean Sturgeon Lake Subaqueous Caldera complex, Northwestern Ontario." Unpublished paper: 1.
314. Huber: 2. See cite 312.
315. Pabian and Zarins: 12. See Cite 16.
316. Simons: 880. See Cite 134.
317. Walger et al: 128. See Cite 106.
318. www.djmcadam.com/agate.html
319. Gauthier, Kevin and Bruce Mueller. Lake Superior Rock Pickers Guide. Ann Arbor, MI: The University of Michigan Press, 2007: 13.
320. www.riverdeep.net/current/20000/12/120700_moon
321. Kile, Daniel. "Occurrence and Genesis of Thunder Eggs Containing Plume and Moss Agate." *Rocks and Minerals*. 77: 4: Jul/Aug 2002: 252.
322. Pabian and Zarins: 6. See Cite 16.
323. Kile: 253. See Cite 321.
324. Pabian, Roger K. "Recognition of Ancient Chalcedony-Filled Spherulites, or in Search of Ancient Thunder Eggs." *Proceedings of the Nebraska Academy of Sciences, 108th Annual Meeting*. Lincoln, NB: Nebraska Wesleyan University, April 24, 1998: 1.
325. Pabian and Zarins: 8, 10. See Cite 16.
326. Kile: 262. See Cite 4.
327. Pabian and Zarins: 9, 10. See Cite 16.
328. Pabian and Zarins: 26. See Cite 16.
329. Clark: 87. See Cite 27.
330. Clark: 67. See Cite 27.
331. Gotze, J, R. Mockel, U. Kempe, I. Kapitonov, and T. Vennemann. "Characteristics and origin of Agates in Sedimentary Rocks from the Dryhead Area, Montana, USA." *Mineralogical Magazine*. 73: 4: August 2009.
332. Clark: 88. See Cite 27.
333. Pabian and Zarins: 26. See Cite 16.
334. Clark: 52. See Cite 27.
335. Clark: 55. See Cite 27.
336. Cross, Brad L. "The Agates and Geodes of Northern Chihuahua, Mexico." *Symposium on Agate and Cryptocrystalline Quartz*. Golden, CO, ept 10-13, 2005: 20-22.
337. Clark, Roger. "Fairburn Agate: History and Mystery." *The Wonderful World of Agates Conference Program*. Menasha, WI, July 10-13, 2008: 5.

338. http://www.globalchange.umich.edu/global-change1/current/lectures/clocks_in_rocks/clocks_in_rocks.html
339. Beaster: 11. See Cite 5.
340. Moxon, Terry and S.J.B. Reed. "Agate and Chalcedony from Igneous and Sedimentary Hosts Aged from 13 to 3480Ma: a Cathodo-luminescence Study." *Mineralogical Magazine.* 70: 5: October 2006: 486.
341. Petranek: 203. See Cite 90.
342. Gotze: 536. See Cite 110.
343. Moxon and Reed: 485. See Cite 340.
344. www.en.wikipedia.org/wiki/Moganite.
345. http://www.turnstone.ca/mogan.htm
346. Wahl, C, G. Miehe, and H. Fuess. "TEM Characterisation and Interpretation of Fabric and Structural Degree of Order in Micro-crystalline Si02 phases." *Contrib Mineral Petrol.* 202: 143: 360.
347. Walger et al: 146-147. See Cite 106.
348. Moxon and Reed: 485. See Cite 340.
349. Moxon et al: 462. See Cite 298.
350. Moxon et al: 461. See Cite 298.
351. Moxon, Terry and Susana Rios. "Moganite and Water Content as a Function of Age in Agates." *European Journal of Mineralogy.* 16: 2: April 2004: 269.
352. Moxon and Reed: 485. See Cite 340.
353. Beaster: 17. See Cite 5.
354. Pabian: 15. See Cite 221.
355. www.agateworld.co.uk/worldagates.html.
356. www.agateworld.co.uk/worldagates.html.
357. www.snr.unl.edu/data/geologysoils/agates/AgateLexicon.asp
358. http://vulcan.wr.usgs.gov/LivingWith/VolcanicPast/Places/volcanic_past_nebraska.html
359. Raines, Ed. "Creede Sowbelly Agate: Banded Amethystine Quartz and Chalcedony." Symposium on Agate and Cryptocrystalline Quartz." Golden, CO, Sept 10-13, 2005: 131.
360. Moxon: 1101. See Cite 108.
361. Petranek: 198. See Cite 90.
362. www.rockhounds.com/rockgem/articles/agates.html
363. Carlson: 36. See Cite 7.
364. www.indiana9fossils.com/Agates/Black-River-Agates.htm
365. Zenz, Johann. Agates. Rainer Bode, Haltern Germany, 2005: 554.
366. Gotze: 690. See Cite 331.
367. Schumacher: 73. See Cite 22.
368. www.buenavistagemworks.com/agates/fairburn.htm
369. www.snr.unl.edu/data/geologysoils/agates/AgateLexicon.asp
370. www.uky.edu/KGS/rocksmn/silicates.htm
371. Moxon and Reed: 494. See Cite 340.
372. www.agateworld.co.uk/worldagates.html.
373. Walger et al: 145. See Cite 106.
374. Wang and Merino: 1627. See Cite 232.
375. Pabian et al: 8. See Cite 9.
376. Hattori et al: 169. See Cite 146.
377. Clark: 90. See Cite 27.
378. Moxon: 1113. See Cite 108.
379. Lee: 1. See Cite 123.
380. Michalski, Thomas C., and Eugene E. Foord. "Seven Causes of Color in Banded Agaes." *Symposium on Agate and Cryptocrystalline Quartz.* Golden, CO: Sept 10-13, 2005: 60.
381. Beaster: 10. See Cite 5.
382. Michalski: 63. See Cite 380.
383. Michalski: 61. See Cite 380.
384. Michalski: 63. See Cite 380.
385. Michalski: 63. See Cite 380.
386. Wolter: 102. See Cite 24.
387. Clark: 65. See Cite 27.
388. Michalski: 60. See Cite 380.
389. Michalski: 65. See Cite 380.
390. Michalski: 65. See Cite 380.
391. Michalski: 65. See Cite 380.
392. http://www.1911encyclopedia.org/Agate
393. www.djmcadam.com/agate.html
394. Pabian and Zarins: 22. See Cite 16.
395. Michalski and Foord: 61. See Cite 380.
396. Clark: 73. See Cite 27.
397. www.reade.com/Particle_Briefings/spec_gra2.html
398. Brodrick: 13. See Cite 2.
399. www.minerals.net/resource/property/luster.htm
400. Weinberger: 43. See Cite 8.
401. Carlson: 20. See Cite 7.
402. Moxon: 25. See Cite 6.
403. www.galleries.com/minerals/sulfates/caledoni/caledoni.htm
404. Pabiean et al: 19. See Cite 9.
405. www.en.wikipedia.org/wiki/Limonite
406. www.djmcadam.com/agate.html
407. Nazari: 38. See Cite 132.
408. Wolter: 102. See Cite 24.
409. Wolter: 10. See Cite 24.
410. www.en.wikipedia.org/wiki/Stromatolite
411. www.en.wikipedia.org/wiki/Binghamite
412. www.mindat.org/min-7622.html, binghamite.
413. www.en.wikipedia.org/wiki/Onyx
414. www.encyclopedia.farlex.com/Mexican+onyx
415. www.en.wikipedia.org/wiki/Rhodochrosite
416. Powers, Eric. *Advanced Rock Cleaning Process.* 2009.
417. Wolter: 112. See Cite 24.
418. Weinberger: 42. See Cite 8.
419. www.en.wikipedia.org/wiki/Botryoidal
420. www.answers.com/topic/breccia
421. Walger et al: 116. See Cite 106.
422. www.en.wikipedia.org/wiki/Carnelian
423. Wolter: 101. See Cite 24.

424. www.snr.unl.edu/data/geologysoils/agates/AgateLexicon.asp

425. Gotze: 528. See Cite 110.

426. www.gemselect.com/other-info/about-dendritic-agate.php

427. www.mindat.org/min-7599.html. Dendritic Agate.

428. Dumariska-Stowik: 255. See Cite 137.

429. Pabian and Zarins: 23. See Cite 16.

430. Pabian et al: 25. See Cite 9.

431. www.mindat.org/min-7596.html. Enhydro Agate.

432. www.rocksinmyheadtoo.com/Enhydros.htm

433. Pabian et al: 12. See Cite 9.

434. Goldenfeld, Nigel. "Theory of Spherulitic Crystallization." *Journal of Crystal Growth.* 84: 1987:601.

435. www.sepmstrata.org/thinsections/caco3-pisolites.html

436. www.en.wikipedia.org/wiki/Ooid

437. Lyklema: 2.27. See Cite 104.

438. Pabian and Zarins: 14. See Cite 16.

439. LaBerge: 149. See Cite 68.

440. Pabian and Zarins: 21. See Cite 16.

441. Pabian and Zarins: 59. See Cite 16.

442. Pabian et al: 27. See Cite 9.

443. www.mindat.org/min-7601.html. Fire Agate.

444. Wolter: 102. See Cite 24.

445. www.fireagate.com/fired_up.htm

446. Pabian et al: 28. See Cite 9.

447. www.cst.cmich.edu/USERS/DIETR1RV/agate.htm

448. Wolter: 101. See Cite 24.

449. Wolter: 56. See Cite 24.

450. Petranek: 195. See Cite 90.

451. Milliken, Kitty Lou. "Geodes." Unpublished paper: 1.

452. Wolter: 101. See Cite 24.

453. www.en.wikipedia.org/wiki/Geode.

454. Cross: 22. See Cite 336.

455. Frondel, Clifford. "Characters of Quartz Fibers." *American Mineralogist.* 63: 1978: 24.

456. http://www.usfacetersguild.org/articles/bob_keller/refractive_index/

457. Moxon: 34. See Cite 35.

458. Rodewald: 22. See Cite 135.

459. Beaster: 9. See Cite 5.

460. Heaney, Peter J., and Andrew m. Davis. "Observation and Origin of self-Organized Textures in Agates." *Science.* 269:5320: September 1995: 1562.

461. www.mindat.org/min-7610.html. Iris agate.

462. www.mindat.org/min-52.html. Agate-Jasper.

463. Kile: 259. See Cite 321.

464. Wolter: 58. See Cite 24.

465. Conway: 14. See Cite 6.

466. www.en.wikipedia.org/wiki/Hornblende

467. Pabian et al: 32. See Cite 9.

468. Pabian: 40. See Cite 133.

469. Wolter: 56. See Cite 24.

470. Wolter: 106. See Cite 24.

471. Wolter: 10. See Cite 24.

472. Kile: 259. See Cite 321.

473. www.cst.cmich.edu/USERS/DIETR1RV/agate.htm

474. Pabian and Zarins: 16. See Cite 16.

475. Pabian and Zarins: 14. See Cite 16.

476. www.mindat.org/min-26405.html Plume agate

477. Carlson: 36. See Cite 7.

478. www.en.wikipedia.org/wiki/Pseudomorph

479. Pabian et al: 24. See Cite 9.

480. Wolter: 59. See Cite 24.

481. Carlson: 7. See Cite 7.

482. Carlson: 12. See Cite 7.

483. Pabian and Zarins: 16. See Cite 16.

484. Wolter: 61. See Cite 24.

485. Wolter: 104. See Cite 24.

486. www.all-that-gifts.com/se/onyx.html

487. www.bluelaceagate.net

488. Weinberg: 45. See Cite 8.

489. Sukow, Wayne W. "The Lake Superior 'Shadow' Agate." *Rock and Gem.* July 1999: 44.

490. Weinberger: 44. See Cite 8.

491. Weinberger: 44. See Cite 8.

492. Wolter: 102. See Cite 24.

493. www.snr.unl.edu/data/geologysoils/agates/AgateLexicon.asp

494. Pabian and Zarins: 10. See Cite 16.

495. Pabian and Zarins: 8. See Cite 16.

496. Kile: 262. See Cite 321.

497. Kile: 252. See Cite 321.

498. Kile: 258. See Cite 321.

499. Pabian and Zarins: 10. See Cite 16.

500. www.en.wikipedia.org/wiki/Thunderegg.

501. Pabian et al: 35. See Cite 9.

502. Wolter: 59. See Cite 24.

503. Pabian and Zarins: 15. See Cite 16.

504. Petranek: 202. See Cite 90.

505. Walger: 115. See Cite 106.

506. Petranek: 195. See Cite 90.

507. http://minerals.usgs.gov/minerals/pubs/commodity/gemstones/sp14-95/chalcedony.html

508. Zenz: 490. See Cite 365.

509. www.kentuckyagaterocks.com

510. Pabian et al: 8. See Cite 9.

511. Gauthier and Mueller: 11. See Cite 319.

512. Barron, Bob. "Diving for Agates in Lake Superior." *The Wonderful World of Agates Conference Program.* Menasha, WI, July 10-14, 2008: 3.

513. Wolter: 1. See Cite 24

514. Schoolcraft, Henry R. *Narrative Journal of Travels from Detroit Northwest Through the Great Chin of American Lakes to the Source of the Mississippi River in the Year 1820.* Albany, NY: EKE Hosford, 1821: 180.

515. Wolter: 4. See Cite 24.

516. Wolter: 9. See Cite 24.

517. Weinberger: 42. See Cite 8.
518. www.snr.unl.edu/data/geologysoils/agates/ AgateLexicon.asp
519. www.snr.unl.edu/data/geologysoils/agates/ AgateLexicon.asp
520. Zenz: 512. See Cite 365.
521. www.harmons.net/Montana_Agate.html
522. Zenz: 521. See Cite 365.
523. Michalski and Foord: 63. See Cite 380.
524. Zenz: 535. See Cite 365.
525. www.snr.unl.edu/data/geologysoils/agates/ AgateLexicon.asp
526. Clark: 56. See cite 27.
527. Clark: 5. See Cite 337.
528. Clark: 55. See Cite 27.
529. Clark: 35. See Cite 27.
530. Zenz: 553-554. See Cite 365.
531. Clark: 51. See Cite 27.
532. www.snr.unl.edu/data/geologysoils/agates/ AgateLexicon.asp
533. www.rockhounds.com/rockgem/articles/agates.html
534. Zenz: 325. See Cite 365.
535. Howard: 4. See Cite 138.
536. Moxon and Reed: 494. See Cite 340.
537. Moxon et al: 247. See Cite 41.
538. Zenz: 583. See Cite 365.
539. Zenz: 613. See Cite 365.
540. www.djmcadam.com/agate.html
541. Carlson: 38. See Cite 7.
542. Carlson: 36. See Cite 7.
543. Carlson: 36. See Cite 7.
544. Petranek: 196. See Cite 90.
545. Cordua: 1. See Cite 303.
546. Petranek: 198. See Cite 90.
547. Zenz: 573. See Cite 365.
548. www.engravedstones.net/engraved-stones-collection.htm
549. Zenz: 399. See Cite 365.
550. Cross: 22. See Cite 336.

Figure 265
This is an intricately banded Lake Superior agate. It has fortification bands with extreme color changes that are different varieties of microcrystalline quartz.

INDEX

MUSEUM INFORMATION

For almost 25 years (1954-1978) Axel Niemi, the founder of the Gitche Gumee Museum, entertained people with his music, stories, and knowledge about agates. He sporadically allowed people in the museum for a few years after that, before moving to Ontonagon in the mid 1980s. In 1990 Ron Marshall purchased the museum from Axel. Although he never reopened the museum, he did make some repairs to the building. I met Ron in 1991 and told him how important Axel and the museum were to me. In exchange for a couple of Axel's agates, I wrote a poem for Ron about the museum. After reading the poem, he decided that if he were ever to sell the museum, he would sell it to me. Finally, in 1997 while agate hunting together, Ron asked me if I wanted to purchase the museum. It took me a year to scrape together the money and another year to renovate the building, sort the collection, and build the displays. After being closed for 21 years, the museum was reopened on July 4, 1999.

At first the museum was open only a few hours a day in the summer. At that time I was also co-owner of the Lake Superior Brewing Company in Grand Marais. In 2001 I left that business to commit full time to the Gitche Gumee. Since then, work on the museum and the gift shop has continued. Every year new improvements or expansions are implemented. In 2004 the first agate book Understanding and Finding Agates was published to help museum visitors to "think like an agate." Around that same time, a line of unique agate products was introduced that are now sold at the museum and at juried art shows and mineral club meetings. In the last few years rock hounding classes and lectures were developed that are conducted in Grand Marais as well as off site.

The museum hours have expanded every year, Please go to www. agatelady.com to find out the current hours. The web site also has information about agates, Grand Marais, mineral art products, classes, lectures, and our art and mineral show schedule.

Figure 265
The Gitche Gumee Museum is located at E21739 Brazel Street in Grand Marais, Michigan. For more information about the museum go to www.agatelady.com.

HOW TO VOTE FOR YOUR FAVORITE PHOTOGRAPH

A lot of time and effort went into selecting and photographing the rocks for this book. We are curious which agate photos are your favorite. If you would like to voice your opinion, there are two ways you can vote. In both cases, please select your THREE favorite photos:

First Favorite . . . . .Figure _____

Second Favorite . . . . .Figure _____

Third Favorite . . . . . . .Figure _____

To vote, you can either send an email to: Karen@agatelady.com

OR

You can go to the website www.agatelady.com. On the home page, click on the link "Vote For Your Favorite Agate Book Photo" and cast your ballot. Each time the web page is updated (usually every month) the tally of votes will be posted. Thanks in advance for giving us your opinion!

INFORMATION ABOUT AGATE DVDs & OTHER PRODUCTS

While working on the manuscript, we reviewed the photographs on a big screen TV that was connected to a computer. We enjoyed looking at the images in this big format so much, that we decided to produce DVDs so that others can enjoy the photos in this large format, too. Our preliminary thought is to produce two DVDs. One will include images of agates, and perhaps other minerals, that will be choreographed to music. The second will be a narrated version with photographic images and diagrams to summarize the information in this book. Please go to the web page www.agatelady.com for updated information about these and other mineral art products.

ROCK HUNTING LOG

Rock Identification	Location Found	Date Found

NOTES. . .